A special issue of

The European Journal of Cognitive
Psychology

Face Recognition

Edited by

Vicki Bruce

*Department of Psychology, University
of Nottingham, U.K.*

 LAWRENCE ERLBAUM ASSOCIATES, PUBLISHERS
Hove and London (UK)   Hillsdale (USA)

Lawrence Erlbaum Associates Ltd., Publishers
27 Palmeira Mansions
Church Road
Hove
East Sussex, BN3 2FA
U.K.

British Library Cataloguing in Publication Data

Face recognition: a special issue of the European journal of cognitive psychology.
   1. Humans. Memory (Mental processes)
   I. Bruce, Vicki II. European journal of cognitive psychology
   153.132

ISBN 0-86377-173-4

Cover designed by Joyce Chester
Index compiled by Caroline Sheard
Typeset by Acorn Bookwork, Salisbury

Printed in Great Britain by BPCC Wheatons Ltd, Exeter

Contents

EUROPEAN JOURNAL OF COGNITIVE PSYCHOLOGY, 1991, *3* (1) 1–3

Editor's Introduction

The perception and recognition of faces forms a topic that interests cognitive psychologists for a number of reasons. First, our individual abilities to recognise several hundreds (perhaps thousands) of faces demonstrates the extraordinary power and sensitivity of our visual memory system. Secondly, due to the uniqueness of facial appearance, the face plays the same key role as the fingerprint in forensic identification, yet we have no simple way to reveal the image of the face in witnesses' minds. Cognitive psychologists have an important role to play in determining the most effective ways of eliciting this hidden knowledge. Thirdly, the face mediates a wider variety of cognitive/social activities than any other kind of visual object: we recognise our friends from their faces, but also whether they look tired or sad, whether or not they are listening to us, and their lip movements help us to understand the words they speak. Faces play a truly central role in our social cognitions and people who lose the ability to comprehend and recognise faces experience a profound effect on their social lives.

In reviewing the field of face recognition in 1975, Ellis deplored the lack of any broad theoretical framework within which the disparate findings in the field could be brought together. The last decade has seen a rapid change as researchers interested in face recognition began to develop the same kinds of empirical and theoretical approaches to face recognition that had already proved fruitful in the study of visual word and object recognition. Much of this development has taken place within Europe, and so it seemed particularly appropriate that a special issue of this new journal should be devoted to this topic.

The issue comprises eight articles that demonstrate quite well the methodological diversity and theoretical coherence that now characterises the field. The first article by Young and Bruce is a critical review of the theoretical framework (as exemplified by Bruce & Young, 1986) that unifies much current work in the area. We suggest areas in which further work, or a shift in theoretical orientation, may be needed in the future. De Haan, Young and Newcombe then present a case study of a patient whose deficiencies in retrieving semantic information about faces lend further support to the "Bruce and Young" model, particularly a slight modification of the model recently developed and implemented by Burton, Bruce and Johnston (1990). Most work on face processing deficiencies has concentrated on disorders acquired as a result of brain damage in adulthood. De Gelder, Vroomen and van der Heide review research which suggests that autistic children may have deficiencies in processing faces, and go on to explore the abilities of such children to recognise faces and to lip-read.

One of the striking aspects of face recognition is its robustness given certain manipulations of the image. A face can be recognised from a "coarsely quantised" set of blocks (as in Harmon's, 1973, famous "Abraham Lincoln" portrait) or when distorted as in caricature. The study of the effects of such distortions helps us to elucidate the nature of the visual representations that allow us to discriminate between faces. Using coarsely quantised images, Bachmann demonstrates that facial recognition seems to be particularly disrupted by a very small shift in the number of square pixels used to depict the facial image. Benson and Perrett produce photographic caricatures of famous faces and provide evidence that there may be some advantage for a small degree of caricature in recognising the face, suggesting that a photograph can be made to look more like a person than the person does him or herself! Caricatures seem to operate by exaggerating "distinctive" aspects of the face, and provide further evidence for the importance of the dimension of "distinctiveness" in face recognition. Shepherd, Gibling and H. Ellis show that the advantage in memory for distinctive faces does not interact with exposure duration or delay, a finding that constrains certain interpretations of the distinctiveness effect.

The face is only one route into the person identification system. We can recognise people from their voices, clothing or gait, and of course by their name. When we hear or read the headline "Bush takes root in desert", we may have different interpretations of it, depending on whether we take "Bush" to mean a shrubby tree, or an American president. In the next paper, Valentine, Bredart, Lawson and Ward describe their experiments aimed at exploring the organisation of processes which allow proper names to gain access to the person identification system.

The majority of papers in this issue use conventional experimental techniques to study the processing of faces or names by normal subjects, and in developmental and acquired disorders. However, face recognition is one of the many areas of cognition where computer simulation is allowing us to develop and test theoretical ideas more rigorously than before (cf. Burton et al., 1990). The issue concludes with a paper by Schreiber, Rousset and Tiberghien who explore the potential of a parallel distributed processing model to account for how we learn new face patterns under different contextual conditions.

August 1990   Vicki Bruce

REFERENCES

Bruce, V. & Young. A. (1986). Understanding face recognition. *British Journal of Psychology, 77*, 305–327.

Burton, A. M., Bruce, V. & Johnston, R. A. (1990). Understanding face recognition with an interactive activation model. *British Journal of Psychology, 81*, 361–380.

Ellis, H. D. (1975). Recognising faces. *British Journal of Psychology, 66*, 409–426.

Harmon, L. D. (1973). The recognition of faces. *Scientific American, 227* (November), 71–82.

EUROPEAN JOURNAL OF COGNITIVE PSYCHOLOGY, 1991, *3* (1), 5–49

Perceptual Categories and the Computation of "Grandmother"

Andrew W. Young

Department of Psychology, University of Durham, Science Laboratories, Durham, U.K.

Vicki Bruce

Department of Psychology, University of Nottingham, University Park, Nottingham, U.K.

Recent theoretical approaches to understanding face recognition have used converging evidence from studies of normal face processing, everyday errors and patterns of neuropsychological impairment to suggest how different face processing modules are related to each other. This paper discusses four issues that arise from this body of work. These concern the nature of representations involved in face recognition, the existence of parallel pathways for processing different types of information, the relationship between recognition and awareness, and the question of how faces become familiar. Current research provoked by these issues is reviewed in the paper and suggestions are made about the ways in which such research will help refine theories of face processing.

INTRODUCTION

The story of Little Red Riding Hood is instructive. This unfortunate young woman mistook a wolf for her grandmother. She could see that the wolf's eyes, nose, and especially its teeth, were larger than her grandmother's.

Requests for reprints should be addressed to Andrew W. Young, Department of Psychology, University of Durham, Science Laboratories, South Road, Durham DH1 3LE, U.K.

This paper is a revised version of one originally prepared for the Trieste Encounters in Cognitive Science (June 1989). Its preparation has been supported in part by an ESRC programme award for a multi-centred investigation into face recognition (funded as grants XC15250001 to Vicki Bruce at Nottingham University; XC15250002 to Ian Craw at Aberdeen University; XC15250003 to Hadyn Ellis at the University of Wales, Cardiff; XC15250004 to Andy Ellis and Andy Young at Lancaster University; XC15250005 to David Perrett at St Andrews University). We thank Jacques Mehler and John Morton for inspiring us with its title, and Andy Ellis and John Morton for their comments on an earlier draft of the manuscript.

But she failed to give due weight to these observations because the wolf was in her grandmother's house, wearing her grandmother's clothes and sitting in her grandmother's bed. This seemingly overwhelming contextual evidence was sufficient to overrule what Little Red Riding Hood could see.

Studies of everyday errors show that all of us make such mistakes from time to time (Young, Hay & A. Ellis, 1985a), though they do not always have such potentially disastrous consequences. Visual recognition itself usually takes place automatically, but it can be subject to intentional cross-checking if some aspect of context or appearance doesn't quite fit. For some neuropsychiatric patients, the cross-checking process seems to become disordered, as in Frégoli syndrome (de Pauw, Szulecka & Poltock, 1987; H. Ellis & Young, 1990; Young, H. Ellis, Szulecka & de Pauw, 1990). Frégoli patients are convinced that they are pursued by cunningly disguised enemies. The condition was first described by Courbon and Fail (1927), and takes its name from the actor Leopoldo Frégoli, whose speciality was to contort his face into different appearances.

Face and Object Recognition

Even in a world in which it is now the wolf that has become endangered, we rely greatly on accurate recognition of the people we know. Without it, social interaction would be impossible. We need to recognise the appearances of familiar people in order to access approprite semantic information concerning our knowledge of each individual. Appearance alone might be sufficient to determine that the person standing behind you in the chip shop queue is a middle-aged woman, but it is only access to previously stored information specific to this individual that can tell you that she works in the pet shop. This point led Bruce and Young (1986) to make a distinction between *visually derived* semantic codes, which can be inferred from a person's appearance, and the *identity-specific* semantic codes that are dependent on accessing stored information about that particular person. Identity-specific semantic codes may be accessed from numerous sources including faces, voices and names. Context and clothing led Little Red Riding Hood to the identity-specific semantic codes specifying "grandmother", and this led her to ignore the visually derived semantic information that might otherwise have warned her to flee.

It is useful to pause for a moment to reflect on the demands of person recognition, and especially face recognition. Because people may change their clothing, and because we do not always hear their voices or have them introduced to us by name, we rely heavily on face recognition. As Galton (1883) pointed out, however, faces form a visual stimulus category that contains many similar items; each with two eyes, nose, mouth and so on in roughly the same general arrangement. But recognising a face *as a face* does not get us very far. Instead, we need to know *which individual's* face we are looking at, and the smallest of differences may be crucial in determining this.

These demands are interestingly different to those usually considered to be involved in recognising everyday objects. Objects often need to be assigned to relatively broad categories that maximise the visual and functional similarity between exemplars. Thus it is important to us to know that a particular object is a hammer, or a suitcase. Rosch and her colleagues refer to this property of everyday object recognition as involving recognition at the basic category level (Rosch, 1978; Rosch et al., 1976). Knowing *which* hammer or *which* suitcase it might be is not always necessary.

Nevertheless, faces are not the only kind of object that need to be discriminated within a basic level category. Most of us can probably distinguish one kind of car from another, and many of us will be used to spotting our own cars, and those of our colleagues, in the car park at work. Farmers and pet owners may become adept at identifying particular, individual animals. Even individual suitcase recognition becomes both important and skilful at the baggage return at an airport. All these examples, including face recognition, require discrimination of subtle aspects of the configurations of objects. All faces, all cars and all suitcases share the same general configuration, because they must all fulfil similar functions, whether natural or manufactured. For example, eyes and ears need to be spaced appropriately so that we can localise objects. All suitcases must be similar because they are portable containers that need to stack neatly into cars, and so forth. Recognition of "individuals" requires that we discriminate differences between these same basic configurations. Individual exemplars must therefore vary at the level of relationships between the elements that define this general configuration – this is what Diamond and Carey (1986) termed "second-order" configural information. Faces form the most important class of objects for which such discrimination skills are developed, and the only class where such skills must be developed in everybody. Such skills are also developed at an early age for faces (within the first year of life; see review by Flin & Dziurawiec, 1989).

Why Faces are Important

One of the things that helps to make faces particularly important to us is the wealth of different types of social information that we derive from them. We use them not only to recognise the people we know, but also to infer moods and feelings, to regulate social interaction through eye contact and facial gestures, to assist in speech comprehension (e.g. when lip-reading; McGurk and MacDonald, 1976, have demonstrated that even people with normal hearing do this), to determine age and sex, and even to attribute characteristics on the basis of social stereotypes.

These uses of facial information are well developed early in infancy, and are probably built up from a basis of innately specified components, since we know that newly born babies show precocious face processing abilities. They are, for instance, attentive to faces (Goren, Sarty & Wu, 1975), they can perceive different emotional expressions (Field, Woodson, Greenberg & Cohen, 1982), and they will imitate both emotional (Field et al., 1982) and relatively conventional facial gestures (Meltzoff & Moore, 1977; 1983; Vinter, 1985).

Given this background, we should perhaps be less surprised than many of us have been to find that the cerebral cortex contains many neurons that are apparently dedicated to face processing (Perrett, Rolls & Caan, 1982; Perrett et al., 1984; 1985; Rolls, 1984; in press). A number of separate studies have shown that there are substantial numbers of cells in the superior temporal sulcus of the macaque temporal cortex that respond preferentially to faces and show little if any response to other simple objects (such as clocks) or arousing objects (such as snakes). Within those cells selective for faces, there is further selectivity for particular facial features, viewpoints and identities (Perrett et al., 1984; 1985). Although the cells themselves show a high degree of selectivity for faces, and some degree of selectivity for individual faces, or particular viewpoints, the cortical areas in which these cells are found also contain cells responsive to other objects, particularly other parts of the body. Face-specific cells do not seem to be confined to an exclusive faces "centre", and it may be for this reason that prosopagnosia (an inability to recognise faces which may result from brain injury) is only rarely observed in the absence of some other subtle recognition deficit (H. Ellis & Young, 1989).

To summarise, face recognition requires the discrimination of subtle differences in the basic configuration of the face. Faces are important because of the diversity of social skills within which face perception plays a role. Their importance seems to be reflected in the facts that infants seem predisposed to attend to and respond to faces, and specialised neural networks in the cortex are involved in facial processing.

What this Paper is about

Until the late 1970s, the psychological literature on face processing was dominated by an almost exclusively empirical approach which sought to identify the effects of different subject and treatment "variables" (H. Ellis, 1975; Young, 1987a): age, sex, presentation time, memory interval, and so on.

This type of work is, of course, useful in a number of ways, but it inevitably tended to give rise to a complicated and fragmented collection of "facts", rather than a coherent body of knowledge. Dissatisfaction (in Britain, at least) with this state of affairs was responsible for three significant changes in research strategy. To a large extent, these changes resulted from a deliberate attempt to emulate developments in studies of word recognition, and especially those inspired by later versions of Morton's (1969; 1979; 1984) "logogen" model. This attempt involved a shift in emphasis from studies of remembering unfamiliar faces to studies of *familiar face recognition*.

The first change involved the use of explicit theoretical models to pose questions for and to interpret the results of empirical investigations. Secondly, the introduction of a more eclectic, and in many respects more sophisticated, collection of investigative procedures for studies of normal subjects. Thirdly, the use of neuropsychological data as an important additional source of evidence concerning the functional organisation of face processing.

This new research strategy leans heavily on the view that much cerebral organisation is primarily "modular" in nature (Fodor, 1983). Modular organisation is considered a useful solution to the need to keep nerve connections as "tidy" as possible, and to be able to modify part of a complex process without disrupting other stages (Cowey, 1985; Marr, 1982). The implication of the hypothesis of functional modularity is that by studying the effects of brain injuries, and also the patterns of breakdown occasionally observed in normal performance, we will gradually be able to piece together the "functional architecture" of human cognition. Moreover, our attempts to do this can be guided by theoretical models developed independently in experimental psychology and, in addition, cognitive neuropsychological studies can in turn be used to refine such models. The underlying assumption here is that, if modular organisation obtains, then an adequate model of the functional architecture of normal cognition must be able to predict the patterns of breakdown that can occur. Care is usually also taken to seek converging evidence from different types of study pointing towards the same conclusion. Although this enterprise can be criticised in so far as it is unlikely to lead to a full understanding of how each of the identifiable modular components actually achieves its purposes (Seidenberg, 1988), there is no doubt that much important information can none the less be revealed (A. Ellis & Young, 1988; Shallice, 1988), and that such information can be used to set constraints on explicitly computational theories. Indeed, as we will explain later, Burton, Bruce and Johnston (1990) have already successfully constructed a simulation of a model with many of the properties we describe.

A number of groups in Britain are pursuing this new research strategy, and the framework that we summarise here is essentially a joint perspec-

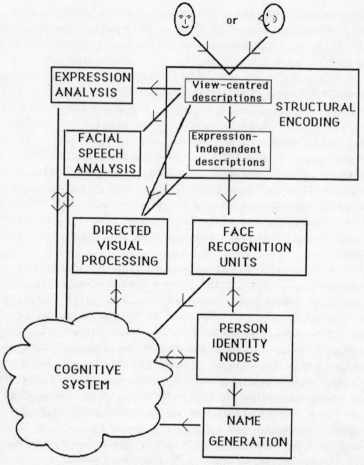

Fig. 1.   A framework for understanding face recognition (from Bruce & Young, 1986).

tive. A number of recent reviews of this work are available (Bruce & Young, 1986; Bruce, 1988; Bruyer, 1987; A. Ellis, Young & Hay, 1987b; H. Ellis, 1986; Young, 1987a; 1988; Young & H. Ellis, 1989a), so it is only necessary to sketch the main points here.

By way of summary, Fig. 1 describes the functional "model" (more appropriately "framework") which we published a few years ago (Bruce & Young, 1986) and which outlines the functional independence of certain stages or modules of face processing and the sequential dependence of others. Briefly, the model indicates that identification proceeds *in parallel with* expression analysis and lip-reading ("facial speech"). Identification itself involves stages of perceptual classification (via the "face recognition units"), semantic classification (at the "person identity nodes") and name retrieval. The face recognition units allow the classification of a novel view of a known face as familiar, and are thought (possibly) to contain view-specific representations of each known face. The person identity nodes, unlike the face recognition units, are domain-independent; they can be accessed by faces, voices, names and so forth, and they provide access to identity-specific semantic information, but are distinct from name retrieval. Another component in the model is "directed visual processing", which includes any non-obligatory (task-specific) visual processing of faces. We have more to say about this below. The final component is the "cognitive system", which is cloudy but self-explanatory.

We do not intend here to rehearse the evidence that led us to devise such a framework. However, since its publication, evidence has accumulated in favour of the sequential model of familiar face recognition. Bruce and Young's (1986) model followed Hay and Young (1982) in suggesting that there was a *sequential* relationship between components labelled face recognition units, person identity nodes and names in Fig. 1. Recent studies of the difficulties in person identification and the relative utility of different kinds of cue in resolving such difficulties have lent strong support to this sequential arrangement (Brennen, Baguley, Bright & Bruce, 1990; Hanley & Cowell, 1988; Hay, Young & A. Ellis, in press).

Rather than discuss other evidence which supports this framework, here we propose to move on a little, in order to concentrate on more recent studies and on four issues arising from this body of work that seem to us of central importance, and that are not yet definitively resolved. These concern the nature of representations involved in face perception, the existence of parallel pathways for processing different types of facial information, recognition and awareness, and how faces become familiar. As we will show, further investigation of these issues promises to refine our understanding of face-processing mechanisms considerably.

REPRESENTATIONS INVOLVED IN FACE PERCEPTION

Many of us suspect that the key to understanding how we do many of the wonderful things we can do with seen faces lies in understanding the visual representations involved. Because of the combination of the characteristic demands of face processing, the complexity of the face as a three-dimensional structure, and its capacity for both rigid and non-rigid movement, it is tempting to conclude that a unique type of visual representation might be required in order to solve the computational problems involved.

There is as yet, however, no direct evidence to support this speculation. What does seem to us to be clear is that some of the traditional approaches to understanding how visual information is represented in the brain are unlikely to have much to contribute in understanding the representation of facial information. It does not, for instance, seem to take us very far to learn that different studies have shown the importance of low, intermediate and high spatial frequencies in face recognition (Harmon, 1973; Tieger & Ganz, 1979; Fiorentini, Maffei & Sandini, 1983, respectively). Claims that face *recognition* depends more or less on one band of spatial frequencies rather than another still leave us mystified as to how recognition is actually achieved. (This is not to deny that different spatial scales may be more or less useful for different tasks, e.g. that a coarser scale representation may suffice for judging the sex of a face compared with deciding its identity: Sergent, 1986.)

Further to confound the issue, Table 1 shows summary details concerning three men with missile wound injuries from the series studied by Newcombe, de Haan, Ross and Young (1989a). Spatial contrast sensitivity functions have been plotted for each person, and performance on a simple face perception task (reaction time to decide whether or not a stimulus is a properly organised face, or a non-face containing scrambled features). As can be seen, cases TC and BS (both drawn from the group of patients with left cerebral hemisphere lesions) show impaired contrast sensitivity without any corresponding impairment of face perception, whereas case PG (from the right hemisphere group) performs very poorly on the face perception task and yet has unimpaired contrast sensitivity for all spatial frequencies. Hence a double dissociation is evident between face processing and contrast sensitivity impairments.

TABLE 1

Cases Drawn from Newcombe et al.'s (1989a) Study, Demonstrating Dissociable Impairments of Face Perception and Contrast Sensitivity

RT (msec) for Face Perception Task		Contrast Sensitivity (2-$\log_{10}$ contrast)					
		00.72 cpd	01.43 cpd	02.88 cpd	05.80 cpd	10.10 cpd	17.40 cpd
Missile wound cases							
TC	1443	158.6[a]	187.6[a]	185.5[a]	159.7[a]	100.3[a]	000.0[a]
BS	854	151.7[a]	192.1[a]	217.2	208.5	120.0	031.5[a]
PG	2220[a]	191.6	255.1	287.6	278.9	225.0	150.6
Controls							
Mean	1098	189.5	236.0	263.8	238.5	188.5	119.5
S.D.	210	11.3	13.7	20.5	19.4	31.5	33.7

[a]Performances falling more than 2.5 standard deviations below those of the control subjects.

The reason for these essentially negative findings concerning spatial frequency is almost certainly that higher-order representations that can pool information derived from a wide range of spatial frequencies are involved in face perception. This suggestion is consistent with Rolls, Baylis and Leonard's (1985) demonstration that "face" cells in the monkey's cerebral cortex respond both to high- and low-pass filtered faces, and to Rolls and Baylis's (1986) finding that these cells are also tolerant of changes in size and contrast.

What could these "higher-order" representations be based upon? Recent theories of representations for object recognition seem more appropriate for discriminating basic level categories (first-order configurations) than for discriminating within such categories. For example, the axis-based descriptions that Marr (1982) suggested might be involved in object recognition are inappropriate to the task of recognising faces (Bruce & Young, 1986), because broadly similar three-dimensional structures obtain for all members of the stimulus class "faces". Instead, what is required is some form of representation that can capture the *differences* between the faces we encounter.

Can we offer any promising directions for the further understanding of the visual representation of faces? One observation that seems interesting and relevant is that faces are more readily recognised as belonging to particular individuals if they are more "distinctive" in appearance than if they are typical in appearance. Valentine and Bruce (1986a; 1986b) compared the latencies in a "face familiarity decision task" (where subjects must decide whether each face they see is familiar or unfamiliar to them: cf. the lexical decision task) to familiar faces whose facial appearances varied in rated distinctiveness. Distinctive faces were classified as familiar more quickly than typical faces (e.g. see Table 2a) and this result was found whether the faces were personally familiar (faces of members of staff in the subjects' department: Valentine & Bruce, 1986a) or famous (Valentine & Bruce, 1986b). Valentine and Bruce (1986a; 1986b) suggested that this result would be expected if faces were encoded in terms of their deviation *from* a basic or prototypical face representation. If so, then distinctive faces should be *harder* to classify *as faces*. In a task where subjects had to distinguish intact faces from faces whose features were jumbled, Valentine and Bruce (1986b) indeed found distinctive faces were at a disadvantage, whether familiar or unfamiliar to the subjects (see Table 2b). Such results would also be expected if incoming faces were compared with all known face instances, i.e. there is no need to postulate the formation of an *explicit* prototype. We return to this issue again later in the section on learning new faces.

Representations for face recognition must in some way capture the way in which each face differs from the norm, and this may explain why

TABLE 2

Mean Latencies (msec) to Categorise Distinctive and Typical Familiar Faces (a) as Familiar (Distractors were Unfamiliar Faces) and (b) as Faces (Distractors were Jumbled Faces)[a]

	Distinctive	Typical
(a)	661	707
(b)	608	561

[a]Data from Valentine and Bruce (1986b).

caricatures, which are non-veridical representations of the metric proportions of a face, can nevertheless be highly recognisable. Brennan (1985) devised an automatic "caricature generator" that works by comparing the locations of a large set of specified reference points for a particular face with the stored "average" locations of each reference point from a large set of faces. The caricature is produced by exaggerating differences between each target reference point and the norm, in proportion to their initial difference. Rhodes, Brennan and Carey (1987) have shown that caricatures produced by this system are more recognisable than the original line drawings from which the caricatures were derived, and Benson and Perrett (this issue) report an interesting extension of this work to *photographic* caricatures.

Such examples of distinctiveness and caricature serve to highlight the way in which faces must be represented as *second-order* configurations – but these demonstrations say little of the possible bases for such a representation. Brennan's caricature generator "represents" faces as the locations of a set of contour reference points, standardised to fixed interocular distance. It seems unlikely that the visual system adopts such a method. Indeed, Brennan's system illustrates a common feature of face processing theories, which is to consider the face as though it were a flat pattern, with individuating differences captured by distances within the picture plane. A more promising direction for the future may come from a proper "computational theory" of the nature of the input to be represented, and the constraints which may be exploited in the representation and processing of faces (e.g. Bruce, 1988; 1989; Bruce & Burton, 1989). Faces are not flat patterns, but three-dimensional surfaces that grow on skulls. Understanding the nature of the facial surface has already proved important in devising new edge-finding algorithms that can automatically "sketch" a moving face for telecommunications purposes (e.g. Pearson & Robinson, 1985).

Such an understanding may also prove fruitful for suggesting the perceptual "primitives" which form the basis of the representations used for face recognition. Research on the relative salience of different features or dimensions of the face has manipulated similarities between faces by interchanging or moving features in the picture plane (e.g. see Haig, 1986; Sergent, 1984; and Shepherd, Davies & Ellis, 1981, for a review of earlier studies of feature salience). Recent work has investigated the perceptual effects of global and local deformations to a three-dimensional *surface* of the face, with the aim of developing a more adequate basis for psychophysical experiments on feature salience (for examples of this work, see Bruce, Burton, Doyle & Dench, 1989; Bruce, Burton & Doyle, in press a). Bruce and her colleagues have also been investigating the extent to which our visual representations of faces encode surface *shape*, in addition to surface markings (Bruce et al., submitted b). Of some relevance here is the observation that line drawings of faces are much more readily recognised when they contain cues to three-dimensional structure as well as two-dimensional structure (Bruce et al., submitted a).

We believe that such a "computational" level of theorising will prove an essential ingredient of future theories of face recognition, whatever the fruitfulness of instance-based approaches (particularly PDP) to understanding how representations of familiar faces are derived (see last section). We must still understand what kind of representations are derived by any PDP network, and how they may be derived from initial grey-level inputs from each encountered instance. Attempts to automate face recognition using such neural network modelling have until very recently used only single-layer nets with either grey levels (e.g. Kohonen, Lehtio & Oja, 1981; Stonham, 1986) or edge segments (Millward & O'Toole, 1986) as inputs, and it will be interesting in the future to investigate connectionist implementations of more plausible computational schemes.

PARALLEL PATHWAYS

One of the most important claims made by all current functional models of face processing is that different types of information are extracted *in parallel* from the faces we see. Bruce and Young (1986), for instance, argued that identity, expression, lip-reading and directed visual processing can all be independently achieved. Such claims run strikingly counter to most peoples' intuitions. Consider, for instance, that it is claimed that one does not need to work out a person's facial expression in order to lip-read, or to determine a person's sex in order to recognise their identity.

These claims of heterarchic organisation derive primarily from two types of evidence, involving an examination of the different patterns of impairment that can follow brain injury, or an investigation of the ways in which experimental manipulations may affect one type of performance but not another for normal subjects.

We do not intend to dispute such claims, which we have often advanced ourselves, and believe to be at least in essence correct. But we do want to draw attention to the fact that the supporting evidence is not yet as overwhelmingly convincing or as complete as one would ideally like. All form clear cases where further investigation is needed to fully explore the reported phenomena. To demonstrate this, we will examine four of these putative dissociations in turn. These involve the independence of familiar face recognition and unfamiliar face matching, identity and expression, sex and identity, and lip-reading from identity and expression.

Familiar and Unfamiliar Faces

The independence of familiar face *recognition* and unfamiliar face *matching* was initially a somewhat serendipitous finding, arising from studies begun in the 1960s. These had often assumed that tests requiring the ability to determine whether or not photographs showed faces of the same or different people would be sufficiently sensitive to detect mild forms of face recognition impairment. This assumption was brought into question when Warrington and James (1967) demonstrated that impairments affecting the processing of familiar or unfamiliar faces were associated with different lesion sites, and especially when Assal (1969), Benton and van Allen (1972) and Tzavaras, Hécaen and Le Bras (1970) all reported finding that prosopagnosic patients (who cannot recognise familiar faces) were successfully able to perform face matching tasks. A number of subsequent reports of accurate matching of unfamiliar faces by prosopagnosic patients have been published (e.g. Bauer, 1982; Bruyer et al., 1983; Tranel, Damasio and Damasio, 1988, case 1).

Such results led Benton (1980) to conclude that identification of familiar faces and discrimination of unfamiliar faces involve different cerebral mechanisms. This view has been supported by the later work of Malone, Morris, Kay and Levin (1982), who described two patients with different patterns of recovery. The first patient was initially unable to recognise familiar faces, but had regained this ability by the time that formal neuropsychological tests were given. Yet he was still impaired on tests requiring the matching of views of unfamiliar faces. The second patient showed the opposite pattern, with ability to match unfamiliar faces recovering while an impairment affecting the recognition of familiar faces persisted.

The problem with reaching the straightforward conclusion of an independence between familiar and unfamiliar face processing on the basis of this evidence alone has been highlighted by Newcombe (1979). Newcombe's prosopagnosic patient also performed face matching tasks quite accurately, but she noticed that he took a long time and seemed to rely on rather unusual strategies. The importance of these observations was confirmed when Newcombe asked the patient to perform a matching task in which the hairlines were masked by an oval frame, thus eliminating his preferred (hair) matching strategy. His performance accuracy then deteriorated dramatically. Young and H. Ellis (1989b) have also been able to study a prosopagnosic girl who performed well on some face matching tasks by carefully using idiosyncratic methods, and in fact some of the original reports of preserved matching in prosopagnosia also drew attention to slow response times (Assal, 1969) or unusual strategies (Tzavaras et al., 1970).

Newcombe (1979) thus emphasised that to demonstrate satisfactorily a neuropsychological dissociation between familiar face recognition and unfamiliar face matching, it is essential to show not only that prosopagnosic patients can match unfamiliar faces successfully, but that they achieve this in the "normal" way. Recording response times as well as overall accuracy would be one way of providing more convincing evidence of this (see Sergent & Poncet, 1990). One might also turn the point round, and argue that it is also important to show that the patients who are poor at unfamiliar face matching and yet can recognise familiar faces also show normal reaction times for familiar face recognition (de Haan, personal communication).

Since we none the less consider that familiar and unfamiliar face processing *do* dissociate, on what basis could such a dissociation occur? The literature on normal face processing offers three differing (and not necessarily mutually exclusive) possibilities. First, Bruce (1982) and Davies and Milne (1982) both reported that accuracy of recognition memory for familiar faces was unaffected by changes of view between study and test, whereas recognition memory for unfamiliar faces was severely impaired by such changes. Additionally, Davies and Milne (1982) showed that recognition memory for familiar faces was unimpaired by changing the context against which each face was pictured, again in contrast with results for unfamiliar faces (see Memon & Bruce, 1985, for a review). Here it seems that the dissociations between familiar and unfamiliar face processing arise because of the different sources of information that can mediate recognition of the different classes of face. For familiar faces, an episodic recognition decision can be mediated via semantic and/or verbal coding ("I remember seeing the prime-minister's face") and these codes will remain invariant across viewpoint. Unfamiliar faces cannot be matched at the level of "identity-specific" semantic codes, and even the "visually derived" semantic codes formed to unfamiliar faces ("looks intelligent", "looks friendly", and so forth) may depend upon a particular view and expression. Thus the recognition of familiar faces could dissociate from the matching of unfamiliars when a patient could rely on semantic codes for the tasks involving familiar faces that were unavailable for unfamiliars.

There is a second way in which the visual processing of familiar and unfamiliar faces could dissociate from each other, if we suggest that familiar faces are normally encoded and recognised "automatically" via a *mandatory* processing module (a possibility that we discuss in more detail later). If known faces are usually recognised irrespective of our particular cognitive set, any faces (known or unknown) may additionally be scrutinised in a more flexible, if attention-demanding, way. Thus, for example, while we may obligatorily recognise the face of a friend, we may also optionally examine their face for signs of the ravages of age or alcohol. It is this kind of "optional" visual processing of faces that we labelled "directed visual processing" in our model (Bruce & Young, 1986; see Fig. 1), and it may be these kinds of processes that can allow a prosopagnosic patient to compare laboriously two unfamiliar faces to decide whether or not they match.

Evidence for a distinction between "directed visual processing" and obligatory semantic processing was found by Bruce (1979) in experiments on visual search. In these experiments, the subject's task was to decide whether or not each encountered face belonged to one of the last four prime ministers of the U.K. The nature of distractor faces was varied: Of the familiar distractors, half were politicians and half were non-political celebrities, and within each semantic group half the faces were rated as visually similar to one or more of the targets. Both visual similarity and semantic similarity slowed rejection latency, but in an *additive* fashion. This pattern is not consistent with a model in which visual analysis must precede semantic analysis (as this would predict effects of semantic similarity only on those faces that were visually similar to targets), suggesting instead that visual and semantic analyses proceeded in parallel. However, some form of visual analysis is clearly needed prior to retrieval of the semantic identity of a face and this logical argument would place visual and semantic analysis in series. The key to this apparent paradox is to recognise that the visual analysis needed to *recognise* a face (via the "mandatory" processing route) may not be the same as the visual analysis needed to *decide* whether a face has the visual characteristics of a particular target. We may go to the station to meet someone's grandmother – and hence be searching for short white-haired old ladies (with small teeth) – but we would still be able to recognise our spouse alighting from the same train. Thus "directed visual processing" can be separable from "familiar face recognition", and this may account for the apparent dissociations reported in the clinical literature. For example, a patient who has an impairment to the "mandatory" processing route for the recognition of familiar faces, may have preserved "directed visual processing" and therefore be able to match unfamiliar faces.

A final possible basis for a dissociation between familiar and unfamiliar face processing lies in H. Ellis, Shepherd and Davies's (1979) finding that somewhat different facial features are involved. They demonstrated better recognition of familiar faces from internal than external features, yet there was no corresponding difference for unfamiliar faces, which were recognised equally well from internal or external features. The finding has been replicated with Japanese subjects and Japanese faces by Endo, Takahashi and Maruyama (1984), and differential salience of the internal features of familiar faces has also been found using a face matching task by Young et al. (1985b) and de Haan and Hay (1986). It is thus clear that as a face becomes familiar, differential importance accrues to the internal features, either because these are the ones that remain unaffected by changes in hairstyle or because of the attention paid to them because of their expressive characteristics. Any deficit which rendered a person selectively deficient at processing particular parts of the face could therefore contribute to a dissociation between the processing of familiar and unfamiliar faces. We will return to the topic of differences between familiar and unfamiliar faces in a later section of this paper concerned with the question of how faces become familiar.

Identity and Expression

Neuropsychological findings were the first to suggest an independence between the processing of identity and expression. Although it would seem that a number of prosopagnosic patients show impaired processing of both identity and expression from faces, there are none the less some prosopagnosic patients who remain able to understand emotional facial expressions, despite their inability to recognise familiar faces (Bruyer et al., 1983; Hécaen & Angelergues, 1962; Shuttleworth, Syring & Allen, 1982; Tranel et al., 1988). Some of these studies provide quite detailed documentation in support of this finding, and we see no reason to query it.

The opposite dissociation was first reported by Bornstein (1963), who noted that some of his prosopagnosic patients showed a degree of recovery of ability to identify familiar faces while remaining unable to interpret facial expressions. Similarly, Kurucz and Feldmar (1979) and Kurucz, Feldmar and Werner (1979) found that a group of patients with diffuse brain injuries found it difficult to interpret facial emotions and yet were still able to identify photographs of American presidents. Unfortunately, however, none of these studies probed very deeply into the exact nature of the impairments observed. They did not, for instance, adequately rule out the possibility that these patients may simply have failed to comprehend the meaning of terms used to describe emotional states, thus leaving open the possibility that the impairments on expression tasks might not be linked to a problem with facial expression *per se*. A more detailed investigation of a patient with this type of problem would be most useful. It has been suggested that autistic patients may also be deficient at processing expressions (see de Gelder, Vroomen & van der Heide, this issue). However, as de Gelder et al. point out, most studies of autistic patients have not made careful studies of whether expression processing and identity processing dissociate in this population.

Again, though, studies of normal subjects also support the claim of independence between identity and expression processing, with both Bruce (1986a) and Young, McWeeny, Hay and A. Ellis (1986a) finding no difference between familiar and unfamiliar faces on tasks requiring expression analysis (i.e. no influence of face familiarity on expression processing).

Neurophysiological studies of cells responsive to faces in the monkey's temporal cortex are also consistent with the idea of separable brain mechanisms for analysing expression and identity. Neurons that have been found to be sensitive to the identity of faces are insensitive to facial expression, whereas neurons that are sensitive to facial expression tend to generalise across face identity (Perrett et al., 1984). The identity-sensitive cells tend to occur in different cortical areas to the expression-sensitive cells (Hasselmo, 1987). There does here seem to be strong converging evidence for the independence of processing of facial expressions and identities.

Sex and Identity

The relation between the processing of sex and identity provides a neat illustration of the value of functional models in generating testable research hypotheses. Because sex can readily be determined from most unfamiliar faces, Bruce and Young (1986) tended to consider this as independent from establishing the person's identity. H. Ellis (1986), however, offered the simpler alternative suggestion that recognition of familiar faces may be achieved through a kind of perceptual hierarchy, in which increasingly precise classifications are made. On this view, faces would be classified as male or female *in order* to make the more precise discriminations within these categories that led to the determination of individual identity.

It is easy to think of differing predictions that allow us to test the usefulness of these two theoretical positions. At present, the evidence favours Bruce and Young's (1986) view of independence between the processing of sex and identity. For example, Bruce, H. Ellis, Gibling and Young (1987) reasoned that if subjects had to determine the sex of faces before identifying them, then faces whose sex was difficult to determine should be slower to classify as familiar than faces whose sex was easy to

TABLE 3
Mean Latencies (msec) to Categorise
High-masculinity and Low-masculinity
Familiar Faces (a) as Male Faces and (b)
as Familiar Faces[a]

	Rated Masculinity	
	High	Low
(a)	558	682
(b)	911	883

[a]Data from Bruce et al. (1987).

determine, as the relatively androgynous faces should take longer at the earlier, sex classification stage. Bruce et al. (1987) had subjects rate the apparent masculinity of both famous and unfamiliar male faces, and were able to construct groups of familiar and unfamiliar male faces that were either "high" or "low" in apparent masculinity. These faces were inter-mixed with familiar and unfamiliar female faces, and the subjects were asked either to make speeded sex classification decisions or speeded face familiarity decisions. All faces were clean-shaven, and the females had hair trimmed, to make the sex judgement task relatively difficult even for those items rated as very high in masculinity.

The results of this study are shown in Table 3, where we see that while the apparent masculinity of the faces had a large and highly significant effect on the time taken to classify the sex of each familiar male face, it had no effect on the time taken to judge their familiarity. A second experiment replicated and extended this finding, by showing that even when the sex judgement task was made relevant to the face familiarity decision task (i.e. when subjects were asked to respond positively only when the faces were both male *and* familiar), the rated masculinity of the faces had no effect on the response time. The detailed results were accounted for by a model in which there were two independent components, with the output of the sex judgement component usually, though not always, achieved faster than the output of the identification module.

Further evidence for the dissociation between sex and familiarity judge-ments comes from Roberts and Bruce (1988), who found differential feature salience for the two tasks. Familiar and unfamiliar faces from Bruce et al.'s (1987) study, above, were presented with eyes, noses or mouths concealed with masks. The results are shown in Table 4. When the task was to judge the familiarity of each face, concealing the eyes had the greatest detrimental effect (in line with other results on feature salience)

TABLE 4

Mean Latencies (msec) to Categorise Familiar Faces (a) as Male or Female Faces and (b) as Familiar Faces, Depending on the Feature Masked[a]

	Feature Masked			
	None	Eyes	Nose	Mouth
(a)	637	710	924	724
(b)	768	798	746	762

[a]Data from Roberts and Bruce (1988).

and concealing the nose had no effect at all. When the task was to judge the sex, however, concealing the nose had the greatest detrimental effect, slowing decisions by over 200 msec relative to the no-mask control. The relative importance of the nose and brow region (nose masks concealed the very top of the nose, which includes a part of the brow region) is consistent with the suggestions of Enlow (1982) that the faces of males and females differ in terms of the shapes of the "muzzle" – with females having concave facial profiles and males having protruberant facial profiles.

It has already been reported that some prosopagnosic patients are correctly able to determine the sex of seen faces (e.g. Bruyer et al., 1983; Tranel et al., 1988). If sex and identity are independently processed, however, there should also be patients who can recognise familiar faces but are impaired at determining the sex of unfamiliar faces. To the best of our knowledge, no such patient has been described. This might be because our position is incorrect, and such a dissociation cannot exist. Or it might be because people have not looked for it. There are so many other cues to gender (hairstyle, clothing, etc.) that a person with an impaired ability to determine this from facial features alone might well not experience much in the way of everyday difficulties, and so would be unlikely to seek help for this particular symptom.

Lip-reading

A dissociation between the ability to "lip-read" speech from seen movements of the mouth and tongue and the processing of facial expression and identity has been demonstrated in a neuropsychological study of two contrasting patients by Campbell, Landis and Regard (1986). One patient (with a posterior lesion of the right cerebral hemisphere) was unable to recognise familiar faces and could not categorise facial expressions correctly. She could none the less correctly judge what phonemes were being mouthed in photographs of faces, and she was susceptible to the illusion described by McGurk and MacDonald (1976), in which a mismatch between heard and seen phonemes results in the perceiver "blending" the two. The second patient (with a posterior lesion of the left hemisphere) was impaired at making phoneme judgements to face stimuli and was not susceptible to McGurk and MacDonald's (1976) illusion, yet had no difficulties in recognising faces or facial expressions.

Campbell et al.'s (1986) neuropsychological data are convincing concerning this dissociation. Our only reservation is that it would be useful to demonstrate the same independence of lip-reading from other aspects of face processing in studies of normal subjects. De Gelder, Vroomen and van der Heide (this issue) find evidence of correlations between lip-reading and face identification in normal subjects, though interestingly there does not appear to be such an association in autistic subjects.

To sum up, while there is good, converging evidence for the independence of identification processes from expression classification, the evidence for independence of other modules is less overwhelming, though we believe that the "parallel processing" position is in essence correct. It will be worth investing research effort into clarifying these relationships, since the overall modular structure may provide important constraints upon the microstructure of each module.

RECOGNITION AND AWARENESS

Despite the occurrence of occasional errors of the type made by Little Red Riding Hood, as we have already pointed out visual recognition usually proceeds quite automatically. We cannot look at a familiar face and decide not to recognise it. The processes involved are not open to introspection or conscious intervention. Only the product of the recognition process (i.e. the sense that it is person X) enters awareness.

A number of useful techniques for examining these automatic aspects of recognition have been developed by experimental psychologists. We will consider three here: repetition priming, associative priming and interference effects, and the relation between them. We will then look at how these and other techniques have been used to investigate the breakdown of awareness of recognition in cases of prosopagnosia and semantic memory impairment.

Repetition Priming

Repetition priming tasks investigate the facilitatory effect of having previously encountered a particular stimulus on subsequent recognition. These facilitatory effects are usually long-lasting, and can be measured across intervals of several minutes, days or even longer.

A particularly interesting feature of repetition priming effects is that they do not cross stimulus domains (Clarke & Morton, 1983; Warren & Morton, 1982; Winnick & Daniel, 1970). The decision that a particular face is familiar can be made more quickly if that face has been previously seen, but is unaffected by having seen the person's name or even his or her (clothed) body (Bruce & Valentine, 1985; A. Ellis, Young, Flude & Hay, 1987a). Although the influence of repetition priming is specific to the primed stimulus domain, however, there is as yet no evidence of any difference in the *form* of repetition priming effects found in different stimulus domains (i.e. faces behave in very much the same way as visually presented objects or words in repetition priming tasks).

An important implication of this domain-specificity of repetition priming effects is that they cannot be based on subjects deliberately remembering which people have been encountered in the experiment. Explicit memory would be little different across faces, names or bodies, yet it is only seeing faces that affects subsequent reaction times for face recognition. Thus there is an independence between repetition priming and explicit memory for the items that have been seen, which is consistent with their relatively "automatic" origin (see also Schacter, 1987).

One reason why repetition priming effects are domain-specific is probably that they are based on the degree of physical similarity between prime and test items. A. Ellis et al. (1987a) showed that repetition priming will transfer from one photograph of a face to another, but only in proportion to the degree of similarity between the two views. Thus names and bodies may not prime later recognition of the same people's faces because their names and bodies do not look like their faces.

Our initial reaction to these "graded-similarity" effects was to conclude that repetition priming does not necessarily arise in the recognition system itself, but might instead be a product of the re-creation of stimulus encoding operations or previous processing episodes, as Kolers (1975; 1976) and Jacoby (1983a; 1983b) have consistently maintained (A. Ellis et al., 1987a). This was rather disappointing to us, because our interest in repetition priming had been as a tool to probe the properties of hypothetical face recognition units based on analogy with Morton's (1969; 1979) logogens. Fortunately, A. Ellis et al.'s (1987a) conclusion turned out to be wrong. Subsequent work has made us confident that the locus of the repetition priming effects found in our preferred "familiarity decision" task (which involves deciding whether a seen face is that of a known or an unfamiliar person; an analogue of the lexical decision task often used in studies of word recognition) can be located in the recognition system.

Table 5, for example, shows data from an experiment in which repetition priming was investigated in both sex (male *vs* female face) and familiarity decision tasks (A. Ellis, Young & Flude, 1990, Experiment 3). The

TABLE 5

Reaction Times (msec) to Familiar Faces from the Second Phase of A. Ellis et al. (1990, Experiment 3), for Sex Decision and Familiarity Decision to Faces Seen (Primed) or Not Seen (Unprimed) in the First Phase of the Experiment

First-phase task:	Sex Decision	Familiarity Decision	Sex Decision	Familiarity Decision
Second-phase task:	Sex Decision	Sex Decision	Familiarity Decision	Familiarity Decision
Primed	525	564	616	640
Unprimed	530	575	711	777

experiment involved two phases. In the first phase, the subjects made either familiarity decisions or they made sex decisions to a series of seen faces. In the second phase of the experiment, some of the original stimulus faces were repeated ("primed" faces) and some were new to the experiment ("unprimed" faces), with the subjects again making familiarity decisions or sex decisions. As Table 5 shows, faster responses to primed than unprimed faces were only found for the familiarity decision task, for which they were observed regardless of the task that the subjects performed in the experiment's first phase. This demonstrates that priming is not simply due to the repetition of previous encoding operations, which would either have affected all tasks equally or led to maximal priming whenever the first- and second-phase tasks were the same. Instead, repetition priming does seem to arise from the recognition system itself, and hence is only evident for the familiarity decision task. The recognition system operates automatically, and thus produces priming of familiarity decisions even when the subjects were not initially asked about the items' familiarity. A. Ellis et al. (1990) also showed that there is no priming for expression decisions, which are also thought not to require access to the recognition system, and that the priming found for familiarity decisions is not a direct consequence of the fact that these often take longer to make than decisions about sex or expression (i.e. it is not simply that only the slowest decisions can be primed).

Our current view is thus that priming effects are located in the face recognition system (see also Brunas, Young & A. Ellis, 1990). In order to account for graded-similarity effects, however, we will probably have to conclude that this system operates in a way that allows it to store records of previously encountered *instances* (cf. McClelland & Rumelhart, 1985), rather than the relatively "abstractive" conception we had initially put forward (Bruce & Young, 1986; Hay & Young, 1982).

Associative Priming

Associative priming tasks examine the influence of one stimulus on the recognition of a related stimulus; for instance, the effect of seeing Raisa Gorbachev's face on recognition of Mikhail Gorbachev. Substantial priming effects are found, but unlike repetition priming effects they dissipate rapidly (Bruce, 1986b; Dannenbring & Briand, 1982). Associative priming effects are also unlike repetition priming effects in that they will readily cross stimulus domains. Thus associative priming can be found between object and word recognition, or between face and name recognition (Sperber, McCauley, Ragain & Weil, 1979; Young, Hellawell & de Haan, 1988a).

This effect is often referred to as "semantic" priming (e.g. Bruce, 1983; Bruce & Valentine, 1986; Dannenbring & Briand, 1982; Young et al., 1988a), but we now prefer the term "associative" priming because it seems to capture more precisely the nature of the underlying mechanism, which is probably based on associative connections rather than semantic category membership (Lupker, 1984). Fodor (1983) argued for associative connections in the word recognition system, on the grounds that they would help a stupid system to behave as if it were smart, and his argument has been extended to object recognition by Lupker (1985) and to face recognition by A. Ellis et al. (1987b) and Young and H. Ellis (1989a). It may be useful to build up associative connections that can allow us to recognise Mikhail Gorbachev more quickly after we have seen Raisa Gorbachev's face, or read her name in a newspaper. These associative connections would serve the purpose of making the recognition system prepared for what it is likely to encounter next. Such explanations assume that associative priming is "useful". Later in this section we consider an alternative explanation of associative priming, which sees it as an accidental by-product of the organisation of the person recognition system.

A popular paradigm for investigating associative priming involves presenting a prime stimulus (to which no response is made) before the target stimulus to which subjects make their response (Neely, 1976; 1977). This allows one to examine the effects of prime–target stimulus onset asynchrony (SOA), and whether the priming effect involves facilitation of responses with related primes or inhibition from unrelated primes (or both). Posner and Snyder (1975) argued that purely "automatic" priming will produce facilitation even at short SOAs, whereas conscious anticipatory strategies would be more effective at longer SOAs and would also lead to inhibition (slower responses) for unrelated prime–target pairs.

Bruce and Valentine (1986) used this prime–target paradigm, and found facilitation of face and name recognition by related primes, even at SOAs as short as 250 msec. As they point out, such SOAs can be considered too short to support an intentional use of the prime, as latencies for overt recognition are much longer (Young, McWeeny, A. Ellis & Hay, 1986b). Again it would seem that automatic aspects of the recognition system are implicated. A further reason in support of this conclusion is that other studies of normal subjects have found that associative priming effects can occur even with prime presentation times that are too brief for overt recognition of the prime stimuli (Carr, McCauley, Sperber & Parmelee, 1982; McCauley, Parmelee, Sperber & Carr, 1980), though this has yet to be demonstrated for face recognition. We suspect that such a finding could easily be made for faces, because there is no evidence of any difference in the form of associative priming effects found for words, objects, faces and names.

Interference Effects

Interference effects can be found in variations of the Stroop (1935) paradigm in which objects and words or faces and names are simultaneously presented. To investigate face–name interference, we have developed a technique that involves presenting a photograph of a face with a printed name alongside it, and asking subjects to make a response either to the face (ignoring the name distractor) or to the name (ignoring the face distractor).

The purpose of this approach is to examine the "cross-talk" between face and name recognition systems, and to compare their properties to those already well-established for object and word recognition. It has been demonstrated (Young et al., 1986c; Young, Flude, Ellis & Hay, 1987) that *distractor names interfere with face naming*, but have little effect on face categorisation. Conversely, *distractor faces interfere with name categorisation*, but have no effect on naming tasks. Hence the direction of interference effects between faces and names is task-dependent. The pattern is closely comparable to that found for object–word interference (Lupker, 1985; Rosinski, Golinkoff & Kukish, 1975; Smith & Magee, 1980), with faces showing the same properties as visually presented objects and names showing the same properties as other words.

To account for this pattern of findings, A. Ellis et al. (1987b) extended McLeod and Posner's (1984) concept of "privileged loops", and suggested that access to semantic representations from familiar faces and access to phonological representations from familiar names can be considered to have such "privileged" status. In essence, although the subject is instructed to try to ignore the distractor in such experiments, this is simply not possible, because the operations involved in visual recognition are mandatory, and are automatically executed. Interference paradigms can thus be considered to be variants of dual-task experiments, and an interesting topic for future research will be to explore the usefulness of this conception. If correct, it should be possible to integrate interference experiments into the dual-task literature.

A further unresolved issue concerns the relation between interference and associative priming (La Heij, van der Heijden & Schreuder, 1985). We have taken the view that these are not simply different variants of the same underlying phenomenon, because effects that are genuinely linked to semantic category membership can be found in interference tasks (Rosinski, 1977; Young et al., 1986c; 1987), and because the pattern of interference effects observed differs between faces and words (or between objects and words). In both respects, interference is *not* like associative priming. It would be useful to explore the parallels and divergences between interference and associative priming effects more thoroughly.

Relation Between Priming and Interference Effects

As we have seen, repetition priming, associative priming and interference effects all seem to reflect automatic aspects of recognition mechanisms. There are, however, differences between the effects themselves. Repetition priming effects are long-lasting but domain-specific, whereas associative priming effects dissipate rapidly but do readily cross stimulus domains. Unlike associative priming effects, interference can be based on semantic category membership *per se*.

These differences suggest that, although they may all be "automatic" in nature, these priming and interference effects probably originate in different ways. An important task is thus to trace the different loci at which they exert their influences on visual recognition. Various ideas have been proposed, including the suggestions that repetition priming reflects activation of domain-specific recognition units, whereas associative priming affects decision thresholds (Young & de Haan, 1988; Young & H. Ellis, 1989a), or, in more "connectionist" terms, that repetition priming results from altering the connection strengths between nodes, whereas associative priming results from activity at the level of the nodes themselves (Burton, Bruce & Johnston, 1990; Humphreys & Bruce, 1989).

Our thinking on associative and repetition priming effects has recently been helped considerably by a formal simulation of aspects of Bruce and Young's framework, recast in terms of an interactive activation model (Burton et al., 1990). In Burton et al.'s (1990) model, there are distinct pools of units that correspond to different components in Bruce and Young's (1986) original framework. There are "feature" units, activated by particular, hypothetical features or dimensions of faces, which correspond approximately to the structural encoding component of Fig. 1. These feature units are linked to "face recognition units" (FRUs), which are

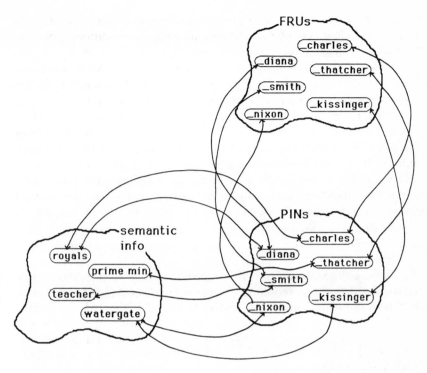

Fig. 2.   Three of the pools of units in Burton et al.'s (1990) interactive activation model.

activated maximally by specific patterns of feature activity. Face recognition units are linked to "person identity nodes" (PINs), which are also activated by inputs from names, via "name recognition units". Semantic information is stored within a separate set of "semantic units". Figure 2 shows the way in which FRUs, PINs and semantic units are interlinked. In this implementation, both the face recognition units and the person identity units act as *nodes*, but do not themselves *contain* information about visual or semantic features. A difference from Bruce and Young's (1986) model, though, is that for the purposes of simulation in Burton et al.'s model, it is assumed that familiarity decisions are taken at the *PINs* rather than at the level of the face or name recognition units.

As in McClelland and Rumelhart's (1981) interactive activation model, there is excitation between pools of units, but inhibition within pools, so that, for example, each PIN inhibits each other. Associative priming can occur, despite within-pool inhibition, because excitation passes between the PINs of associated people via shared semantic features. A PIN that has been excited via spreading activation in this way reaches the threshold of activation needed for a familiarity decision more quickly than one that has not been primed. Burton et al. (1990) describe simulations of associative priming, and show how in such a system associative priming will cross input domains (e.g. from a face input to a name input) but will be abolished by an intervening item – consistent with the rapid dissipation of associative priming effects. By assuming that when a face is recognised there is a strengthening of the links between FRUs and PINs, a distinct mechanism for repetition priming is created, which is domain-specific, and whose persistence depends entirely on the decay parameters fed into the system. Burton et al. (1990) discuss how this model can also account for other findings, such as distinctiveness effects and the fan effect.

The model does not currently have a component corresponding to name output, and therefore we cannot at present attempt to simulate the full range of interference effects. However, the fact that certain central features of Bruce and Young's model can be implemented in this way is likely to be of importance to future work, because it demonstrates that the model does have many of the properties claimed for it, provides a more precise (implemented) specification of the mechanisms held to underlie priming effects, and has the potential to predict patterns of findings that can be confirmed or falsified in future studies.

Breakdown of Awareness of Recognition in Prosopagnosia

Prosopagnosic patients report that, following brain injury, they are no longer able to recognise familiar faces. They can still see well enough to identify a face as a face, to point to or describe individual facial features (eyes, nose, mouth, etc.), and as we have already noted they may be able to determine sex and expression and to match views of unfamiliar faces. Yet even the most familiar people can remain unrecognised from their faces alone, including friends, family and the patient's own face when seen in a mirror (Hécaen & Angelergues, 1962). In order to recognise familiar people, the patients rely on non-facial cues, such as voices.

Autopsied cases of prosopagnosia usually show bilateral occipitotemporal lesions (Damasio, Damasio & van Hoesen, 1982; Meadows, 1974), but a number of cases in which neuroradiological evidence suggests an exclusively right hemisphere lesion have recently been described (e.g. de Renzi, 1986a; Landis et al., 1986).

The failure of overt recognition experienced by prosopagnosic patients is so striking that it surprised many of us when Bauer (1984) demonstrated that a prosopagnosic patient could show skin conductance responses which differentiated between correct and incorrect pairings of faces and names, even though the patient could not consciously distinguish the correct from the incorrect pairs. A similar finding was made by Tranel and Damasio

(1985), who noted a difference between skin conductance responses to "unrecognised" familiar and unfamiliar faces. Rizzo, Hurtig and Damasio (1987) showed a difference in eye movement scan-paths when patients with impaired overt face recognition ability viewed familiar and unfamiliar faces.

Such findings profoundly alter our conception of the nature of prosopagnosia, as they show that it is inadequate to think of it as simply involving loss of recognition mechanisms. Instead, at least some degree of recognition does take place; what the patient has lost is *awareness of recognition*.

More recently, behavioural measures have been used to explore this phenomenon in more detail, especially with the prosopagnosic patient PH (de Haan, Young & Newcombe, 1987a; 1987b; Young & de Haan, 1988; Young, Hellawell & de Haan, 1988a). The focus of interest has been to determine which tasks will and will not produce evidence of "covert" recognition, and to compare the phenomena revealed to those that are thought to reflect automatic aspects of the operation of the normal recognition system.

One of the principal requirements for demonstrating preserved ("covert") recognition is that recognition is tested *indirectly*, in terms of its effect on some other ability. In contrast, PH performs at chance level on *direct* tests (i.e. tests that overtly demand recognition as part of the instructions), such as choosing which of two simultaneously presented photographs of faces (one of a famous person, and one of an unfamiliar person) is familiar. Table 6 shows the performance of PH and two other patients, who will be discussed later, on this task. PH scored 65 out of 128 correct (chance = 64/128), yet when the task was repeated using printed names as stimuli, he scored 118 out of 128 correct, showing that he does know the people involved (Young & de Haan, 1988).

The indirect tests that have been used to date with PH involve variants of *matching, interference, associative priming* and *learning* paradigms. In matching tasks, he showed faster matching of familiar than unfamiliar faces

TABLE 6
Forced-choice Familiarity Decision to Faces and Names by MS (Newcombe et al., 1989b), PH (Young & de Haan, 1988) and BD (Hanley et al., 1989)

	Faces	Names
MS	67/128	116/128
PH	65/128	118/128
BD	97/128	101/128

TABLE 7
Reaction Times (msec) for PH's Correct Responses to
Target Names of Familiar People Preceded by Related,
Neutral or Unrelated Face or Name Primes[a]

	Related	Neutral	Unrelated
Face primes	1016	1080	1117
Name primes	945	1032	1048

[a]Data from Young et al. (1988a).

(with face stimuli drawn from the direct test described above, on which he performed at chance level), and this faster matching of familiar faces only obtained when the matches had to be based on the faces' internal (rather than external) features (de Haan et al., 1987b). These patterns of reaction times correspond to those found for normal people by Young et al. (1985b; 1986a).

PH's faster matching of familiar than unfamiliar faces shows that some information about known faces as familiar visual patterns is preserved, even if he cannot access it overtly. By using interference tasks, however, de Haan et al. (1987a; 1987b) also demonstrated that information about the semantic category to which a face belonged was covertly accessed by PH. In these tasks, PH was asked to classify printed names as those of politicians or non-politicians. His reaction times for name classification were longer when the names were accompanied by distractor faces drawn from the opposite semantic category than when a distractor face was not present, or came from the same semantic category. The same pattern of interference of faces on name classification is found for normal subjects (Young et al., 1986c) but, unlike normal subjects, PH could not achieve accurate overt classification as politicans or non-politicians of the distractor faces used.

Table 7 shows the reaction times from an associative priming task in which PH was asked to determine whether or not printed names were those of familiar (famous) people. Each name target was preceded by a related, neutral or unrelated prime at 500 msec SOA, with either faces or names used as the prime stimuli. Only the data for familiar name targets are presented. PH showed equivalent associative priming from face and name primes, despite his inability to identify most (18/20) of the faces used. The nature of the priming found in each case (facilitation of responses to related pairs, with no inhibition for unrelated pairs) was that thought to characterise a purely "automatic" effect (see Posner & Snyder, 1975).

A question that naturally arises concerns whether or not such findings will hold for all patients with severely impaired overt face recognition ability. The answer is that they do not; patients who fail to show "covert"

TABLE 8
Reaction Times (msec) for MS's Correct Responses to
Target Names of Familiar People Preceded by Related,
Neutral or Unrelated Face or Name Primes[a]

	Related	Neutral	Unrelated
Face primes	1260	1276	1264
Name primes	1178	1370	1439

[a]Data from Newcombe et al. (1989b).

recognition have already been described (Bauer, 1986; Newcombe, Young & de Haan, 1989b; Sergent & Villemure, 1989; Young & H. Ellis, 1989a). Table 8, for instance, shows the reaction times to name targets preceded by related, neutral or unrelated face or name primes for the patient MS (Newcombe et al., 1989b). MS's overt face recognition abilities are as badly impaired as those of PH (see Table 6), but unlike PH he shows no evidence of covert recognition of familiar faces. Only the name primes, which MS can recognise overtly, produce any facilitation of his responses.

Evidently, then, there are different forms of prosopagnosia, and indirect tests may well prove useful in establishing this. Patients like MS show clear signs of higher-order perceptual impairment (Ratcliff & Newcombe, 1982), which probably affects the structural encoding of faces sufficiently to genuinely prevent any form of recognition. This is consistent with the distinction between perceptual and mnestic forms of prosopagnosia emphasised in some clinical studies (de Renzi, 1986; Hécaen, 1981; but see McNeill & Warrington, in press).

Considering cases like PH as involving a domain-specific memory impairment for familiar faces, or mnestic prosopagnosia, may also be useful in that it emphasises the parallel with the findings of implicit memory from studies of amnesia (Schacter, 1987; Warrington & Weiskrantz, 1968; 1970). But the locus of the covert recognition effects remains to be determined. We have found learning tasks particularly useful in this respect.

Bruyer et al. (1983) found that their prosopagnosic patient learned "true" pairings of faces and names more readily than he learned "untrue" combinations. That is, when shown a particular face, he could learn to associate the correct name to it more easily than someone else's name. This was also true for PH, and it even applied to the faces of people who had only become known to PH since his accident (de Haan et al., 1987b), demonstrating that his recognition system has continued to build up representations of faces of the people he meets, even though he has never recognised them overtly.

The particular advantage of this learning paradigm is that it is easy to

TABLE 9
Summary of Results of Learning Tasks for PH (de Haan
et al., 1987b; Young & de Haan, 1988) and BD (Hanley
et al., 1989)

Type of Material to be Associated with Unrecognised Stimulus	Better Learning of True than Untrue Pairings	
	PH	BD
Full names	Yes	Yes
Occupational categories	Yes	Yes
"Precise" semantic information	No	Yes
First names	No	No

vary the type of material to be learned. Table 9 shows the results of doing this with PH (de Haan et al., 1987b; Young & de Haan, 1988). The interesting point is that whether or not PH shows better learning of true than untrue pairings is dependent on the type of material to be learned. Better learning of true pairings was found for full names and for occupational categories ("politican", "actor", etc.), but was *not* found for first names ("Jim", "Bob", etc.) or for relatively "precise" semantic information (such as the political parties and backgrounds associated with a group of politicians, or the specific sports associated with a group of sportsmen).

Our current interpretation of these findings is that the system(s) responsible for covert recognition by PH does not encompass name retrieval, as he does not learn true pairings of faces and people's first names any better than untrue pairings (the better learning of true pairings of faces and full names is attributed to the possibility of accessing occupational categories from the names), and may not include normal access to what Bruce and Young termed "person identity nodes", because he shows no benefit from precise semantic information in these learning tasks. We are impressed by the parallel between PH's preserved abilities on implicit tests and those aspects of recognition that seem to operate automatically for normal people. Young and de Haan (1988) have argued that his condition can be seen as involving disconnection of the output of an otherwise adequately functioning face recognition system from whatever processes are needed to support awareness of recognition. The result is a curious disorder of awareness, in which there is no global alteration of consciousness, but one specific aspect (awareness of recognition) is lost. The parallel with other types of neuropsychological impairment that can also be seen as involving different types of defective access to consciousness is an intriguing one that we are keen to pursue (Schacter, McAndrews & Moscovitch, 1988; Young, 1988; Young & de Haan, 1990).

Semantic Memory Impairment

One of the defining characteristics of prosopagnosia is that recognition of familiar people by non-facial means remains relatively intact. This can be contrasted with cases in which the recognition of people is impaired regardless of input domain (e.g. A. Ellis, Young & Critchley, 1989), and the patient shows impaired recognition from faces, voices or names. Recently, there has also been the opportunity to study a post-encephalitic patient, BD, who is poor at recognising familiar people from face, name or voice (Hanley, Young & Pearson, 1989). We must emphasise again that BD is *not* prosopagnosic. Instead, it is probably more useful to conceptualise his problems as involving a form of semantic memory impairment (Hanley et al., 1989), and they occur in the context of a more general semantic memory impairment affecting living things (cf. Warrington & Shallice, 1984).

Table 6 shows BD's ability to recognise faces and names in forced-choice familiarity decision tasks. Notice that he is impaired for both faces and names, but that the impairment for faces is not as severe as that experienced by PH or MS, and he remains able to recognise a proportion of familiar people. This makes it relatively tricky to investigate "covert" recognition, but it was possible to investigate BD's performance in learning tasks using faces or names of people he failed to identify at the time. Better learning of true than untrue pairings of faces and full names was found even when both the face and the name were "unfamiliar" to BD on overt testing. The pattern of his performance on learning tasks is shown in Table 9, alongside that for PH.

The most interesting feature of BD's learning task performance is that unlike PH he *did* show better learning of true than untrue combinations of faces and precise semantic information (Hanley et al., 1989, task 4) and, similarly, he also showed better learning of true than untrue combinations of names and precise semantic information (Hanley et al., 1989, task 5).

This pattern is perhaps as one might expect on the view that, because BD's impairment affects faces, voices and names, it must be sited more "deeply" in the recognition system than PH's, at a point where domain-specific representations are no longer involved. Bruce and Young's (1986) "person identity nodes" form obvious candidates, and it is in this respect interesting that BD does not show evidence of "covert" name retrieval from faces in face + first name learning tasks.

Our work with BD makes it clear that different patterns of preserved abilities on indirect tests can follow different types of brain injury. Our working hypothesis is that awareness of recognition may break down in different ways following damage at different loci in the face processing system (Young & de Haan, 1990; Young, de Haan & Newcombe, in press a), and we have shown that this will fit the data collected to date. Further studies of covert recognition hold great promise for understanding the cerebral mechanisms that underlie awareness.

LEARNING NEW FACES

The question of how faces become familiar is one that should probably have received more attention from those of us who have argued for differences between familiar and unfamiliar face processing. Hay and Young (1982) had maintained that one role of directed visual processing was the creation of new recognition units. Such a position emphasises a discontinuity between the processing of familiar and unfamiliar faces. However, later functional models have tended to view recognition units as a more or less inevitable by-product of sufficient encounters. On such a view, apparent discontinuities between the processing of familiar and unfamiliar faces would be seen as emerging from underlying quantitative effects. One way to think of face recognition units emerging as a by-product of discrete encounters is to think of their microstructure in instance-based terms. In this section, we will present some evidence for and against such a position.

In an earlier section we described how the processing of familiar faces seemed to be weighted towards the internal facial features when compared with the processing of unfamiliar faces. A PDP or other instance-based model could accommodate such effects by arguing that the external visual features are more variable than the internal features because hairstyles change, people are seen wearing hats and scarves in the winter, and so forth. The features that will remain invariant across all these instances are the internal ones. Of course, the internal features themselves vary, as facial expressions and lip movements are constantly changing. However, such non-rigid distortions of the particular individual face might actually serve to *enhance* the representation of its own particular, "second-order" configuration, as we will now explain.

Recent experiments have shown how readily subjects can learn the prototypical configuration from a series of slightly different facial variants (Bruce, Doyle, Dench & Burton, in press b). In these experiments, the subjects were presented with a series of line drawn faces prepared using the "Mac-a-Mug" electronic facial composite system (see Fig. 3). Each of a series of 10 different individual faces appeared once, in each of four or five slightly different versions (depending on experiment) produced by altering the relative placements of the internal features of the face (see Fig. 3), and the subjects were asked to rate the apparent age and sex of each face. In a later, unexpected test of memory, the subjects were asked to choose which member of a test pair they had rated earlier. The subjects usually chose the "prototype" of each individual face they had seen from pairs containing

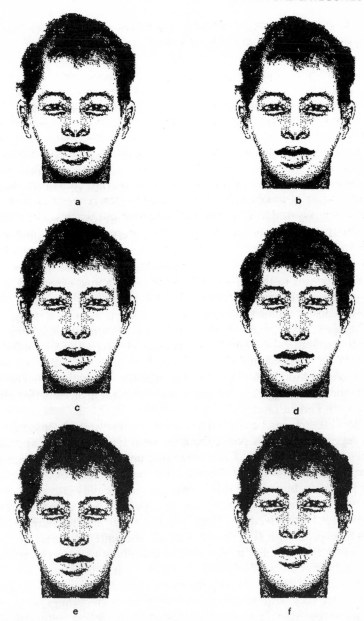

Fig. 3.   Examples of slightly different facial variations produced using the Mac-a-Mug Pro™ composite generator. Subjects shown versions (a), (b), (c) and (d) will later choose version (e) (the unseen "prototype" from which (a) to (d) were constructed) as familiar on about 80% of trials when paired with version (f) (which differs from any of those studied). When given pairs such as (d) (a studied instance) and (f) (a new distractor), they will opt for (d) on about 70% of trials. (cf. Bruce et al., in press b). (Mac-a-Mug Pro is a trademark licensed to Shaherazam, P.O. Box 26731, Milwaukee, WI 53226 U.S.A.)

the prototype plus an unseen distractor which was a further slightly different variant on the same basic configuration. This preference was maintained *even when the prototype had itself not been studied*. Further experiments showed that subjects could also discriminate an actually studied "extreme" instance (see Fig. 3) from a distractor that was slightly different from any of those studied, though performance was not as high as it was when the test pairs included the prototype. These experiments seem to show that subjects can learn the "prototypical" second-order configuration characterising a particular individual face from a very few instances, while still retaining some sensitivity to the actual instances seen. Such findings are reminiscent of properties of certain kinds of instance-based memory models (e.g. McClelland & Rumelhart, 1985).

One interesting property of PDP models that must learn non-orthogonal patterns across shared units is that under certain circumstances noise in the learning trials actually *enhances* responses to prototypical patterns. It remains to be seen whether this is true of human face recognition (i.e. whether responses to the prototypical faces in the above experiments are actually better following exposure to variant instances compared with repeated exposure to the prototype itself), but the possibility is intriguing. We have spent many years assuming that face recognition is a "harder" task than recognition of other objects because (1) second-order configurations must be encoded and (2) they must be encoded from non-rigidly transforming instances. Perhaps the non-rigid transformations themselves *facilitate* the encoding of the second-order configural invariants that characterise each known face.

Further research will be needed to explore the theoretical consequences of this suggestion. At this point, the most we can say is that an approach that sees the properties of "face recognition units" as emerging from the "automatic" superposition of discrete instances of faces looks promising. One appeal of such models is that they could quite readily also account for the effects of repetition priming we described earlier, and they could accommodate distinctiveness effects *without* requiring that any explicit overall face prototype (i.e. average of all encountered faces) be constructed and stored. Such a view would also allow us to accommodate Tranel and Damasio's (1985) and de Haan et al.'s (1987b) findings of covert recognition effects for patients who had *only* encountered the faces involved since they sustained their brain injuries. Such findings favour the view that recognition units may be created more or less automatically, rather than as a result of an explicit decision to create a new unit.

On the other hand, however, there are arguments against the idea that face recognition units simply "emerge" from discrete encounters. First, Endo et al. (1984) have shown that a differential salience accrued more readily to the internal features of faces when subjects learned them using relatively "deep" processing strategies. It is not immediately clear how an instance-based model would account for this. Secondly, the "instance-based" model does not readily accommodate recent observations of a patient who appears unable to assimilate new "instances" of unfamiliar faces, while retaining this ability for familiar ones.

Ross (1980) drew attention to an interesting neuropsychological condition involving what he called loss of visual recent memory, in which the patient shows poor learning of new visual information but does not suffer from more general memory impairment. A detailed case study of someone with this problem, ELD, has been carried out by Hanley, Pearson and Young (1990). ELD was severely impaired on tests of unfamiliar face memory, and showed poor recognition of faces of people who had become famous since her illness in 1985. Her ability to recognise people familiar to her pre-1985 was entirely normal on formal testing, and she could also recognise post-1985 people from their names and perform normally on tests of verbal memory.

ELD's spontaneous complaints concerned her inability to learn new faces and problems in learning her way around in new environments. The latter complaint shows that her problems were not specific to faces. Further testing confirmed this view, and demonstrated a most interesting pattern to her performance.

The results of recognition memory tests involving familiar and unfamiliar objects and faces for ELD are summarised in Table 10 (data from Hanley et al., 1990). Two types of test were used. In one (which ITEM?) type of test, ELD was shown a series of 20 objects or 20 faces to remember, and then shown pairs of different objects or different faces and asked to choose which member of each pair had previously been presented. In the second (which VIEW?) type of test, ELD was again shown a series of 20 objects or 20 faces, but was then asked to choose the particular *view* (i.e. photograph) she had seen earlier from pairs of photographs showing different views of each of the faces or objects. As Table 10 shows, her performance was poor for unfamiliar objects and faces, but unimpaired to familiar objects and faces. This pattern held across both ITEM and VIEW tests.

These results demonstrate that ELD's problem is not really one of visual memory *per se*; her visual memory is quite normal when tested with familiar stimuli, even to the point where she can remember exactly which photographs of a familiar object or person she was previously shown. Instead, it is evident that she can only learn new visual information so long as it relates to a familiar visual form; it is the learning of new visual forms that is impaired. This pattern is difficult to accommodate readily within *either* the instance-based *or* the original account of face recognition units (e.g. Hay & Young, 1982). On the instance-based account, it is not clear

TABLE 10
Performances of ELD and Control Subjects on Recognition Memory Tests for Familiar
and Unfamiliar Objects and Faces[a]

	Familiar		Unfamiliar	
	Objects (max = 20)	Faces (max = 20)	Objects (max = 20)	Faces (max = 20)
Tested for which ITEM seen?				
ELD	19.0	19.0	17.0	16.0
Controls				
Mean	19.5	19.7	19.9	19.1
S.D.	0.67	0.64	0.30	1.45
Tested for which VIEW seen?				
ELD	20.0	16.0	13.0	10.0
Controls				
Mean	17.0	16.3	17.2	16.7
S.D.	2.30	2.57	1.72	1.55

[a]Data from Hanley et al. (1990).

what kind of mechanism would lead to the retention of instances only when some certain critical mass of instances were already stored. The original conception of face recognition units as holding some set of "abstract" visual structural descriptions must appeal to a separate visual or pictorial memory system – e.g. the "pictorial codes" of Bruce (1982) and Bruce and Young (1986) – to explain the retention of instances. Thus both accounts need to postulate additional mechanisms to account for ELD's deficits.

CONCLUDING REMARKS

In this paper, we have discussed both macrostructural and microstructural issues that have arisen from recent attempts to produce functional models of face recognition. Experimental and neuropsychological research in the areas we have discussed is ongoing, supplemented by attempts at simulation of some of these processes, and we anticipate that increasingly refined models will result from these efforts.

We have here concentrated mainly on recognition and semantic identification of faces, rather than on *name retrieval* which forms a distinct and final stage in the process of person identification. Names are difficult to retrieve not just because their phonology must be accessed (phonology must also be accessed when we describe a person's occupation). When response demands are equated so that subjects must decide whether or not two faces are both politicians (semantic condition) or both called John (naming condition), and when the faces are drawn from a small set of repeated items whose visual appearance cannot be used as a clue to semantic category, semantic decisions to faces are made more quickly than name decisions (Young, A. Ellis & Flude, 1988b).

Converging evidence for a distinction between names and semantic information has been obtained in a study of naming difficulties in an anomic aphasic (Flude, A. Ellis & Kay, 1989), and the specificity of processing the names of familiar individuals is further highlighted by a recent case of anomia confined to facial expressions *without* any accompanying difficulties in familiar name retrieval (Rapcsak, Kaszniak & Rubens, 1989). Hence the reason why names are difficult to retrieve is not straightforward (Johnston & Bruce, 1990, and McWeeny, Young, Hay & A. Ellis, 1987, present studies which refute common suggestions about why names are difficult), and the relationship between semantic information and proper names is currently a topic of research in its own right.

It may be partly because of our difficulties in retrieving names that so many story-book characters are given names which are in some way linked to their appearance, to ease the burden on children's memories. Little Red Riding Hood and Goldilocks are both examples of this tendency, though the clearest example is seen in the names given to the Seven Dwarfs (Sleepy, Grumpy, etc.). Unfortunately, in the real world, we cannot tell someone's name from their appearance, and we can only guess at their occupation. The arbitrary relationship between a face's appearance and a person's identity, combined with the large number of faces we encounter in today's societies, make our usual facility at face recognition a remarkable achievement.

Manuscript received September 1989
Revised manuscript received June 1990

REFERENCES

Assal, G. (1969). Régression des troubles de la reconnaissance des physionomies et de la mémoire topographique chez un malade opéré d'un hématome intracérébral pariéto-temporal droite. *Revue Neurologique, 121*, 184–185.

Bauer, R. M. (1982). Visual hypoemotionality as a symptom of visual–limbic disconnection in man. *Archives of Neurology, 39*, 702–708.

Bauer, R. M. (1984). Autonomic recognition of names and faces in prosopagnosia: A neuropsychological application of the guilty knowledge test. *Neuropsychologia, 22*, 457–469.

Bauer, R. M. (1986). The cognitive psychophysiology of prosopagnosia. In H. D. Ellis, M. A. Jeeves, F. Newcombe & A. Young (Eds), *Aspects of face processing*, pp. 253–267. Dordrecht: Martinus Nijhoff.

Benton, A. L. (1980). The neuropsychology of facial recognition. *American Psychologist, 35*, 176–186.

Benton, A. L. & van Allen, M. W. (1972). Prosopagnosia and facial discrimination. *Journal of the Neurological Sciences, 15*, 167–172.

Bornstein, B. (1963). Prosopagnosia. In L. Halpern (Ed.), *Problems of dynamic neurology*, pp. 283–318. Jerusalem: Hadassah Medical School.

Brennan, S. E. (1985). The caricature generator. *Leonardo, 18*, 170–178.

Brennen, T., Baguley, T., Bright, J. and Bruce, V. (1990). Resolving semantically induced tip-of-the-tongue states for proper nouns. *Memory and Cognition, 18*, 339–347.

Bruce, V. (1979). Searching for politicians: An information processing approach to face recognition. *Quarterly Journal of Experimental Psychology, 31*, 373–395.

Bruce, V. (1982). Changing faces: Visual and nonvisual coding processes in face recognition. *British Journal of Psychology, 73*, 105–116.

Bruce, V. (1983). Recognising faces. *Philosophical Transactions of the Royal Society of London, B302*, 423–436.

Bruce, V. (1986a). Influences of familiarity on the processing of faces. *Perception, 15*, 387–397.

Bruce, V. (1986b). Recognising familiar faces. In H. D. Ellis, M. A. Jeeves, F. Newcombe & A. Young (Eds), *Aspects of face processing*, pp. 107–117. Dordrecht: Martinus Nijhoff.

Bruce, V. (1988). *Recognising faces*. London: Lawrence Erlbaum Associates Ltd.

Bruce, V. (1989). The structure of faces. In A. W. Young & H. D. Ellis (Eds), *Handbook of research on face processing*. Amsterdam: North Holland, 101–106.

Bruce, V. & Burton, M. (1989). Computer recognition of faces. In A. W. Young & H. D. Ellis (Eds), *Handbook of research on face processing*. Amsterdam: North Holland, 487–506.

Bruce, V., Burton, M. & Doyle, T. (in press a). Faces as surfaces. In V. Bruce & M. Burton (Eds), *Processing images of faces*. Norwood, N.J.: Ablex.

Bruce, V., Burton, M., Doyle, T. & Dench, N. (1989). Further experiments on the perception of growth in three dimensions. *Perception and Psychophysics, 46*, 528–536.

Bruce, V., Doyle, A., Dench, N. & Burton, M. (in press b). Remembering facial configurations. *Cognition*.

Bruce, V., Ellis, H., Gibling, F. & Young, A. (1987). Parallel processing of the sex and familiarity of faces. *Canadian Journal of Psychology, 41*, 510–520.

Bruce, V., Hanna, E., Dench, N., Healey, P. & Burton, M. (submitted a). Further evidence for the importance of "line" and "mass" in drawings of faces.

Bruce, V., Healey, P., Burton, M., Doyle, T., Coombes, A. & Linney, A. (submitted b). Recognising facial surfaces.

Bruce, V. & Valentine, T. (1985). Identity priming in the recognition of familiar faces. *British Journal of Psychology, 76*, 363–383.

Bruce, V. & Valentine, T. (1986). Semantic priming of familiar faces. *Quarterly Journal of Experimental Psychology, 38A*, 125–150.

Bruce, V. & Young, A. (1986). Understanding face recognition. *British Journal of Psychology, 77*, 305–327.

Brunas, J., Young, A. W. & Ellis, A. W. (1990). Repetition priming from incomplete faces: Evidence for part to whole completion. *British Journal of Psychology, 81*, 43–56.

Bruyer, R. (1987). *Les mecanismes de reconnaissance des visages*. Grenoble: Presses Universitaires de Grenoble.

Bruyer, R., Laterre, C., Seron, X., Feyereisen, P., Strypstein, E., Pierrard, E. & Rectem, D. (1983). A case of prosopagnosia with some preserved covert remembrance of familiar faces. *Brain and Cognition, 2*, 257–284.

Burton, A. M., Bruce, V. & Johnston, R. A. (1990). Understanding face recognition with an interactive activation model. *British Journal of Psychology, 81*, 361–380.

Campbell, R., Landis, T. & Regard, M. (1986). Face recognition and lipreading: A neurological dissociation. *Brain, 109*, 509–521.

Carr, T. H., McCauley, C., Sperber, R. D. & Parmelee, C. M. (1982). Words, pictures, and priming: On semantic activation, conscious identification, and the automaticity of information processing. *Journal of Experimental Psychology: Human Perception and Performance*, 8, 757–777.

Clarke, R. & Morton, J. (1983). Cross modality facilitation in tachistoscopic word recognition. *Quarterly Journal of Experimental Psychology*, *35A*, 79–96.

Courbon, P. & Fail, G. (1927). Syndrome d'illusion de Frégoli et schizophrénie. *Bulletin de la Société Clinique de Médicine Mentale*, *15*, 121–125.

Cowey, A. (1985). Aspects of cortical organization related to selected attention and selective impairments of visual perception: A tutorial review. In M. I. Posner & O. S. M. Marin (Eds), *Attention and performance*, *XI*, pp. 41–62. Hillsdale, N.J.: Lawrence Erlbaum Associates Inc.

Damasio, A. R., Damasio, H. & van Hoesen, G. W. (1982). Prosopagnosia: Anatomic basis and behavioral mechanisms. *Neurology*, 32, 331–341.

Dannenbring, G. L. & Briand, K. (1982). Semantic priming and the word repetition effect in a lexical decision task. *Canadian Journal of Psychology*, *36*, 435–444.

Davies, G. M. & Milne, A. (1982). Recognising faces in and out of context. *Current Psychological Research*, 2, 235–246.

de Haan, E. H. F. & Hay, D. C. (1986). The matching of famous and unknown faces, given either the internal or the external features: A study on patients with unilateral brain lesions. In H. D. Ellis, M. A. Jeeves, F. Newcombe & A. Young (Eds), *Aspects of face processing*, pp. 302–309. Dordrecht: Martinus Nijhoff.

de Haan, E. H. F., Young, A. & Newcombe, F. (1987a). Faces interfere with name classification in a prosopagnosic patient. *Cortex*, *23*, 309–316.

de Haan, E. H. F., Young, A. & Newcombe, F. (1987b). Face recognition without awareness. *Cognitive Neuropsychology*, 4, 385–415.

de Pauw, K. W., Szulecka, T. K. & Poltock, T. L. (1987). Frégoli syndrome after cerebral infarction. *Journal of Nervous and Mental Disease*, *175*, 433–438.

de Renzi, E. (1986a). Prosopagnosia in two patients with CT scan evidence of damage confined to the right hemisphere. *Neuropsychologia*, *24*, 385–389.

de Renzi, E. (1986b). Current issues in prosopagnosia. In H. D. Ellis, M. A. Jeeves, F. Newcombe & A. Young (Eds), *Aspects of face processing*, pp. 243–252. Dordrecht: Martinus Nijhoff.

Diamond, R. & Carey, S. (1986). Why faces are and are not special: An effect of expertise. *Journal of Experimental Psychology: General*, *115*, 107–117.

Ellis, A. W. & Young, A. W. (1988). *Human cognitive neuropsychology*. London: Lawrence Erlbaum Associates Ltd.

Ellis, A. W., Young, A. W. & Critchley, E. M. R. (1989). Loss of memory for people following temporal lobe damage. *Brain*, *112*, 1469–1483.

Ellis, A. W., Young, A. W. & Flude, B. M. (1990). Repetition priming and face processing: Priming occurs within the system that responds to the identity of a face. *Quarterly Journal of Experimental Psychology*, *39A*, 193–210.

Ellis, A. W., Young, A. W., Flude, B. M. & Hay, D. C. (1987a). Repetition priming of face recognition. *Quarterly Journal of Experimental Psychology*, *39A*, 193–210.

Ellis, A. W., Young, A. W. & Hay, D. C. (1987b). Modelling the recognition of faces and words. In P. E. Morris (Ed.), *Modelling cognition*, pp. 269–297. Chichester: John Wiley.

Ellis, H. D. (1975). Recognizing faces. *British Journal of Psychology*, *66*, 409–426.

Ellis, H. D. (1986). Processes underlying face recognition. In R. Bruyer (Ed.), *The neuropsychology of face perception and facial expression*, pp. 1–27. Hillsdale, N.J.: Lawrence Erlbaum Associates Inc.

Ellis, H. D., Shepherd, J. W. & Davies, G. M. (1979). Identification of familiar and unfamiliar faces from internal and external features: Some implications for theories of face recognition. *Perception, 8,* 431–439.

Ellis, H. D. & Young, A. W. (1989). Are faces special? In A. W. Young & H. D. Ellis (Eds), *Handbook of research on face processing,* pp. 1–26. Amsterdam: North Holland.

Ellis, H. D. & Young, A. W. (1990). Accounting for delusional misidentification. *British Journal of Psychiatry, 157,* 239–248.

Endo, M., Takahashi, K. & Maruyama, K. (1984). Effects of observer's attitude on the familiarity of faces: Using the difference in cue value between central and peripheral facial elements as an index of familiarity. *Tohoku Psychologica Folia, 43,* 23–34.

Enlow, D. H. (1982). *Handbook of facial growth.* Philadelphia: W. B. Saunders.

Field, T. M., Woodson, R., Greenberg, R. & Cohen, D. (1982). Discrimination and imitation of facial expressions by neonates. *Science, 218,* 179–181.

Fiorentini, A., Maffei, L. & Sandini, G. (1983). The role of high spatial frequencies in face perception. *Perception, 12,* 195–201.

Flin, R. & Dziurawiec, S. (1989). Developmental factors in face processing. In A. W. Young & H. D. Ellis (Eds), *Handbook of research on face processing,* pp. 335–378. Amsterdam: North Holland.

Flude, B., Ellis, A. & Kay, J. (1989). Face processing and name retrieval in an anomic aphasic. *Brain and Cognition, 11,* 60–72.

Fodor, J. (1983). *The modularity of mind.* Cambridge, Mass.: MIT Press.

Galton, F. (1883). *Inquiries into human faculty and its development.* London: Macmillan.

Goren, C. G., Sarty, M. & Wu, P. Y. K. (1975). Visual following and pattern discrimination of face-like stimuli by newborn infants. *Pediatrics, 56,* 544–549.

Haig, N. D. (1986). Investigating face recognition with an image-processing computer. In H. D. Ellis, M. A. Jeeves, F. Newcombe & A. Young (Eds), *Aspects of face processing,* pp. 410–426. Dordrecht: Martinus Nijhoff.

Hanley, J. R. & Cowell, E. S. (1988). The effects of different types of retrieval cue on the recall of names of famous faces. *Memory and Cognition, 16,* 545–555.

Hanley, J. R., Pearson, N. & Young, A. W. (1990). Impaired memory for new visual forms. *Brain, 113,* 1131–1148.

Hanley, J. R., Young, A. W. & Pearson, N. (1989). Defective recognition of familiar people. *Cognitive Neuropsychology, 6,* 179–210.

Harmon, L. D. (1973). The recognition of faces. *Scientific American, 229,* 71–82.

Hasselmo, M. (1987). *The representation and storage of visual information in the temporal lobe.* D.Phil. thesis, Oxford University.

Hay, D. C. & Young, A. W. (1982). The human face. In A. W. Ellis (Ed.), *Normality and pathology in cognitive functions,* pp. 173–202. London: Academic Press.

Hay, D. C., Young, A. W. & Ellis, A. W. (in press). Routes through the face recognition system. *Quarterly Journal of Experimental Psychology.*

Hécaen, H. (1981). The neuropsychology of face recognition. In G. Davies, H. Ellis & J. Shepherd (Eds), *Perceiving and remembering faces,* pp. 39–54. London: Academic Press.

Hécaen, H. & Angelergues, R. (1962). Agnosia for faces (prosopagnosia). *Archives of Neurology, 7,* 92–100.

Humphreys, G. W. & Bruce, V. (1989). *Visual cognition: Computational, experimental and neuropsychological perspectives.* London: Lawrence Erlbaum Associates Ltd.

Jacoby, L. L. (1983a). Perceptual enhancement: Persistent effects of an experience. *Journal of Experimental Psychology: Learning, Memory and Cognition, 9,* 21–38.

Jacoby, L. L. (1983b). Remembering the data: Analyzing interactive processes in reading. *Journal of Verbal Learning and Verbal Behavior, 22,* 485–508.

Johnston, R. A. & Bruce, V. (1990). Lost properties? Retrieval differences between name codes and semantic codes for familiar people. *Psychological Research, 52,* 62–67.

Kohonen, T., Lehtio, P. & Oja, E. (1981). Storage and processing of information in distributed associative memory systems. In G. Hinton & J. A. Anderson (Eds), *Parallel models of associative memory*, pp. 105–143. Hillsdale, N.J.: Lawrence Erlbaum Associates Inc.

Kolers, P. A. (1975). Memorial consequences of automatized encoding. *Journal of Experimental Psychology: Human Learning and Memory*, *1*, 689–701.

Kolers, P. A. (1976). Pattern analyzing memory. *Science*, *191*, 1280–1281.

Kurucz, J. & Feldmar, G. (1979). Prosopo-affective agnosia as a symptom of cerebral organic disease. *Journal of the American Geriatrics Society*, *27*, 225–230.

Kurucz, J., Feldmar, G. & Werner, W. (1979). Prosopo-affective agnosia associated with chronic organic brain syndrome. *Journal of the American Geriatrics Society*, *27*, 91–95.

La Heij, W., van der Heijden, A. H. C. & Schreuder, R. (1985). Semantic priming and Stroop-like interference in word-naming tasks. *Journal of Experimental Psychology: Human Perception and Performance*, *11*, 62–80.

Landis, T., Cummings, J. L., Christen, L., Bogen, J. E. & Imhof, H.-G. (1986). Are unilateral right posterior cerebral lesions sufficient to cause prosopagnosia? Clinical and radiological findings in six additional patients. *Cortex*, *22*, 243–252.

Lupker, S. J. (1984). Semantic priming without association: A second look. *Journal of Verbal Learning and Verbal Behavior*, *23*, 709–733.

Lupker, S. J. (1985). Context effects in word and picture recognition: A reevaluation of structural models. In A. W. Ellis (Ed.), *Progress in the psychology of language*, Vol. 1, pp. 109–142. London: Lawrence Erlbaum Associates Ltd.

McCauley, C., Parmelee, C., Sperber, R. & Carr, T. (1980). Early extraction of meaning from pictures and its relation to conscious identification. *Journal of Experimental Psychology: Human Perception and Performance*, *6*, 265–276.

McClelland, J. L. & Rumelhart, D. E. (1981). An interactive activation model of context effects in letter perception: Part 1. An account of basic findings. *Psychological Review*, *88*, 375–407.

McClelland, J. L. & Rumelhart, D. E. (1985). Distributed memory and the representation of general and specific information. *Journal of Experimental Psychology: General*, *114*, 159–188.

McGurk, H. & MacDonald, J. (1976). Hearing lips and seeing voices. *Nature*, *264*, 746–748.

McLeod, P. & Posner, M. I. (1984). Privileged loops from percept to act. In H. Bouma & D. G. Bouwhuis (Eds), *Attention and performance*, *X*, pp. 55–66. Hillsdale, N.J.: Lawrence Erlbaum Associates Inc.

McNeill, J. E. & Warrington, E. K. (in press). Prosopagnosia – a reclassification. *Quarterly Journal of Experimental Psychology*.

McWeeny, K. H., Young, A. W., Hay, D. C. & Ellis, A. W. (1987). Putting names to faces. *British Journal of Psychology*, *78*, 143–151.

Malone, D. R., Morris, H. H., Kay, M. C. & Levin, H. S. (1982). Prosopagnosia: A double dissociation between the recognition of familiar and unfamiliar faces. *Journal of Neurology, Neurosurgery, and Psychiatry*, *45*, 820–822.

Marr, D. (1982). *Vision*. San Francisco, Calif.: Freeman.

Meadows, J. C. (1974). The anatomical basis of prosopagnosia. *Journal of Neurology, Neurosurgery, and Psychiatry*, *37*, 489–501.

Meltzoff, A. N. & Moore, M. K. (1977). Imitation of facial and manual gestures by human neonates. *Science*, *198*, 75–78.

Meltzoff, A. N. & Moore, M. K. (1983). Newborn infants imitate adult facial gestures. *Child Development*, *545*, 702–709.

Memon, A. & Bruce, V. (1985). Context effects in episodic studies of verbal and facial memory: A review. *Current Psychological Research and Reviews*, *4*, 349–369.

Millward, R. & O'Toole, A. (1986). Recognition memory transfer between spatial-frequency analysed faces. In H. D. Ellis, M. A. Jeeves, F. Newcombe & A. Young (Eds), *Aspects of face processing.* Dordrecht: Martinus Nijhoff, 34–44.

Morton, J. (1969). Interaction of information in word recognition. *Psychological Review, 76,* 165–178.

Morton, J. (1979). Facilitation in word recognition: Experiments causing change in the logogen model. In P. A. Kolers, M. Wrolstad & H. Bouma (Eds), *Processing of visible language,* Vol. 1, pp. 259–268. New York: Plenum Press.

Morton, J. (1984). Naming. In S. Newman & R. Epstein (Eds), *Dysphasia,* pp. 217–230. Edinburgh: Churchill Livingstone.

Neely, J. H. (1976). Semantic priming and retrieval from lexical memory: Evidence for facilitatory and inhibitory processes. *Memory and Cognition, 4,* 648–654.

Neely, J. H. (1977). Semantic priming and retrieval from lexical memory: Roles of inhibitionless spreading activation and limited-capacity attention. *Journal of Experimental Psychology: General, 106,* 226–254.

Newcombe, F. (1979). The processing of visual information in prosopagnosia and acquired dyslexia: Functional versus physiological interpretation. In D. J. Oborne, M. M. Gruneberg & J. R. Eiser (Eds), *Research in psychology and medicine,* Vol. 1, pp. 315–322. London: Academic Press.

Newcombe, F., de Haan, E. H. F., Ross, J. & Young, A. W. (1989a). Face processing, laterality, and contrast sensitivity. *Neuropsychologia, 27,* 523–538.

Newcombe, F., Young, A. W. & de Haan, E. H. F. (1989b). Prosopagnosia and object agnosia without covert recognition. *Neuropsychologia, 27,* 179–191.

Pearson, D. E. & Robinson, J. A. (1985). Visual communication at very low data rates. *Proceedings of the IEEE, 73,* 795–812.

Perrett, D. I., Rolls, E. T. & Caan, W. (1982). Visual neurones responsive to faces in the monkey temporal cortex. *Experimental Brain Research, 47,* 329–342.

Perrett, D. I., Smith, P. A. J., Potter, D. D., Mistlin, A. J., Head, A. S., Milner, A. D. & Jeeves, M. A. (1984). Neurones responsive to faces in the temporal cortex: Studies of functional organization, sensitivity to identity and relation to perception. *Human Neurobiology, 3,* 197–208.

Perrett, D. I., Smith, P. A. J., Potter, D. D., Mistlin, A. J., Head, A. S., Milner, A. D. & Jeeves, M. A. (1985). Visual cells in the temporal cortex sensitive to face view and gaze direction. *Proceedings of the Royal Society of London, B223,* 293–317.

Posner, M. I. & Snyder, C. R. R. (1975). Facilitation and inhibition in the processing of signals. In P. M. A. Rabbitt & S. Dornic (Eds), *Attention and performance, V,* pp. 669–682. London: Academic Press.

Rapcsak, S. Z., Kaszniak, A. W. & Rubens, A. B. (1989). Anomia for facial expressions: Evidence for a category specific visual–verbal disconnection syndrome. *Neuropsychologia, 27,* 1031–1041.

Ratcliff, G. & Newcombe, F. (1982). Object recognition: Some deductions from the clinical evidence. In A. W. Ellis (Ed.), *Normality and pathology in cognitive functions,* pp. 147–171. London: Academic Press.

Rhodes, G., Brennan, S. & Carey, S. (1987). Identification and ratings of caricatures: Implications for mental representations of faces. *Cognitive Psychology, 190,* 473–497.

Rizzo, M., Hurtig, R. & Damasio, A. R. (1987). The role of scanpaths in facial recognition and learning. *Annals of Neurology, 22,* 41–45.

Roberts, T. & Bruce, V. (1988). Feature saliency in judging the sex and familiarity of faces. *Perception, 17,* 475–481.

Rolls, E. T. (1984). Neurons in the cortex of the temporal lobe and in the amygdala of the monkey with responses selective for faces. *Human Neurobiology, 3,* 209–222.

Rolls, E. T. (in press). The processing of face information in the primate temporal lobe. In V. Bruce and M. Burton (Eds), *Processing Images of Faces*. Norwood, N.J.: Ablex.

Rolls, E. T. & Baylis, G. C. (1986). Size and contrast have only small effects on the responses to faces of neurons in the cortex of the superior temporal sulcus of the monkey. *Experimental Brain Research, 65*, 38–48.

Rolls, E. T., Baylis, G. C. & Leonard, C. M. (1985). Role of low and high spatial frequencies in the face-selective responses of neurons in the cortex in the superior temporal sulcus in the monkey. *Vision Research, 25*, 1021–1035.

Rosch, E. (1978). Principles of categorization. In E. Rosch & B. Lloyd (Eds), *Cognition and categorization*, pp. 27–48. Hillsdale, N.J.: Lawrence Erlbaum Associates Inc.

Rosch, E., Mervis, C. B., Gray, W. D., Johnson, D. M. & Boyes-Braem, P. (1976). Basic objects in natural categories. *Cognitive Psychology, 8*, 382–439.

Rosinski, R. R. (1977). Picture–word interference is semantically based. *Child Development, 48*, 643–647.

Rosinski, R. R., Golinkoff, R. M. & Kukish, K. S. (1975). Automatic semantic processing in a picture–word interference task. *Child Development, 46*, 247–253.

Ross, E. D. (1980). Sensory-specific and fractional disorders of recent memory in man: 1. Isolated loss of visual recent memory. *Archives of Neurology, 37*, 193–200.

Schacter, D. L. (1987). Implicit memory: History and current status. *Journal of Experimental Psychology: Learning, Memory and Cognition, 13*, 501–518.

Schacter, D. L., McAndrews, M. P. & Moscovitch, M. (1988). Access to consciousness: Dissociations between implicit and explicit knowledge in neuropsychological syndromes. In L. Weiskrantz (Ed.), *Thought without language*, pp. 242–278. Oxford: Oxford University Press.

Seidenberg, M. S. (1988). Cognitive neuropsychology and language: The state of the art. *Cognitive Neuropsychology, 5*, 403–426.

Sergent, J. (1984). An investigation into component and configural processes underlying face recognition. *British Journal of Psychology, 75*, 221–242.

Sergent, J. (1986). Microgenesis of face perception. In H. D. Ellis, M. A. Jeeves, F. Newcombe & A. Young (Eds), *Aspects of face processing*. Dordrecht: Martinus Nijhoff, 17–33.

Sergent, J. & Poncet, M. (1990). From covert to overt recognition of faces in a prosopagnosic patient. *Brain, 113*, 989–1004.

Sergent, J. & Villemure, J.-G. (1989). Prosopagnosia in a right hemispherectomised patient. *Brain, 112*, 975–995.

Shallice, T. (1988). *From neuropsychology to mental structure*. Cambridge: Cambridge University Press.

Shepherd, J. W., Davies, G. M. & Ellis, H. D. (1981). Studies of cue saliency. In G. Davies, H. D. Ellis & J. W. Shepherd (Eds), *Perceiving and remembering faces*. London: Academic Press.

Shuttleworth, E. C. Jr, Syring, V. & Allen, N. (1982). Further observations on the nature of prosopagnosia. *Brain and Cognition, 1*, 307–322.

Smith, M. C. & Magee, L. E. (1980). Tracing the time course of picture–word processing. *Journal of Experimental Psychology: General, 109*, 373–392.

Sperber, R. D., McCauley, C., Ragain, R. D. & Weil, C. M. (1979). Semantic priming effects on picture and word processing. *Memory and Cognition, 7*, 339–345.

Stonham, J. (1986). Practical face recognition and verification with WISARD. In H. D. Ellis, M. A. Jeeves, F. Newcombe & A. Young (Eds), *Aspects of face processing*. Dordrecht: Martinus Nijhoff, 426–441.

Stroop, J. R. (1935). Studies of interference in serial verbal reactions. *Journal of Experimental Psychology, 18*, 643–662.

Tieger, T. & Ganz, L. (1979). Recognition of faces in the presence of two-dimensional sinusoidal masks. *Perception and Psychophysics*, *26*, 163–167.

Tranel, D. & Damasio, A. R. (1985). Knowledge without awareness: An autonomic index of facial recognition by prosopagnosics. *Science*, *228*, 1453–1454.

Tranel, D., Damasio, A. R. & Damasio, H. (1988). Intact recognition of facial expression, gender, and age in patients with impaired recognition of face identity. *Neurology*, *38*, 690–696.

Tzavaras, A., Hécaen, H. & Le Bras, H. (1970). Le problème de la specificité du déficit de la reconnaissance du visage humain lors des lésions hémisphériques unilaterales. *Neuropsychologia*, *8*, 403–416.

Valentine, T. & Bruce, V. (1986a). Recognising familiar faces: The role of distinctiveness and familiarity. *Canadian Journal of Psychology*, *40*, 300–305.

Valentine, T. & Bruce, V. (1986b). The effects of distinctiveness in recognising and classifying faces. *Perception*, *15*, 525–536.

Vinter, A. (1985). La capacité d'imitation à la naissance: Elle existe, mais que signifie-t-elle? *Canadian Journal of Psychology*, *39*, 16–33.

Warren, C. & Morton, J. (1982). The effects of priming on picture recognition. *British Journal of Psychology*, *73*, 117–129.

Warrington, E. K. & James, M. (1967). An experimental investigation of facial recognition in patients with unilateral cerebral lesions. *Cortex*, *3*, 317–326.

Warrington, E. K. & Shallice, T. (1984). Category specific semantic impairments. *Brain*, *107*, 829–854.

Warrington, E. K. & Weiskrantz, L. (1968). New method of testing long-term retention with special reference to amnesic patients. *Nature*, *217*, 972–974.

Warrington, E. K. & Weiskrantz, L. (1970). Amnesia: Consolidation or retrieval? *Nature*, *228*, 628–630.

Winnick, W. A. & Daniel, S. A. (1970). Two kinds of response priming in tachistoscopic recognition. *Journal of Experimental Psychology*, *84*, 74–81.

Young, A. W. (1987a). Face recognition. In H. Beloff & A. M. Colman (Eds), *Psychology survey*, Vol. 6, pp. 28–54. Leicester: British Psychological Society.

Young, A. W. (1987b). Finding the mind's construction in the face. *Cognitive Neuropsychology*, *4*, 45–54.

Young, A. W. (1988). Functional organization of visual recognition. In L. Weiskrantz (Ed.), *Thought without language*, pp. 78–107. Oxford: Oxford University Press.

Young, A. W. & de Haan, E. H. F. (1988). Boundaries of covert recognition in prosopagnosia. *Cognitive Neuropsychology*, *5*, 317–336.

Young, A. W. & de Haan, E. H. F. (1990). Impairments of visual awareness. *Mind and Language*, *5*, 29–48.

Young, A. W., de Haan, E. H. F. & Newcombe, F. (1990). Unawareness of impaired face recognition. *Brain and Cognition*, *14*, 1–18.

Young, A. W. & Ellis, H. D. (1989a). Semantic processing. In A. W. Young & H. D. Ellis (Eds), *Handbook of research on face processing*, pp. 235–262. Amsterdam: North Holland.

Young, A. W. & Ellis, H. D. (1989b). Childhood prosopagnosia. *Brain and Cognition*, *9*, 16–47.

Young, A. W., Ellis, A. W. & Flude, B. M. (1988b). Accessing stored information about familiar people. *Psychological Research*, *50*, 111–115.

Young, A. W., Ellis, A. W., Flude, B. M., McWeeny, K. H. & Hay, D. C. (1986c). Face–name interference. *Journal of Experimental Psychology: Human Perception and Performance*, *12*, 466–475.

Young, A. W., Ellis, H. D., Szulecka, T. K. & de Pauw, K. W. (1990). Face processing impairments and delusional misidentification. *Behavioural Neurology*, *3*, 153–168.

Young, A. W., Flude, B. M., Ellis, A. W. & Hay, D. C. (1987). Interference with face naming. *Acta Psychologica*, *64*, 93–100.

Young, A. W., Hay, D. C. & Ellis, A. W. (1985a). The faces that launched a thousand slips: Everyday difficulties and errors in recognising people. *British Journal of Psychology*, *76*, 495–523.

Young, A. W., Hay, D. C., McWeeny, K. H., Flude, B. M. & Ellis, A. W. (1985b). Matching familiar and unfamiliar faces on internal and external features. *Perception*, *14*, 737–746.

Young, A. W., Hellawell, D. & de Haan, E. H. F. (1988a). Cross-domain semantic priming in normal subjects and a prosopagnosic patient. *Quarterly Journal of Experimental Psychology*, *40A*, 561–580.

Young, A. W., McWeeny, K. H., Ellis, A. W. & Hay, D. C. (1986b). Naming and categorising faces and written names. *Quarterly Journal of Experimental Psychology*, *38A*, 297–318.

Young, A. W., McWeeny, K. H., Hay, D. C. & Ellis, A. W. (1986a). Matching familiar and unfamiliar faces on identity and expression. *Psychological Research*, *48*, 63–68.

EUROPEAN JOURNAL OF COGNITIVE PSYCHOLOGY, 1991, *3* (1) 51–67

A Dissociation Between the Sense of Familiarity and Access to Semantic Information Concerning Familiar People

Edward H. F. de Haan

MRC Neuropsychology Unit, Radcliffe Infirmary, Oxford and Department of Psychology, University of Durham, Science Laboratories, Durham, U.K.

Andrew W. Young

Department of Psychology, University of Durham, Science Laboratories, Durham, U.K.

Freda Newcombe

MRC Neuropsychology Unit, Radcliffe Infirmary, Oxford, U.K.

Functional models that describe the underlying processes involved in normal face perception and recognition postulate separate stages for the classification of a face as familiar and for the retrieval of semantic information concerning the bearer of the face. On the assumption that these stages can be selectively affected by neurological disease, the models predict the existence of brain-injured patients who may remain able to decide whether a face is familiar or not, but who cannot access person information such as occupation, etc. This possibility is investigated in a patient, ME, with a pure amnesic syndrome including severe anterograde and retrograde long-term memory loss. Performance on tasks requiring the matching of unfamiliar faces and judging the familiarity of faces or names was normal for ME, but she was very poor at giving relevant semantic information to identify faces or names she found familiar. These findings support current neuropsychological *and* simulation models of face processing.

Requests for reprints should be addressed to Edward H. F. de Haan, Department of Psychology, University of Durham, Science Laboratories, Durham DH1 3LE, U.K.

This work was supported by MRC Grant G 8904698N to Edward de Haan and Andy Young. We would like to thank Andy Ellis, Rick Hanley and Alan Allport for their suggestions and helpful comments, and John Leddingham for referring this interesting patient.

INTRODUCTION

A number of different impairments in the perception and recognition of faces have been described in neurological patients. Most notably, deficits in the ability to match unfamiliar faces (e.g. Benton, 1980), to analyse facial expressions (e.g. Kurucz & Feldmar, 1979), to interpret lip movements for the understanding of speech (Campbell, Landis & Regard, 1986) and to recognise the identity of familiar people from the face (e.g. Damasio, Damasio & van Hoesen, 1982; de Renzi, 1986; Hécaen & Angelergues, 1962) have been well documented.

A recent development in this field of research has been the introduction of information processing models that attempt to incorporate the available clinical data and the findings from studies with normal subjects, in order to describe the functional processes that underlie face perception and recognition in the healthy brain (e.g. Bruce & Young, 1986; Ellis, 1986; Hay & Young, 1982). These models are broadly similar, and all identify a number of separate processing stages and the nature of their interconnections.

An important aspect of these models for the neuropsychological investigation of brain-injured patients is that they make clear predictions about the functional deficits which are theoretically possible, and thus provide a "checklist" of functions that can be selectively impaired or preserved after brain disease. The analysis of face perception disorders along the lines suggested by such models has two important advantages. First, it promotes a more theory-based exploration of neuropsychological breakdown and, secondly, it allows for direct testing of the hypotheses derived from the models.

The model put forward by Bruce and Young (1986) will be used here as a representative of the general class of contemporary models of face perception. When a face is seen, the structural encoding processes create two internal descriptions. The first one is thought to be analogous to the particular view of the face (including the information concerning the angle under which the face is seen and the facial expression), while the second one is of a more abstract nature. This latter description is included to allow for recognition of familiar faces via a limited set of stored representations. These stored representations are located in the face recognition units (FRUs). There is a recognition unit for each known face, and the unit will fire once the created representation surpasses a threshold for that face. When an FRU is activated, it will signal that the face is familiar and instigate the retrieval of semantic knowledge concerning the bearer of the face. This semantic information, however, is not part of the FRU-system, but accessed separately via person identity nodes (PINs). Complete recognition is achieved by accessing the name of the bearer of the face. The retrieval of names is again thought to take place in a separate stage.

A number of processors are proposed which deal with other aspects of facial information independent of the mechanisms involved in recognising familiar faces. Inferences concerning the emotional state of a person from the facial expression, the analysis of lip and tongue movements for the understanding of speech, and the extraction of information for the determination of age, sex, etc., are all performed in separate systems. Directed visual processing can also be engaged in tasks where photographs of *unfamiliar* faces have to be matched on identity. The evidence for this theoretical account of face perception has been reviewed by Bruce and Young (1986).

Using this theoretical framework, Flude, Ellis and Kay (1989) studied a patient with an impairment in the last stage of face recognition: retrieval of the name. Their patient, EST, showed a preserved ability to (1) match unfamiliar faces on identity, (2) distinguish between familiar and unfamiliar faces and names and (3) access semantic information from faces and written names of familiar people. However, EST was severely impaired in naming familiar faces. The finding of this selective functional deficit supports the idea that the mechanism dealing with name retrieval (which was severely impaired for EST) is separable from mechanisms responsible for the sense of familiarity and access to appropriate semantic information (which were both well preserved for EST).

Flude et al.'s (1989) investigation of EST, then, demonstrates that name retrieval can be impaired when access to identity-specific semantic information is preserved. However, functional models that describe the underlying processes involved in normal face perception and recognition also postulate separate stages for the classification of a face as familiar and for the retrieval of identity-specific semantic information concerning the bearer of the face. On the assumption that these stages can be selectively affected by neurological disease, the models predict the existence of brain-injured patients who may remain able to decide whether a face is familiar or not, but who cannot access information such as the person's occupation.

This possibility is investigated in the present report with a patient, ME, with a pure amnesic syndrome including severe loss of long-term memories. On formal testing, a substantial loss of knowledge of facts which ME previously must have known was evident. Our aim was to investigate the deficit predicted by Bruce and Young's (1986) model of a preserved ability to recognise faces as familiar in the presence of deficient retrieval of person-related knowledge.

CASE DESCRIPTION

ME is a right-handed female, born on 27 October 1913, with a history of a vasculitic disorder that was first diagnosed in August 1985. The illness presented with fever, rash and arthralgia. Laboratory investigations were unhelpful in pinpointing the cause, and she was treated with antibiotics.

Initially, she made a good recovery, but after a few months she had a relapse, this time with some pulmonary involvement. She was then treated with steroids as well as antibiotics. It was when she was first on steroids that mental problems became apparent. She became rather "retarded, withdrawn and forgetful, and overactive and sleepless at night". Subsequently, her neurological consultant reduced the steroid dosage (Prednisolone) and introduced an immunosuppressant (Cyclophosphamide).

A CT-scan was carried out in November 1986, which showed "mild cerebral atrophy in keeping with the patient's age; no focal infarcts or other abnormalities were demonstrated". ME was referred to the MRC Neuropsychology Unit at the Radcliffe Infirmary in September 1986.

NEUROPSYCHOLOGICAL ASSESSMENT

ME was assessed on standard neuropsychological measures on two separate occasions (September 1986 and October 1987), and whenever possible parallel versions of the same test were used. Comparisons between the two test sessions showed a very consistent performance, and therefore only the most recent test results will be presented here.

Her well-preserved cognitive abilities will be briefly summarised to highlight the highly selective nature of her amnesic deficit. There was no evidence of generalised intellectual deterioration. On the contrary, her performance on a standard I.Q. test (WAIS) was well above average (I.Q. 124), with no difference between the verbal (I.Q. 120) and the performance scales (I.Q. 125). On the Raven's Coloured Progressive Matrices, she scored above the 95th percentile for her age (34/36 correct). There was no evidence of impairments in visuoperceptual and visuospatial perception, and spatial construction. ME made an excellent copy of the Rey-Osterrieth complex figure (copy score: 36/36), and performed well on spatial tasks such as where the subject has to find her way out of a complex maze (Porteus Maze: mean time = 83.7 sec; mean errors = 1.25), where she has to perceive the three-dimensional structure in a two-dimensional line drawing (block counting: score = 29/35), or where a pattern has to be constructed from a picture with coloured blocks (WAIS block design: age scaled score = 15).

Short-term memory was normal both in the verbal [digit span (immediate repetition of digit sequences): forwards = 6; backwards = 6] and nonverbal domains [Corsi span (immediate repetition of spatial position sequences) = 7; Benton visual retention (immediate recognition of geometrical line drawings): score = 29/32]. In contrast, ME's long-term memory was severely impaired for both verbal [Wechsler Memory Scale II story recall: immediate recall, 3 and 4½; delayed (60 min) recall, 0 and 0] and nonverbal material [Rey-Osterrieth test: copy = 36/36; delayed (45 min) recall = 9/36].

Language comprehension (Token test: 0 errors) and production were entirely normal, and her writing was easily legible. Her comprehension of written prose was excellent (Chapman test: time, 148 sec, 0 errors), spelling was in the superior range (oral, 12/12; written, 11/12) and object-naming was within normal limits for her age (Oldfield-Wingfield object-naming test: 30/36). In contrast, ME's performance on verbal fluency tasks (where the subject is asked to produce as many words as possible in 1 min, either exemplars from a category or words beginning with the same letter) was relatively poor (objects, 22; animals, 11; "F", 10) for a person of her superior vocabulary and verbal I.Q.

There was evidence for a loss of general information which she must have possessed previously, despite the fact that ME has always been an avid daily reader of newspapers. For example, her answer to the question "Name three ex-Prime Ministers of Great Britain" (WAIS – Information) was "Baldwin", and when asked how long ago he was a Prime Minister she replied: "about six years". In fact, Baldwin was Prime Minister in the 1920s. ME therefore has a retrograde memory deficit in addition to her problems in retaining new material.

In summary, ME is a highly intelligent woman of 76, with well-preserved language and visuoperceptual abilities, who presents with a remarkably pure impairment of long-term memory. Her condition has remained stable over the last 2–3 years.

EXPERIMENTAL INVESTIGATIONS

The aim of the investigations was to explore the face processing abilities of ME, following the logic of the theoretical model proposed by Bruce and Young (1986). The working hypothesis was that given her pure mnestic deficit, there should be no difficulties in the earlier stages of face processing. With respect to face *recognition*, Bruce and Young's (1986) model postulates a bottom-up processing sequence until the level of perceptual categorisation (FRUs), which predicts that ME should be able to process physiognomic information up to the point of deciding whether a face is familiar or not.

Matching of Unfamiliar Faces on Identity

Three separate tests were used to assess ME's efficiency in perceiving and matching photographs of unfamiliar faces on identity. The first task involved a series of 32 trials in which two photographs were presented sequentially for 4 sec each, with an interstimulus interval of 1 sec. In half of

TABLE 1
Unfamiliar Face Matching[a]

| | Identical Views | | Different Views | |
	"Same"	"Different"	"Same"	"Different"
ME	0.0	0.0	1.0	1.0
Controls				
Mean	0.18	0.63	2.30	1.23
S.D.	0.45	1.25	1.44	1.37

[a]Error scores for the "same" and "different" conditions in tasks requiring matching of identical views or different views for ME and 40 control subjects from the same age range.

the trials, the two photographs were of different people ("different" condition), while in the other half the identical photograph of a face was repeated ("same" condition). ME was instructed to make a "same" *vs* "different" decision, and the task began with eight practice trials.

In terms of Bruce and Young's (1986) model, this task taps the earliest level of structural encoding: the construction of a view-dependent description, and may also require some relatively simple directed visual processing. It is unclear whether the task concerns a specific *face* processing ability, as the use of identical photographs for the "same" pairs allows the subject to treat the stimuli as visual patterns instead of as faces *per se*. A normal performance does indicate, however, that the basic visuoperceptual processes needed to construct an internal image of a seen face are intact.

The second task followed the same procedure as the first one, apart from the manipulation that two different views (either in orientation or in expression) of the same unfamiliar face were used in the "same" condition. This means that a purely pictorial match (Hay & Young, 1982) would be insufficient for accurate performance; the task demands the construction of a more abstract representation of the face, and directed visual processing.

The results of these two tasks are presented in Table 1, together with control data from 40 normal male subjects in the same age range as ME. The control data were gathered for a different study which only involved male subjects, but in the absence of evidence for a substantial sex difference on this kind of task it appears appropriate to use these data here. It is clear from the results that ME had no difficulty with either task.

ME was also given the Benton Facial Recognition test (Benton, van Allen, Hamsher & Levin, 1978) during two separate test sessions. This is a well-standardised simultaneous matching task, using unfamiliar faces and a multiple-choice format. In the first six trials, the identical view to the target face has to be identified among five foils. The remaining 18 items require the subject to select three out of six photographs as being the same person as shown on the target photograph. These photographs differ from the target one in either orientation or in lighting conditions. ME's score was 44 out of 54 on both occasions (1986 and 1987), which is well within the normal range. In addition, there was no indication of the use of idiosyncratic strategies, and the speed with which she completed the test was entirely normal for her age (mean response time per trial: 28.2 sec).

Taken together, the results of these three face matching tasks provide strong evidence for the claim that ME's structural encoding and directed visual processing abilities function normally.

Faces and Names Line-ups

The faces line-up task consists of 60 photographs of faces, presented one at a time, with unlimited exposure duration. The faces were selected from an original item pool of 190 face photographs on the basis of the performance of 12 normal subjects for rating the face's familiarity, remembering the person's occupation and recalling the person's name. The 60 faces are divided into three groups: 20 faces each of high and low familiarity, and 20 unfamiliar faces. In addition, 14 faces from the original pool were used as practice trials. Each face was presented individually for the subject to give three different responses:

1. To rate the familiarity of the face on a 7-point scale (ranging from unknown to very familiar).
2. When the face was rated as familiar, the subject was asked to give the occupation of the bearer of the face (or any other information that would uniquely identify the person).
3. When the face was rated as familiar, the subject was asked to name the bearer of the face.

The faces line-up task was designed to assess the efficiency of the three stages of the recognition process according to Bruce and Young's (1986) model: the sense of familiarity (item 1), access to identity-specific semantic information (item 2) and name retrieval (item 3). A parallel version that employed written names as stimuli was also given to ME on a separate occasion, in order to determine whether possible problems revealed by the faces line-up were restricted to the face recognition system, or whether they reflected a more central impairment. The names used for the 40 familiar items in this names line-up were those of the celebrities included in the faces line-up task, the 20 unfamiliar names were selected from those of obscure actors, local politicians from a different part of the country, etc.

The procedure was identical to the faces line-up task apart from the "name-question" (item 3 above), which was for obvious reasons omitted.

The results of the faces and names line-ups are summarised in Table 2. ME's familiarity ratings for both faces and names of high and low familiarity compared favourably with those of the control subjects. Hence, it can be concluded that she does not have any problems at the level of the FRUs, or at the comparable stage in name recognition. The only way in which ME's familiarity ratings were in any sense abnormal was that she tended to rate some of the unfamiliar names as being of low familiarity, rather than completely unfamiliar. However, it is clear from Table 2 that she still rated these as being much less familiar than names from the low familiarity group of stimuli.

Despite her preserved ability to decide how familiar a person is, ME was extremely poor at identifying the faces or the names by means of semantic information. Both for the high and the low familiarity items she scored far below a cut-off point of the control mean minus 2 standard deviations. It is perhaps useful to mention the difference between the confident way in which she would decide whether a face was familiar or not and the very vague and hesitant manner in which she tried to give some semantic

TABLE 2
Faces and Names Line-up Tasks[a]

	Faces Line-up			Names Line-up		
	ME	Controls		ME	Controls	
		Mean	S.D.		Mean	S.D.
Ratings						
High familiarity	5.7	5.98	0.51	6.2	6.27	0.63
Low familiarity	3.3	4.18	1.02	5.6	5.92	0.92
Unfamiliar	1.5	1.36	0.45	1.6	1.10	0.10
Occupation						
High familiarity	7.0	18.86	1.15	8.0	19.66	0.84
Low familiarity	2.0	13.07	4.54	5.0	19.16	1.14
Name						
High familiarity	7.0	16.25	2.81			
Low familiarity	1.0	9.39	4.44			

[a]The rating score is the mean rating on a 7-point scale (1 = unknown; 7 = very familiar). The occupation and name scores are number correct out of 20 trials. The control data for the names line-up have been taken from Hanley et al. (1989).

information. Only rarely was she able to give anything more than a broad occupational category, such as "politician". The same observation of poor and hesitant performance at providing semantic information was made during the names line-up, emphasising the point that the deficit is located in a mechanism common to both face and name recognition.

Finally, on the faces line-up, ME's performance on the "name-question" (item 3) was, on first impression, also very poor. However, she was able to name nearly all of the faces for which she had been able to give some semantic information. Because all current theoretical models maintain that names are accessed from faces via identity-specific semantic information, there is thus no evidence for a separate name retrieval problem, and ME's deficit in face recognition appears to be confined to the retrieval of identity-specific semantic information.

Deciding Whether Faces (and Names) are Familiar

One of the important features of Bruce and Young's (1986) model is that the categorisation of a face as familiar is set apart from the retrieval of semantic knowledge concerning the bearer of the face. Although the processes necessary for familiar name recognition have not explicitly been described in the model, a similar sequence of stages as for face recognition is suggested up to the point of "name recognition units" (Bruce & Young, 1986; Young & de Haan, 1988). The semantic knowledge store is thought to be common to both face and name recognition (and presumably to all other forms of person recognition).

In the present context, this implies that ME should not have any problem in deciding whether or not a face or a name is familiar, because this does not involve retrieval of semantic knowledge. This hypothesis was confirmed by the line-up tasks, but as a more strict test timed familiarity decision tasks were also employed. The stimuli consisted of 32 photographs of faces (16 familiar and 16 unfamiliar) in one block of trials, and 32 written names (16 familiar and 16 unfamiliar) in a second block of trials. The stimuli were presented on back-projected slides. Each face or name appeared on the screen for 4 sec, and ME was instructed to decide as quickly and as accurately as possible whether the face or name was familiar or not. For a more detailed description of this task, see Newcombe, de Haan, Ross and Young (1989).

ME made two errors in the face familiarity decision condition and one in the name familiarity decision condition (all three false negatives), which is an average performance compared to normal subjects. The mean reaction times of the correct responses in the four experimental conditions for ME and 28 male control subjects are given in Table 3. ME was entirely normal in her speed at deciding whether faces and names are familiar or not.

TABLE 3
Familiarity Decision for Faces and Names[a]

	Faces		Names	
	Familiar	Unfamiliar	Familiar	Unfamiliar
ME	1279	1252	1102	1234
Controls				
Mean	1169	1323	1186	1439
S.D.	193	340	213	299

[a]Mean reaction times (msec) of the correct responses for ME and 28 control subjects.

Matching Faces and Names of Famous People

The previous experiments have clearly demonstrated that ME could extract a sense of familiarity from faces and names of familiar people, but she was very poor at retrieving semantic information. It now becomes intriguing whether her preserved abilities would allow her to match the correct name to a familiar face. That is, will the information she can extract from a name and a face input be enough to decide whether the name and the face belong to the same person, despite the absence of semantic information? This question has important theoretical implications, because if ME can do this, then it must be concluded that she can process face and name information to a level which is common to both recognition systems.

This experiment commenced with a screening task to select items which were familiar to ME, both from the face and the name, but for which she was unable to produce any autobiographical facts either from the name or the face. The initial item pool consisted of 62 photographs of faces of famous people. These were presented to ME individually, and she was asked whether the face looked familiar, and if so to identify the person by giving autobiographical information (e.g. occupation). Of the 62 items, two were classified as unfamiliar, for 11 she was able to produce correct albeit meagre semantic information, and for 14 she gave very vague information in the correct semantic field. The application of a strict selection criterion, so that only those faces for which ME produced no or incorrect semantic information were available for the main task, yielded 35 remaining items. Subsequently, the names of these celebrities were presented to her, using the same procedure as with the faces. None of the names were unfamiliar to her, and she produced correct semantic information to five names. In addition, she gave very vague descriptions which could perhaps indicate a degree of semantic knowledge to four of the names. Using, again, a strict selection criterion, we were left with 26 items for the main task.

For each face ME was given an array of three orally stated names: the correct name, an incorrect name of a celebrity from the same occupational category, and an incorrect unrelated name. ME was asked to select the name of the person whose face was shown in the photograph, and to guess if she was unsure. She was very accurate on this task (23/26 correct). Of the three errors, one was a semantically related foil, and the other two were unrelated alternatives.

Thus, ME's preserved face and name recognition abilities do allow her to match on *identity* the face and the name of a familiar person whose face and name do not elicit any overt semantic knowledge regarding that person. Two important theoretical conclusions can be drawn from this finding. First, in contrast to the hypothesis put forward by Damasio et al. (1982), the experience of a sense of familiarity is independent of accessing semantic information. Secondly, the functional locus of ME's deficit must lie after the point where the face and the name recognition systems converge.

Analysis of Facial Expressions

An independent route is postulated by Bruce and Young (1986) for the processes involved in expression analysis, which implies that this function can be selectively affected. Two different tasks (a matching and a labelling task) were employed to investigate this possibility for ME, both using faces from Ekman and Friesen's (1975) series as stimuli.

The first task involved a simultaneous matching test, in which a photograph of the target face displaying one of six possible emotions (anger, sadness, happines, disgust, surprise, fear) had to be matched against four alternatives (another view of the target emotion, and three distractors selected from the remaining possibilities). All five photographs (target + alternatives) were of faces of five different people, and mounted in a vertical arrangement on a sheet of paper. ME was instructed to point to the face which showed the same expression as the target face, and the task began with four practice trials, followed by 18 experimental trials (three using each of the six emotions as target).

In the second task, ME was shown a photograph of a face displaying one of the six possible emotional expressions (anger, sadness, happiness, disgust, surprise, fear). The six emotion labels were printed below the photograph in a vertical alignment, with the order of the labels randomised across trials. ME was asked to choose the emotion that best described the facial expression. There were 6 practice trials and 24 experimental trials (four for each of the six emotions).

TABLE 4
Matching and Labelling of Facial Expressions[a]

	Matching		Labelling	
	Score	Mean Time	Score	Mean Time
ME	13.0	9.7	17.0	4.6
Controls				
Mean	16.2	5.6	21.1	3.7
S.D.	1.7	2.0	1.7	1.3

[a]Data for ME and 34 control subjects. Times are given in seconds, and the scores are number correct out of 18 (matching) and 24 (labelling) trials.

The results of the facial expression tasks are presented in Table 4, together with control data from 34 healthy male subjects from the same age range as ME. Unexpectedly, she performed poorly. On the expression matching task, her accuracy score was almost two standard deviations below the control mean, and her responses were made slowly. On the labelling task, her accuracy score was more than two standard deviations below the control mean. Despite her normal ability to match faces on identity, which suggests that she can construct an adequate internal representation of a seen face, ME clearly has problems in extracting information concerning the emotional tone of facial expressions.

DISCUSSION

ME could accurately determine if two photographs of unfamiliar faces were of the same person or not, irrespective of whether two identical or two different photographs of the same person were used for the "same person" match. This suggests a normal ability to construct an internal representation of a seen face, and in terms of Bruce and Young's (1986) model implies adequate structural encoding and directed visual processing abilities. Proficient visuoperceptual abilities are also indicated by her normal performance on reading, object recognition and visuospatial tasks.

When presented with a series of familiar and unfamiliar faces (or written names), ME was fast and accurate in deciding which ones were known to her. Moreover, her familiarity ratings for faces of high or low familiarity were comparable to those of age-matched control subjects. These findings provide a strong indication that her face recognition system is unimpaired to the level of FRUs.

In contrast, however, ME was very poor at producing semantic information for the faces which she recognised as familiar. The point we want to stress is thus that there is a clear difference between her preserved ability to decide whether a face is familiar and her markedly impaired ability to identify "who" that person is. Hécaen and Angelergues (1962) give a brief, anecdotal description of a patient with a similar face recognition deficit.

The observation that a sense of familiarity can be achieved from a face while the identity of the person remains obscure has also been made in normal subjects. Young, Hay and Ellis (1985) asked healthy people to keep a diary of everyday face recognition mistakes, and they found this "familiar only" experience to be a frequent occurrence. This finding has been replicated in a laboratory setting by Hanley and Cowell (1988) and Hay, Young and Ellis (in press). Evidence from reaction time studies of normal subjects (Young, McWeeny, Hay and Ellis, 1986a) also points to differences between the sense of familiarity and access to identity-specific semantic information.

Our findings that ME had a preserved sense of familiarity for both faces and names, yet was often unable to access appropriate semantic information, are consistent with this normal pattern. ME's condition is thus apparently an exaggerated form of a more common difficulty in accessing semantic information from faces which have been recognised as familiar.

An important theoretical question concerns the level in the recognition system at which the sense of familiarity is achieved. According to Bruce and Young (1986), familiarity is determined at the level of the domain-specific recognition unit systems, in which case ME's impairment would reflect defective access to the person identity nodes (PINs), or damage to the PINs themselves.

Recently, however, Burton, Bruce and Johnston (1990) have suggested an alternative conception. Burton et al. (1990) have produced a simulation of part of Bruce and Young's (1986) model, couched in interactive activation terms. In order to achieve a workable simulation, Burton et al. (1990) followed a suggestion made by Young et al. (1985), which was that the PINs might provide the point at which different domain-specific person recognition systems converge. Burton et al. (1990) suggest that it could be the activation of a person's PIN, either through the face or the name, that allows one to become aware that the person is familiar. Semantic information concerning the person in question would, however, not necessarily be stored in the PINs, but instead held in a separate store accessed via the PINs. Thus, PINs serve as common access points to identity-specific semantic information from domain-specific analysers of faces, names, etc.

Two features of our findings with ME support Burton et al.'s (1990) view that familiarity is determined at the PIN rather than the FRU level. First, her inability to access identity-specific semantic information was found both for face and name inputs. In Bruce and Young's (1986) original conception, this would have to be accounted for by the somewhat unparsimonious suggestion of exactly parallel impairments affecting face and name recognition units. If familiarity is determined at the PINs, however, the finding would be expected. Secondly, and more importantly, the finding that ME can match faces and names of familiar people, while she is unable to produce any correct semantic information to either the name or the face, clearly supports the view that she accesses PINs. There is no other mechanism in Bruce and Young's (1986) or Burton et al.'s (1990) models for making such a match between face and name inputs.

ME's case thus supports Burton et al.'s (1990) conception that familiarity is determined at the PIN level, and that PINs act as a kind of gateway to semantic information, rather than storing semantic information themselves. In this view, ME's impairment can be seen as an access problem from the PINs to the semantic information store, or a degradation of the semantic information store itself.

Other reports of patients with severe long-term memory deficits who, in addition to an impairment in accessing semantic information, are also unable to distinguish between faces and names of familiar and unfamiliar people (e.g. Ellis, Young & Critchley, 1989; Hanley, Young & Pearson, 1989), can be incorporated in this theoretical account. In these cases, the PINs must have been compromised as well as the semantic information store.

Definitive resolution of the issue concerning the level in the recognition system at which the sense of familiarity is achieved will depend on further empirical or theoretical advances. For now, the important point established by our investigation of ME is that it provides an additional converging source of evidence pointing to a difference between the sense of familiarity and access to identity-specific semantic information.

In Bruce and Young's (1986) model, the final stage of face recognition involves name retrieval. It was observed that for those faces for which ME could give some identity-specific semantic information, the name could usually be retrieved. Thus, ME's retrograde memory impairment selectively concerns semantic information for familiar people, and implies either a disruption of the information store or problems in accessing it (cf. Shallice, 1987). In contrast, the processes involved in name retrieval itself appear to be preserved; name retrieval is still possible when some semantic information concerning the person can be accessed.

The report by Flude et al. (1989) on the anomic patient EST provides instructive points of comparison with our investigation of ME. Flude et al. (1989) found that EST could recognise familiar people equally well from their faces, voices, and spoken and written names. On the line-up tasks with faces and names, EST (like ME) performed well within the normal range on rating the familiarity of the celebrities, and (unlike ME) he was able to access relevant semantic information for these people. EST, however, was virtually unable to produce the name when presented with the face or the voice of a familiar person. Therefore, EST's problem was thought to be a selective impairment in name retrieval, or a disconnection of that process from the person information system.

One important common finding between EST and ME is that the recognition deficit is *not* domain-specific. This is markedly different to the domain-specific impairments found in cases of prosopagnosia, where the problem in face recognition is not usually accompanied by any corresponding disturbance of voice recognition or name recognition (de Renzi, 1986; Hécaen & Angelergues, 1962). EST, though, experienced difficulty in naming both faces and voices, and ME is severely impaired at accessing semantic information both from faces and from names. These observations are consistent with the theoretical position that the semantic information store and name output store are common to *all* of the input systems (faces, voices, names, etc.) involved in recognising familiar people, as suggested in Bruce and Young's (1986) model.

Unexpectedly, ME showed an impairment in the matching and labelling of facial expressions. Evidence for independent systems involved in processing faces for identity and expression judgements comes from two sources. First, reaction time studies of normal subjects. Young, McWeeny, Hay and Ellis (1986b) showed that while familiar faces are matched faster than unfamiliar faces on identity, no such interaction was apparent when subjects were instructed to match the same stimuli on emotional expression. Similarly, Bruce (1986) found no effect of face familiarity on decisions concerning the face's expression. Secondly, a neuropsychological double dissociation is evident for identity and expression processing. Patients with selective deficits in the analysis of facial expressions have been described (e.g. Bowers, Bauer, Coslett & Heilman, 1985; Etcoff, 1984; Kurucz & Feldmar, 1979; Kurucz, Feldmar & Werner, 1979), whereas other patients show face recognition deficits in the absence of expression recognition problems (e.g. Shuttleworth, Syring & Allen, 1982).

ME's poor performance on the expression tasks thus suggests that she has a separate recognition deficit for facial expressions, in addition to her retrograde memory impairment. Further investigations of similar cases involving relatively pure long-term memory impairment will be needed to establish whether we are correct in supposing that this additional expression processing impairment is coincidental in ME's case.

In conclusion, then, our investigation of ME demonstrates that neurological disease can leave a brain-injured patient with an intact sense of the familiarity of known people, but severely impaired knowledge of their identities. The deficit is one which has not been described in detail before, but whose existence is clearly predicted by Bruce and Young's (1986) model of face processing. The results of our investigation, however, show that Burton et al.'s (1990) revision of Bruce and Young's (1986) model, which locates the sense of familiarity at the PIN rather than the FRU level, provides a better description of ME's problem in recognising familiar people.

Manuscript received August 1989
Revised manuscript received July 1990

REFERENCES

Benton, A. L. (1980). The neuropsychology of facial recognition. *American Psychologist*, *35*, 176–186.

Benton, A. L., van Allen, M. W., Hamsher, K. de S. & Levin, H. S. (1978). *Test of facial recognition, Form SL*. Iowa City: Department of Neurology, The University of Iowa Hospitals.

Bowers, D., Bauer, R. M., Coslett, H. B. & Heilman, K. M. (1985). Processing of faces by patients with unilateral hemisphere lesions. 1. Dissociations between judgements of facial affect and facial identity. *Brain and Cognition*, *4*, 258–272.

Bruce, V. (1986). Influences of familiarity on the processing of faces. *Perception*, *15*, 387–397.

Bruce, V. & Young, A. (1986). Understanding face recognition. *British Journal of Psychology*, *77*, 305–327.

Burton, A. M., Bruce, V. & Johnston, R. A. (1990). Understanding face recognition with an interactive activation model. *British Journal of Psychology*, *81*, 361–380.

Campbell, R., Landis, T. & Regard, M. (1986). Face recognition and lipreading: A neurological dissociation. *Brain*, *109*, 509–521.

Damasio, A. R., Damasio, H. & van Hoesen, G. W. (1982). Prosopagnosia: Anatomic basis and behavioral mechanisms. *Neurology*, *32*, 331–334.

de Renzi, E. (1986). Current issues on prosopagnosia. In H. D. Ellis, M. A. Jeeves, F. Newcombe & A. W. Young (Eds), *Aspects of face processing*, pp. 243–252. Dordrecht: Martinus Nijhoff.

Ekman, P. & Friesen, W. V. (1975). *Pictures of facial affect*. Palo Alto, Calif.: Consulting Psychologists Press.

Ellis, A. W., Young, A. W. & Critchley, E. M. R. (1989). Loss of memory for people following temporal lobe damage. *Brain*, *112*, 1469–1483.

Ellis, H. D. (1986). Processes underlying face recognition. In R. Bruyer (Ed.), *The neuropsychology of face perception and facial expression*. pp. 1–27. Hillsdale, N.J.: Lawrence Erlbaum Associates Inc.

Etcoff, N. L. (1984). Selective attention to facial identity and facial emotion. *Neuropsychologia*, *22*, 281–295.

Flude, B. M., Ellis, A. W. & Kay, J. (1989). Face processing and name retrieval in an anomic aphasic: Names are stored separately from semantic information about people. *Brain and Cognition*, *11*, 60–72.

Hanley, J. R. & Cowell, E. (1988). The effect of retrieval cues on the recall of names and famous faces. *Memory and Cognition*, *16*, 545–555.

Hanley, J. R., Young, A. W. & Pearson, N. A. (1989). Defective recognition of familiar people. *Cognitive Neuropsychology*, *6*, 179–210.

Hay, D. C. & Young, A. W. (1982). The human face. In A. W. Ellis (Ed.), *Normality and pathology in cognitive functions*, pp. 173–202. London: Academic Press.

Hay, D. C., Young, A. W. & Ellis, A. W. (in press). Routes through the face processing system. *Quarterly Journal of Experimental Psychology*.

Hécaen, H. & Angelergues, R. (1962). Agnosia for faces (prosopagnosia). *Archives of Neurology*, *7*, 92–100.

Kurucz, J. & Feldmar, G. (1979). Prosopo-affective agnosia as a symptom of cerebral organic disease. *Journal of the American Geriatrics Society*, *27*, 225–230.

Kurucz, J., Feldmar, G. & Werner, W. (1979). Prosopo-affective agnosia associated with chronic organic brain syndrome. *Journal of the American Geriatrics Society*, *27*, 91–95.

Newcombe, F., de Haan, E. H. F., Ross, J. & Young, A. W. (1989). Face processing, laterality, and contrast sensitivity. *Neuropsychologia*, *27*, 523–538.

Shallice, T. (1987). Impairments of semantic processing: Multiple dissociations. In M. Coltheart, G. Sartori & R. Job (Eds), *The cognitive neuropsychology of language*, pp. 111–127. London: Lawrence Erlbaum Associates Ltd.

Shuttleworth, E. C., Syring, V. & Allen, N. (1982). Further observations on the nature of prosopagnosia. *Brain and Cognition*, *1*, 302–332.

Young, A. W. & de Haan, E. H. F. (1988). Boundaries of covert recognition in prosopagnosia. *Cognitive Neuropsychology*, *5*, 317–336.

Young, A. W., Hay, D. C. & Ellis, A. W. (1985). The faces that launched a thousand slips: Everyday difficulties and errors in recognizing people. *British Journal of Psychology*, *76*, 495–523.

Young, A. W., McWeeny, K. H., Hay, D. C. & Ellis, A. W. (1986a). Access to identity-specific semantic codes from familiar faces. *Quarterly Journal of Experimental Psychology*, *38A*, 271–295.

Young, A. W., McWeeny, K. H., Hay, D. C. & Ellis, A. W. (1986b). Matching familiar and unfamiliar faces on identity and expression. *Psychological Research*, *48*, 63–68.

EUROPEAN JOURNAL OF COGNITIVE PSYCHOLOGY, 1991, 3 (1) 69–86

Face Recognition and Lip-reading in Autism

Beatrice de Gelder, Jean Vroomen and Lucienne van der Heide

Department of Psychology, University of Tilburg, Tilburg, The Netherlands

Autistic children individually matched for mental age with normal subjects were tested on memory for unfamiliar faces and on lip-reading ability. The results show that autistic children are poorer than controls in memory for faces but comparable to controls in lip-reading. Autistic children show little influence on their auditory speech perception from visual speech. The results are discussed in relation to Bruce and Young's (1986) model of face recognition. The independence between facial speech and memory for faces is in accordance with this model but is only observed in autistic subjects.

INTRODUCTION

Faces play an important role in social interaction. There are least three aspects to the perception of faces that need to be considered. A very obvious aspect is that faces carry information about a person's identity. Equally important is the fact that face perception allows inferences about a person's states of mind. Finally, the face is a source of linguistic information. What we read on someone's lips contributes much more to decoding linguistic messages than has been suspected until recently.

Ever since Kanner's (1943) first description, it is widely agreed that autism is a deficit that affects subjects' social relations. Subsequent research has clearly underscored the original description which puts social deficits at the core of autism (Rutter, 1978; Volkmar, 1987). Intuitively, there would thus be good reason to suspect that autistic subjects have a

---

Requests for reprints should be addressed to Beatrice de Gelder, Department of Psychology, University of Tilburg, Tilburg, The Netherlands.

We are grateful to P. Nobel for assistance in testing the subjects, to P. Bertelson for permission to use the materials for the FACE test and to K. Keatly for assistance with the manuscript. We would like also to thank R. Campbell and B. Dodd for their insightful comments. Special thanks to those individuals who took part in the study and to the staffs of the schools in Nijmegen, Utrecht and Reek. This research was supported in part by a VF grant from Tilburg University and by a ZWO project to the first author.

---

problem in processing facial information. The issue of face processing ability in autistic children has only been addressed systematically over the last decade (Hobson, 1983; 1986; 1987; 1989; Langdell, 1978; 1980; 1981; Weeks & Hobson, 1987). Research on face perception in autistics is traditionally motivated by the notion of an affective disorder at the core of autism. Because of this concern, the emphasis has been on affective and communicative aspects of faces and on the recognition of facial expressions (Howlin, 1978; Richer, 1976; Rutter, 1978; Wing, 1976). In this sense, studies on face perception in autistics are close to approaches in social psychology where faces are studied in the context of social attributions (Argyle, 1983; Ekman, 1982).

Given that faces play a crucial role in communication, what representations and processes underlie the processing of facial information? An answer to this question is particularly important for understanding what underlies the social competence that normal subjects manifest in making social attributions on the basis of face perception. More to the point here, facial information processing must be understood in order to appreciate the impairments of social competence we witness in cases of autism.

From a logical point of view, the ability to recognise an expression of emotion imposes on the perceptual system a task different from that of recognising a person's identity (Bruce, 1988). At an empirical level, recognition of emotional expression in a face will draw on information sources other than those used in recognition of the identity of a face. Over the last few years, social, experimental and clinical studies have revealed how aspects other than emotion recognition are involved in face perception. Current models of face processing (e.g. Bruce, 1988; Bruce & Young, 1986; Ellis, 1986) are based on findings from those different sources. Models of this kind might have considerable heuristic value in clarifying face recognition in autistics. The present study makes a beginning with this. Bruce and Young (1986) distinguish three major aspects of face perception: recognition of facial identity, of facial expression and of facial speech. The present study examines two of these aspects, which have received little attention in the study of autism so far, i.e. recognition of facial identity and of facial speech.

The Recognition of Facial Expression

Kanner (1943) paraphrased the social impairments of autistics as "inborn disturbances of affective contact with others". Kanner himself noted that some autistic children never looked up at people's faces. Existing approaches have linked the absence of facial communication to a general social inadaptedness characteristic of autism. The notion of disturbed affective contact has motivated most students of face perception in autism to look at affective aspects of face processing, i.e. recognition of facial expression.

In an impressive series of studies, Hobson and associates have looked at the way autistic children perceive facial expressions of emotion (Hobson, 1983; 1986; 1987). It emerges from these studies that autistic children are relatively impaired in the recognition of facial expressions. In contrast with normal children, autistic children do not sort photographs by type of emotional expression but, for example, by type of hat worn or by sex. Autistic children have comparatively great difficulty combining facial expressions in photographs with the corresponding expressions in video-pictures, gestures, vocalisations and contexts. Hobson's results confirm earlier findings on the impaired recognition of facial expressions. Langdell (1980; 1981) presented a task where facial expressions had to be sorted into "sad" or "happy" ones. The subjects were presented with either the whole picture, the upper half or the lower half of the face. Autistic children were less good than normals at telling emotional expressions from the upper part of the face.

The studies just mentioned give no insight into the ability of autistic children to recognise facial identity independently of their ability to process emotional expression. In the absence of an accepted model of face perception, it is difficult to conclude that the observed results follow from a poor ability to recognise facial expression only and not, for example, from a poor ability to recognise facial identity or from both.

Facial Expression *vs* Facial Identity

There is increasing empirical and clinical evidence for the existence of separate processes corresponding to facial identity and facial expression. Experimental studies with normal subjects show that modes of presentation of stimuli (brightness, rotation, movement) influence differentially recognition of identity and of expression (see Bruce, 1988, for an overview). Clinical studies with prosopagnosic patients have documented the existence of a dissociation between recognition of identity and of expression (e.g. Bruyer, 1986). On the basis of such evidence, Bruce and Young (1986) and Bruce (1988) argue for an heterarchic organisation of face recognition abilities. They propose that recognition of identity and of expression and lip-reading may be achieved independently.

In their most recent study, Hobson, Ousten and Lee (1988) address this issue of the relation between recognition of personal identity and recognition of emotional expression. Their study shows that autistics present a divergent profile of face recognition abilities. When presented with full faces, autistics perform as well as controls both in judging identity and emotional expression of faces. When some of the cues to emotion and identity were reduced (e.g. blank mouth, blank forehead), the perform-ance of the autistic subjects declined more for recognition of emotional expression than for recognition of identity.

Facial Speech

We mentioned above that in the view of Bruce and Young (1986) the face perception system might well have separate components for, among others, identity, expression and lip-reading. Studies of eye contact tend to show that autistic children avoid looking at faces and avoid eye contact behaviour (Richer, 1976; Rutter, 1978). No studies of facial speech ability in autistics have been reported so far.

The study by Langdell (1981) offers information that may or may not be relevant. Langdell starts from the fact that children aged 4–10 years find the upper part of the face more helpful for identification than the lower part (Goldstein & Mackenberg, 1966). His own study compares younger and older autistics and finds that, in contrast with normal children, young autistics find the lower features of the face more helpful for peer identifica-tion. Older autistic children show no such preference. When asked to identify faces by looking only at the lower part, they perform at the same level as the younger group, but their identification based on the upper part of the face is as good as that of normal children.

There are reasons to expect that recognition of facial speech in autistic children is within the normal range. Studies of discrimination learning and short-term memory show that autism is not associated with any particular deficits in those areas (see Sigman, Ungerer, Mundy & Sherman, 1987, for an overview). Of immediate relevance for the present issue are the findings that memory for auditory presented stimuli and for written material is adequate (Aurnhammer-Frith, 1969; Frith, 1970a; 1970b; Fyffe & Prior, 1978). We know that in normal subjects the ability to lip-read follows closely the ability for processing language in the auditory modality (Camp-bell, 1989; Massaro, 1987). Yet in subjects with reading disorders in the phonological domain, lip-reading is impaired and exercises less influence on the auditory categorisation of speech sounds (de Gelder & Vroomen, 1988). Those subjects also tend to have worse memory for visual speech information (de Gelder & Vroomen, 1989; 1990). For autistic subjects with no auditory impairment and with reading ability within the normal range, we should expect to observe normal facial speech recognition, and visual influence on auditory speech processing should be at the level predicted by visual speech recognition.

Available research does not allow us to exclude the possibility of an effect of impaired memory for faces on facial speech ability. There is evidence from both clinical and experimental studies that neural mechanisms involved in face recognition are predominantly located in the right hemisphere in contrast with a left hemisphere dominance for linguistic abilities. Neurological damage might selectively affect recognition of facial speech and identity recognition. Campbell, Landis and Regard (1986) have found a dissociation between face recognition and lip-reading in cases of acquired face recognition deficit. The observations fit in with a model as proposed by Bruce and Young (1986; see also Bruce, 1988).

Here also it is difficult to base predictions of developmental phenomena on models of face processing in adults and on cases of acquired disorders. On the basis of clinical data, we would expect to find that impairments in aspects of face processing do not necessarily have an influence on facial speech recognition. But no data from adults or from children are available.

Facial Identity and Facial Speech: The Present Study

The present study might shed light on recognition of facial identity and of facial speech in autistic children and on the possible link between the two processes. None of the studies reviewed above has investigated recognition of facial identity independently of the possible influence of aspects like familiarity, naming and recognition of facial expressions and recognition of degraded facial information. Hobson et al. (1988) studied facial identity using a task where the subjects had to match photographs with one of several simultaneous probes. The paradigm might encourage reliance on non-specific recognition strategies. To obtain insight into recognition of facial identity proper, we have adopted a memory paradigm involving matching different photographs of the same unfamiliar individuals. The difference in presentation guarantees that the extraction of personal identity is mandatory (Bertelson & van Haelen, 1978).

Evidence of a discrepancy between recognition of personal identity and of facial speech would suggest a partial independence between identity and facial speech recognition. Our study might allow us to appreciate the extent to which Bruce and Young's (1986) model, which is based on data from adults and acquired disorders, receives support from the observation of developmental disorders. At the same time, the study of face perception in autism might benefit from investigating a broadened range of hypotheses derived from current face perception models.

A major methodological issue for the study of autistic subjects is the choice of the appropriate control groups. Controls matched on verbal mental age (MA) offer the best chance of unbiased comparisons (Sigman et al., 1987). It guarantees that effects of general-intelligence differences between groups are cancelled out. As complementary measures of intelligence, we administered the RAVEN Progressive Matrices Test (coloured version). To obtain a more specific insight into possible group differences, a task of scene recognition was used as a control task for the face recognition tasks.

METHOD

Subjects

The autistic group consisted of 17 children (16 male, 1 female), aged between 6 years 6 months (6:6) and 16 years 4 months (16:4) (mean = 10:11 years). They had all been diagnosed following Rutter's criteria (Rutter, 1978). The normal group was individually matched with the autistics on the basis of sex and on the raw scores of the Peabody Picture Vocabulary Test (PPVT). Their ages ranged between 6:10 and 11:2 years (mean = 8:6 years). The matching was based on a difference of 5 or less items on the PPVT. The mean raw PPVT scores for autistic and normals was 78.9 and 79.5 respectively.

Raven's Progressive Matrices (coloured version) were also administered. Details of the groups are presented in Table 1. The subjects had no known sensory disorders.

Procedure

The autistic subjects were tested in their daily environment in the presence of a caretaker, whereas the normal subjects were tested in a quiet room in school. Testing lasted about 45 min. The following tests were administered in the order as presented below.

TABLE 1
Details of the Groups

Group	N		Age	PVT Raw Scores	Raven Raw Scores
Autistic	17	Mean	10:11	78.9	26.0
		S.D.	2:4	14.7	4.6
		Range	6:6–16:4	57–121	18–34
Normal	17	Mean	8:6	79.5	25.4
		S.D.	1:4	16.2	5.8
		Range	6:10–11:2	52–125	15–34

1. Kaufman face recognition test for children.   This face recognition test was taken from a neuropsychological battery (Kaufman & Kaufman, 1983). It contains one example and 15 sets of test pictures. Each set consists of (1) a photograph of either one or more target faces and (2) the picture of a group of four or more people. The photographs are coloured, hair and clothes are shown, and facial expressions are neutral. The subjects are shown the sets one by one. The target picture(s) is presented for 5 sec, and then the group picture is shown and the subject is asked to point to the target person(s).

2. Face recognition (FACE).   We constructed the FACE task from a large set of pictures used in an earlier study by Bertelson and co-workers (Bertelson & van Haelen, 1978). The stimuli consisted of: (a) 16 black-and-white passport size photographs presenting 8 male and 8 female young adults. They were presented full face with neutral facial expressions. Hair and clothing were hidden by a black bonnet and a white scarf. (b) Thirty-two photographs in ¾ profile; 16 persons of the (a) group and 16 distractors. In the first round, the subjects were shown the 16 pictures of the (a) set, one photograph after the other for 5 sec each. In the test phase, the subjects were shown two pictures from the (b) set, a ¾ profile picture of a person from the original set and a distractor. The subjects were asked to indicate which of the two persons they had seen before.

3. Facial speech test (FSP).   In the facial speech test (FSP), the subjects watched a video-recording of a female speaker. They were asked to repeat what she said. The speaker had been recorded on U-matic tape while pronouncing a series of VCV syllables. Each syllable consisted of one of the four plosive stops /p, b, t, d/ or a nasal /m, n/ in between the vowel /a/ (e.g. /aba/ or /ana/). There were three presentation conditions: audio-visual, auditory-only and visual-only. In the audio-visual presentation, dubbing operations were performed on the recordings so as to produce a new video-film comprising six different auditory–visual combinations: auditory /p, b, t, d, m, n/ were combined with visual /t, d, p, b, n, m/, respectively. Thus, the visual place of articulation feature never matched the auditory place feature. The dubbing was carried out so as to ensure that there was auditory–visual coincidence of the release of the consonant in each utterance. For the auditory-only condition, the original auditory signal was dubbed onto a video signal from the speaker while sitting quietly. For the visual-only condition, the auditory channel was deleted from the recording, so the subject had to rely entirely on lip-reading. Each presentation condition comprised of three replications of the six possible stimuli. There was a 10-sec gap of blank film between the successive trials. To counterbalance presentation order, each condition was divided into two blocks of nine trials each. The presentation order of these blocks was always audio-visual, auditory-only, visual-only, visual-only, auditory-only, audio-visual. The stimuli were presented on a 19-inch TV screen. The subjects were instructed to watch the speaker and repeat what she had said. References to modality were strictly avoided. The subjects' responses were written down by the experimenter. During the presentation, the experimenter monitored the subjects in order to make sure that they were watching the screen.

4. Luria picture recognition test. In order to obtain a measure of scene and object recognition, a test designed by Luria was administered. The test consisted of a series of 24 black-and-white pictures of everyday scenes. The pictures were presented at a rate of one per 5 sec. Four pictures appeared twice. The subjects were asked to indicate which pictures were repetitions.

RESULTS

The results of two normal subjects on the Kaufman test and two autistic subjects on the FACE task were not entered into the data analysis because of experimenter error. Due to practical reasons, the FSP task was not presented to eight autistic subjects. The percentage of correct responses on the Kaufman test was 72 and 83% for autistic and normal subjects respectively (see Table 2). The difference is significant according to a two-tailed t-test for matched pairs [$t(14) = 2.86$, $P < 0.02$]. Individual analysis showed that for the 15 matched pairs, autistics performed worse than their controls in 12 cases, the subjects performed equally well in two cases, and one autistic subject performed better than his control. The observed difference is significant according to a non-parametric Wilcoxon matched-pairs signed-ranks test ($Z = 2.41$, $P < 0.02$).

The performances on the FACE test are presented in Table 3. The autistics scored 51% correct on the FACE test, whereas the normal subjects scored 62% correct [$t(14) = 2.94$, $P < 0.01$]. A total of 10 autistics performed worse than their controls, three performed equally well, and two autistics performed better than their controls (Wilcoxon: $Z = 2.43$, P

TABLE 2
Percentage of Correct Responses on the
Kaufman Face Recognition Test

Group	Mean	S.D.
Autistic	72%	19.7
Normal	83%	9.7

TABLE 3
Percentage of Correct Responses on the
FACE Test

Group	Mean	S.D.
Autistic	51%	15.7
Normal	62%	9.4

< 0.02). There was a positive correlation between the Kaufman and the FACE test for the autistic group ($r = 0.66$, $P < 0.005$) and the normal group ($r = 0.26$, $P = 0.18$). Thus, the results suggest that autistics performed worse than normal subjects on face recognition tasks.

The results on the two face identity tests were compared with scores on the Luria test in order to have a control on the possible influence of some general visual memory factor. There was no difference between the groups on the Luria test [mean = 77 and 83% correct for autistics and normals respectively: $t(15) = 0.75$, $P = 0.468$]. Individual comparisons showed that four autistics were better than their controls, five pairs performed equally well, and seven autistics performed worse (Wilcoxon: $Z = 0.62$, N.S.). This suggests that the observed results are due to a specific impairment in facial identity recognition and not to a general visual memory deficit.

The results for the facial speech test are presented in Tables 4 and 5. In the audio-visual condition, there were two possible scorings: either lip-reading influenced auditory speech perception or it did not. The influence was measured by calculating the percentage of "fused" and "blended" responses. A fused response is one where visual information of the place of articulation is combined with the auditory information into a single syllable (e.g. ma-auditory/na-lips into a /na/ response), and a blend is a response where the visual place information is added to the auditory information into a two-phonemes composite (e.g. na-auditory/ma-lips into /mna/ response). The mean incidence of fusions and blends in the autistic group was 19% compared to 51% for the normals [$t(8) = 4.60$, $P < 0.005$

TABLE 4
Mean Percentage of Fusions and Blends
in the Audio-visual Condition on the Facial Speech Task (FSP)

Group	Mean	S.D.
Autistic	19%	11
Normal	51%	20

TABLE 5
Mean Percentage of Correct Responses in the Auditory
and Visual Conditions on the Facial Speech Task (FSP)

	Auditory		Visual	
Group	Mean	S.D.	Mean	S.D.
Autistic	97	3	74	24
Normal	91	16	84	16

according to a two-tailed t-test for matched pairs]. A subject analysis showed that, in the audio-visual condition, all nine autistic subjects were less influenced by visual speech than their matched controls (Wilcoxon: $Z = 2.66$, $P < 0.001$).

In the auditory-only condition, a correct response was an accurate repetition of the stimulus. Accuracy in this condition was high for both groups (97 and 90% for autistic and normal subjects respectively) and there was no significant group difference [$t(8) = 1.21$, $P = 0.261$]. For the nine pairs, the autistics performed better than their controls in five cases, equally well in two, and worse in three cases (Wilcoxon: $Z = 1.15$, N.S.). A correct response in the visual-only condition was defined as one that fell in the same category of visually discriminable phonemes as the stimulus. Thus, there were two visually distinct phoneme categories: the bilabials /p, b, m/ and the linguals /t, d, n/ (Binnie, Montgomery & Jackson, 1974; Woodward & Barber, 1960). The percentage of correct responses in the visual-only condition did not differ significantly between the two groups [mean = 74 and 84% for autistic and normal subjects respectively: $t(8) = 0.87$, N.S.]. Five autistics performed better than their controls and four performed worse (Wilcoxon: $Z = 0.29$, N.S.).

The Pearson correlations between visual influence in the audio-visual condition and lip-reading were 0.51 ($P < 0.02$) for the normals and 0.25 ($P > 0.10$) for the autistics. Thus, the hypothesis that better lip-readers would be more influenced by visual information in the audio-visual condition is only significant for normal subjects.

The last aspect of the results concerns the relation between face recognition and lip-reading ability. Pearson correlations between the face recognition tests and the lip-reading tests were calculated to check whether a common factor underlies the observed group differences (see Tables 6 and 7). In the autistic group, correlations between face recognition and lip-reading were low and negative. None of the correlations reached significance (all $P > 0.10$). In the normal group, there were positive correlations between the influence of lip-reading in the audio-visual condition and

TABLE 6
Correlations Between the Face Recognition Tasks, the Facial Speech Task (FSP) and the Luria for the Autistic Group

	Kaufman	FACE	Auditory	Visual	Audio-visual
			FSP		
FACE	0.65[a]				
Auditory	−0.06	−0.50			
Visual	−0.13	−0.07	−0.07		
Audio-visual	−0.21	−0.51	−0.51	0.25	
Luria	−0.01	−0.14	0.00	0.56	0.37

[a]$P < 0.05$.

the Kaufman test ($r = 0.442$, $P < 0.05$), between the influence of lip-reading in the audio-visual condition and the FACE test ($r = 0.442$, $P < 0.05$), and a marginally significant correlation between the percentage correct in the visual/only condition and the Kaufman test ($r = 0.39$, $P < 0.08$).

Multiple regression was used in order to test whether lip-reading could explain the variance of face recognition (measured as the mean proportion of correct responses on the Kaufman test and the FACE test). The classifying variables sex, chronological age, PVT, Raven and Luria were used in addition with the scores on the FSP (auditory, visual and audio-visual). For the autistic group, neither variable contributed significantly to explaining the variance of face recognition (all $P > 0.10$). For the control group, chronological age was entered first in the multiple regression explaining 48% of the variance, followed by the Luria test which contributed another 24% for a total of 72% explained variance. No other variable contributed significantly. Thus, the multiple regressions show that

TABLE 7
Correlations Between the Face Recognition Tasks, the Facial Speech Task (FSP) and the Luria for the Control Group

	Kaufman	FACE	Auditory	Visual	Audio-visual
			FSP		
FACE	0.26				
Auditory	0.05	−0.14			
Visual	0.39	0.20	0.30		
Audio-visual	0.44[a]	0.44[a]	−0.26	0.51[a]	
Luria	0.59[a]	0.49[a]	−0.26	0.34	0.45[a]

[a] $P < 0.05$.

neither lip-reading ability nor the influence of visual input in the audio-visual condition contribute to explaining the variance of face recognition performances. Discriminant analysis was used in order to examine how well each test predicts the autistic/control group division. The visual influence in the audio-visual condition accounted for 47% of the variance. The FACE task added another 5% to the explained variance. None of the other variables contributed significantly. On the basis of the visual influence measure and the performance in the FACE test, 83% of the subjects could correctly be allocated to one of the groups.

DISCUSSION

The present study was conducted to investigate (1) whether autistic children are impaired in their recognition of facial identity and facial speech and (2) whether there might be a link between these. The results suggest that autistic children are impaired in face identity recognition and that no impairment is found as far as the lip-reading ability of autistic children is concerned. Taken together, our results suggest the existence of a dissociation between facial identity and facial speech in autistic children.

To date, defective face processing for identity has not been reported for autistic children. Except for Hobson et al.'s (1988) study, previous studies have all looked for defective understanding of emotion and social cues for faces. Hobson has compared identity recognition across facial expression and vice versa. He found that recognition of facial expression declines in autistic subjects with deterioration of the stimuli. No such tendency was found in the normal group or in the condition of facial identity recognition. Autistic subjects perform as well as normal controls when given full face pictures and asked to judge identity. The fact that no difference is found between the two subject groups might be due to the difference in paradigms. As we noted above, our study uses a memory paradigm, whereas Hobson et al. (1988) used a matching task. Moreover, the subjects tested by Hobson et al. (1988) were much older (mean age 19:4, range 13:4–25:10) than those studied by us.

Does the observed face identity impairment suggest a deficit of a relatively isolated sub-process of the face processing system or might it have links with some other sub-process? Impairments in various aspects of face perception (e.g. recognition of familiar faces, difficulties in judging sex and age) and recognition of facial expression have all been found to exist to some degree in autistics. This convergence of face processing deficits would suggest that some other components of the face perception system are impaired. As we noted, the present picture still needs to be completed and this task is complicated by the fact that available data from autistics suggest developmental changes occurring in the sub-process. For example, some of the processing deficits are much less pronounced in older than in young autistics. No developmental data from normal subjects are available that would give insight into the developmental course of the different aspects of face processing. As to explaining this convergence of face processing deficits, different possibilities must be considered. One might opt for an additive picture of local impairments or one might propose the hypothesis of a common underlying cause. For example, our results about an impairment in face identity as well as earlier results on deficits in recognition of facial expression might have a common origin in a generalised face perception disorder. One possibility might be that there exists a basic disturbance in coding of facedness due to an abnormal development in early infanthood. Findings about preference for face over non-face stimuli in infants (Johnson & Morton, 1989) and about the existence of visual neurones responsive to faces (Perrett et al., 1988) suggest the existence of such a face-specific mechanism (Yin, 1969). This might, for example, result from a disorder in the early development of face processing ability (de Schonen & Mathivet, 1989). The two propositions are compatible with a modular conception of face processing ability. In either case, we are in the presence of a specific face processing deficit which, as indeed our data show, is not due to some general factor responsible for overall poor performance of the autistic group. If so, data on impaired face processing do not by themselves support either a cognitive or an emotion-based explanation of autism.

Our results on the good lip-reading ability of autistics are in agreement with earlier findings on the auditory speech ability of autistics. It has repeatedly been observed that autistic children show good performance in tasks of recalling unstructured material presented auditorially. Lip-reading is a skill that is part of normal speech processing ability. This leads us to expect that the lip-reading ability would also be within the normal range. The results support this prediction.

A surprising finding is that, contrary to earlier findings with normal subjects, in bimodal presentations autistic subjects are much less influenced by visual information than normal subjects. For normal subjects, it is known that the influence of visual information (lip-reading) on auditory information increases with lip-reading ability (Massaro, Thompson, Barron & Laren, 1986). We observed the same link in our normal subjects, because there was a positive correlation between visual influence and lip-reading. For the autistic group, there is considerably less influence from visual speech although there is no difference in lip-reading with normal subjects. This finding contrasts with existing models of audio-visual perception. Massaro's fuzzy logic model predicts that the visual influence in audio-visual speech perception will be the same for both groups, because the informativeness of the auditory-only and visual-only sources are the same for both groups (Massaro, 1987). A model of interactive activation of visual and auditory input predicts also that integration will occur the moment processing in each input modality is normal (Campbell et al., 1988). We have observed other cases where lack of integration does also occur. We found that retarded readers presented with an ambiguous auditory input take less advantage (than is to be expected on the basis of their visual speech capacities alone) from the visual information provided (de Gelder & Vroomen, 1988). Evidence from our facial speech task does not allow us to tell whether this failure to integrate information is a characteristic of audio-visual speech perception in autistic subjects or whether it is limited to the integration of phonemic information from lips outside a speech comprehension context. In the latter restricted case, given the good performance on the silent lip-reading task, the possibility of normal bimodal speech comprehension in autistics remains open (Campbell et al., 1988).

Campbell et al. (1986) have observed a case of developmental prosopagnosia showing some similarities with the results obtained here. Their patient, AB, had a good auditory speech ability and was unimpaired on silent lip-reading tasks but was not susceptible to fusions. The fact that there is no indication of autism is no reason to underestimate the importance of this convergence between different kinds of *developmental* disorders.

The reduced visual influence in the autistic group might signal a lack of integration between linguistic information coming from different modalities. We are not offering this as an explanation of audio-visual speech perception in autism, only as a puzzling fact that theories of bimodal speech perception will need to account for. For that reason, it is unhelpful to link this absence of intramodular integration to the theory that autism is to be characterised as an absence of cohesive force at the level of the central processes (Frith, 1989). There is sufficient evidence of the fact that fusions and blendings of the kind presented in our facial speech task – as is the case for speech perception in general – are not under central control.

We now turn to the more hazardous issue of the relation between observed facial recognition impairment and good facial speech performance. At first sight, facial speech occupies a pivotal position at the intersection of two presumably highly modular domains, competence for language and competence for faces. Very intuitively, a reduced effect of visual speech might be an indication of a processing deficit inside the domain of language – limited to phoneme discrimination or extended to real lip-reading – it might be a symptom of a horizontal interaction, an influence of a face-processing problem on facial speech perception, or facial speech and facial identity recognition might both be impaired due to a common cause. Some suggestions about interactions have been made in earlier developmental studies. The finding of an upper face superiority in normal children might be related to the fact that young children are poor lip-readers. Langdell (1978, p. 265) explains the preference of young children for the lower part of the face by proposing that those children look at the mouth in an effort to compensate for an "inability to extract the full meaning of the auditory component of speech". A similar suggestion is made by Hermelin and O'Connor (1985). Proposals such as these represent an appeal to general factors like meaning and understanding or overall coherence. Given that autistics strike one as often not grasping the full meaning of a situation, one can understand researchers being biased in favour of high-level "cognitive" explanations. But the very fact that autistics as a group do have widely divergent intelligence would seem to rule out central factor theories. Moreover, it has frequently been observed that autistic subjects have very divergent scores on different sub-tests of intelligence batteries. For example, Kaiser (1988) found children with a verbal I.Q. of 70, a social I.Q. of 50 and a visual-spatial I.Q. of 120. The distinction between capacities implemented in modules like face or language processing and central intellectual abilities like concepts, reasoning and problem solving seems crucial for the study of a neurologically based developmental disorder like autism. For that reason, the strategy of trying to look at the effects of autism *per se* and select a population of high-ability autistic children may carry a risk. High-ability and older autistic children are likely to have come up with compensation strategies for their original deficits. For example, notwithstanding the autistic deficit and impaired social skills in everyday life, they perform remarkably well on experimental tasks requiring reasoning about social situations (de Gelder, 1990). Performance on face memory and lip-reading tasks of the kind used in the present experiment are less open to influences from central processes. They are more likely to give insight into specific impairments underlying autistic behaviour. In tasks such as we used here, there is little room for a possible influence from attentional strategies, e.g. ignoring lip-read cues as a way to avoid conflict.

Taken together, the various aspects of our results suggest that facial speech recognition and facial identity recognition might be relatively autonomous. The picture suggested is that of a dissociation between visual speech recognition and facial identity recognition in autistics. The dissociation we observe here in autistic subjects has been observed in a case of an acquired facial identity disorder (Campbell et al., 1986). If so, the findings lend support to a heterarchical model of the functional architecture of face perception as defended by Bruce and Young (1986), where the coding of facial information and recognition of identity proceed in parallel. In our view, this model represents a most welcome framework for further research on face perception disorders in autistics and on the development of face perception in general. The model does commit one to a dissociative picture of the primitive face processing components and to separate modules for face processing and language processing. We do not exclude, though, secondary influences from impairments of face processing to language perception and vice versa. For example, our results of defective integration of auditory and visual information suggest that autistics might have impairments in audio-visual speech perception. This might stimulate the development of attentional strategies like focusing on the lower part of the face. It is important not to mistake such compensatory mechanisms for evidence of interaction occurring at the level of face processing components.

Finally, on the basis of our data, we see no reason to lend support to current competing theories about autism. It is difficult to see how data on face recognition could lend support to an integrative approach to autism, whether formulated as a cognitive theory (Frith, 1989) or as an emotional theory (Hobson, 1989).

Manuscript received September 1989
Revised manuscript received July 1990

REFERENCES

Argyle, I. (1983). *The psychology of interpersonal behaviour*, 4th edn. Harmondsworth: Penguin.

Aurnhammer-Frith, U. (1969). Emphasis and meaning in recall in normal and autistic children. *Language and Speech*, *12*, 29–38.

Bertelson, P. & van Haelen, H. (1978). *Extracting physiognomic invariants*. Paper presented at the meeting of the Experimental Psychology Society, Cambridge, July.

Binnie, C. A., Montgomery, A. A. & Jackson, P. L. (1974). Auditory and visual contributions to the perception of consonants. *Journal of Speech and Hearing Research*, *17*, 619–630.

Bruce, V. (1988). *Recognising faces*. Hillsdale, N.J.: Lawrence Erlbaum Associates Inc.

Bruce, V. & Young, A. (1986). Understanding face recognition. *British Journal of Psychology*, *77*, 305–327.

Bruyer, R. (1986). *The neuropsychology of face perception and facial expression*. Hillsdale, N.J.: Lawrence Erlbaum Associates Inc.

Campbell, R. (1989). Lipreading. In A. W. Young & H. D. Ellis (Eds), *Handbook of research on face processing*, pp. 187–205. Amsterdam: North Holland.

Campbell, R., Landis, T. & Regard, M. (1986). Face recognition and lipreading: A neurological dissociation. *Brain*, *109*, 509–521.

Campbell, R., Garwood, Franklin, Harvard, Regard, M. & Landis, T. (1988, April). *Neuropsychological studies of the fusion illusion*. Paper presented at the EPS meeting, Edinburgh.

de Gelder, B. (1990). The matter of other minds. *Behavioral and Brain Sciences, 13*.

de Gelder, B. & Vroomen, J. (1988). *Bimodal speech perception in young dyslexics*. Paper presented at the 6th Australian Language and Speech Conference. Sydney, August.

de Gelder, B. & Vroomen, J. (1989). *Retention of visual and auditory speech: A common memory?* Paper presented to the annual meeting of the Psychonomic Society, Atlanta, November.

de Gelder, B. & Vroomen, J. (1990). *Poor readers are poor lipreaders.* Paper presented at the Applied Psychology Conference, Kyoto, July.

de Gelder, B. & Vroomen, J. (in press). Phonological deficits: Beneath the surface of reading acquisition. *Psychological Research.*

de Schonen, S. & Mathivet, E. (1989). First come, first served: A scenario about the development of hemispheric specialization in face recognition during infancy. *European Bulletin of Cognitive Psychology, 9,* 3–44.

Ekman, P. (1982). *Emotion in the human face.* Cambridge: Cambridge University Press.

Ekman, P. & Friesen, W. V. (1978). *Slides of facial expression.* Palo Alto, Calif.: Consulting Psychologists Press.

Ellis, H. D. (1986). Processes underlying face recognition. In R. Bruyer (Ed.), *The neuropsychology of face perception and facial expression,* pp. 1–27. Hillsdale, N.J.: Lawrence Erlbaum Associates Inc.

Frith, U. (1970a). Studies in pattern detection in normal and autistic children: I. Immediate recall of auditory sequences. *Journal of Abnormal Psychology, 4,* 413–420.

Frith, U. (1970b). Studies in pattern detection in normal and autistic children: II. Reproduction and production of colour sequences. *Journal of Experimental Child Psychology, 10,* 120–135.

Frith, U. (1989). *Autism: Explaining the enigma.* Oxford: Blackwell.

Frith, U. & Baron-Cohen, S. (1987). Perception in autistic children. In D. J. Cohen, A. M. Donnellan & R. Paul (Eds), *Handbook of autism and pervasive developmental disorders,* pp. 85–102. New York: John Wiley.

Fyffe, C. & Prior, M. (1978). Evidence for language recoding in autistic, retarded, and normal children: A reexamination. *British Journal of Psychology, 69,* 393–402.

Goldstein, A. G. & Mackenberg, E. (1966). Recognition of human faces from isolated facial features. *Psychonomic Science, 6,* 149–150.

Hermelin, B. & O'Connor, N. (1985). Logico-affective states and non-verbal language. In E. Schopler & G. B. Mesibov (Eds), *Communication problems in autism.* New York: Plenum Press.

Hobson, R. P. (1983). The autistic child's recognition of age-related features of people, animals and things. *British Journal of Developmental Psychology, 1,* 343–352.

Hobson, R. P. (1986). The autistic child's appraisal of expressions of emotion. *Journal of Child Psychology and Psychiatry, 27,* 321–342.

Hobson, R. P. (1987). The autistic child's recognition of age- and sex-related characteristics of people. *Journal of Autism and Developmental Disorders, 17,* 63–69.

Hobson, R. P. (1989). Beyond cognition: A theory of autism. In G. Dawson (Ed.), *Autism: New perspectives on diagnosis, nature and treatment,* pp. 22–48. New York: Guilford Press.

Hobson, R. P., Ousten, J. & Lee, A. (1988). What's in a face? The case of autism. *British Journal of Psychology, 79,* 441–453.

Howlin, P. (1978). The assessment of social behaviour. In M. Rutter & E. Schopler (Eds), *Autism: A reappraisal of concepts and treatment.* New York: Plenum Press.

Kaiser, L. H. W. M. (1988). Autisme: symptomen, vroegtijdige onderkenning, oorzaak en behandeling, afl. 1: de symptomen. *Soma and Psyche.*

Kanner, L. (1943). Autistic disturbances of affective contact. *Nervous Child, 2,* 217–250.

Kaufman, A. S. & Kaufman, N. L (1983). *Kaufman Assessment Battery for Children: Face recognition subtest.* Minnesota: American Guidance Service.

Langdell, T. (1978). Recognition of faces: An approach to the study of autism. *Journal of Child Psychology and Psychiatry, 19,* 255–268.

Langdell, T. (1980). *Pragmatic aspects of autism: Or Why is "I" a normal word*. Unpublished paper presented at the BPS Developmental Psychology Conference, Edinburgh.

Langdell, T. (1981). *Face perception: An approach to the study of autism*. Unpublished doctoral dissertation, University of London.

Massaro, D. W. (1987). *Speech perception by ear and eye: A paradigm for psychological inquiry*. Hillsdale, N.J.: Lawrence Erlbaum Associates Inc.

Massaro, D. W., Thompson, L. A., Barron, B. & Laren, E. (1986). Developmental changes in visual and auditory contributions to speech perception. *Journal of Experimental Child Psychology*, *41*, 93–113.

Morton, J. & Johnson, M. (1989). Four ways for faces to be "special". In A. W. Young & H. D. Ellis (Eds), *Handbook of research on face processing*, pp. 49–56. Amsterdam: North Holland.

Perner, J., Frith, U., Leslie, A. & Leekam, S. R. (in press). Exploration of the autistic child's theory of mind: Knowledge, belief and communication. *Child Development*.

Perrett, D. I., Mistlin, A. J., Chitty, A. J., Smith, P. A. J., Potter, D. D., Broennimann, R. & Harris, M. (1988). Specialized face processing and hemispheric asymmetry in man and monkey: Evidence from single unit and reaction time studies. *Behavioral Brain Research*, *29*, 245–258.

Richer, J. (1976). The social avoidance of autistic children. *Animal Behaviour*, *2*, 898–906.

Rutter, M. (1978). Diagnosis and definition of childhood autism. *Journal of Autism and Childhood Schizophrenia*, *8*, 139–161.

Rutter, M. (1983). Cognitive deficits in the pathogenesis of autism. *Journal of Child Psychology and Psychiatry*, *24*, 513–531.

Rutter, M. (1985). Infantile autism and other pervasive developmental disorders. In M. Rutter & L. Hersov (Eds), *Child and adolescent psychiatry: Modern approaches*. Oxford: Blackwell.

Sigman, M., Ungerer, J. A., Mundy, P. & Sherman, T. (1987). Cognition in autistic children. In D. J. Cohen & A. M. Donnellan (Eds), *Handbook of autism and pervasive development disorders*, pp. 103–120. Maryland: Winston and Sons.

Volkmar, F. R. (1987). Social development. In D. J. Cohen, A. M. Donnellan & R. Paul (Eds), *Handbook of autism and pervasive developmental disorders*, pp. 41–60. New York: John Wiley.

Weeks, J. S. & Hobson, R. P. (1987). The salience of facial expressions for autistic children. *Journal of Child Psychology and Psychiatry*, *28*, 137–152.

Wing, L. (1976). *Early childhood autism*. New York: Pergamon Press.

Woodward, M. F. & Barber, C. G. (1960). Phoneme perception in lipreading. *Journal of Speech and Hearing Research*, *3*, 212–222.

Yin, R. K. (1969). Looking at upside-down faces. *Journal of Experimental Psychology*, *81*, 141–145.

EUROPEAN JOURNAL OF COGNITIVE PSYCHOLOGY, 1991, *3* (1) 87–103

Identification of Spatially Quantised Tachistoscopic Images of Faces: How Many Pixels Does it Take to Carry Identity?

Talis Bachmann

Department of Psychology, University of Tartu, Tartu, Estonia, U.S.S.R.

Six images of human faces were quantised into isoluminant square-shaped pixels (16 grey levels) at eight different spatial levels of quantisation. The subjects had to identify the faces that were presented with different exposure durations (from 1 to 200 msec) and with one of two brightness conditions (variable brightness in Experiment 1 or isobrightness in Experiment 2). All finer quantisation levels led to better identification than the most coarse quantisation level (15 pixels per face in the horizontal dimension) at all exposure durations. The observation of an abrupt decrease in identification efficiency on moving from 18 or more pixels per face to 15 pixels per face and the approximate equality in identification efficiency within a broad range of quantisation levels above 18 pixels per face pose some problems for existing theories of face recognition. The implications of these findings for prototype-related, autocorrelational and microgenetic accounts of face and pattern processing are discussed.

INTRODUCTION

Here and there in the face recognition literature, spatially quantised images ("block-portraits") have been employed as stimuli (e.g. Bachmann, 1987; Harmon & Julesz, 1973; Morrone, Burr & Ross, 1983; Sergent, 1986). Mostly, however, the quantisation procedure follows the aim of *demonstration* rather than *measurement*. Systematic analyses have been carried out within the spatial frequency domain (which, of course, is related to the objectives of the spatial quantisation technique: on these matters, see Bruce, 1988; Harmon & Julesz, 1973; Sergent, 1986). However, there has been little research assessing the effects of systematic variation in spatial quantisation level on the efficiency of performance in different pattern recognition tasks, including face recognition (identification, matching, categorisation).

Requests for reprints should be addressed to Talis Bachmann, Department of Psychology, University of Tartu, 78 Tiigi Street, Tartu, Estonia 202400, U.S.S.R.

The following alternative hypotheses can be outlined at the start of systematic research on the effects of spatial quantisation. (1) With moving from coarse to fine spatial quantisation, processing efficiency, correspondingly, will gradually increase. This hypothesis is consistent with both the local feature analysis model (the component model) and the global configuration processing model of recognition, because with moving from coarse to fine pixel structure both local feature adequacy and the adequacy of global configurational measures will increase. (2) With systematic variation of the spatial quantisation level, performance will improve up to a certain point and, beyond this point (i.e. a certain value of the quantisation level), any further increase in the number of pixels per pattern will not yield a substantial increase in recognition efficiency. This hypothesis constrains certain recognition models depending on the exact spatial level where the "catastrophe" (cf. Thom, 1975) in terms of the break-up of face recognition routines takes place. If the break-up border lies close to the coarse quantisation, which leaves the local feature level without any sensible specification (cf. 2–3 pixels per facial element such as mouth, nose or eye), then local feature processing models – or at least straightforward variants of these – prove invalid. If the break-up border lies close to the fine quantisation, then both critical distinctive feature models and global plus local gradual analysis models (with decisive stages of processing left for the final fine-scale analysis: e.g. Sergent, 1986) could be consistent with the data. Our aim was to test these general conjectures in the experiments described below.

Before turning to the empirical work, let us make some additional general comments on the proposed strategy. As for the specification of the independent variables, one can outline trivial measures such as *pixels per face* in horizontal and vertical dimensions and analogous measures for the main distinctive component parts of the face (nose, mouth, eye, eyebrow, iris, etc.). It is not hard to see the potential usefulness of this approach in integrating global-configurational aspects of face recognition problems and local/component-related aspects within a single formal research strategy (including the possibility of formally describing and measuring the global and local spatial levels in the same "vocabulary"). As a special problem, the relative impact of different spatial levels of image elements (or constituents) on *identification* rather than *matching* or *classification* may deserve attention. More generally (and an issue which also has practical aspects), we would ask a simple question: How many pixels does it take for facial identity to be communicated? As we know, to recognise a quantised pattern as a face, a pattern consisting of only 11–12 pixels per face in the horizontal dimension is sufficient to carry relevant information (cf. Morrone et al., 1983; Sergent, 1986). But what about identification?

Besides the question of defining the spatial level of the facial image, we should not overlook the temporal aspect of processing which has received due attention, for example, in the microgenetic approach to pattern recognition (see Bachmann, 1987; 1989; Sergent, 1986). In order to have at least some control over the temporal progression of quantised image processing and, consequently, the relative fullness of representing different scales of image in the percept, tachistoscopic procedures with controlled exposure duration are necessary. But due to the ambiguity of the energetic and temporal factors within the range of exposure durations below 100 msec (cf. Bloch's Law), we need an additional control over the energetic aspect: Experiment 2 is devoted to this aspect.

EXPERIMENT 1

Method

Subjects.   Four students, each of whom had normal vision and were aged between 20 and 22 years, participated in the experiment. They were relatively naive as to the theoretical problems of cognitive psychology, but experienced as subjects in tachistoscopic pattern recognition studies.

Stimuli and Task.   The stimulus materials consisted of six achromatic positive-contrast slides of human faces (A, B, C, D, E, F) in the frontal plane, and respective photographic prints in non-quantised versions (i.e. the "original images"), 24 slides with small (corresponding to approximately 6 min of visual angle at the viewers' distance) Landoldt rings, 6 for each orientation, and 48 slides of computer-quantised images of the "original" versions (each original stimulus quantised at each of the eight spatial levels of quantisation). The quantisation was performed by the computer in a similar fashion to the classic procedure employed by Harmon and Julesz (1973);[1] the display enabled 16 grey levels of the image. Eight spatial levels of quantisation were employed, yielding eight types of quantised facial images: 15 pixels per face (as measured in the horizontal dimension along the straight inter-auricular line), 18, 21, 24, 32, 44 and 74 pixels per face. Figure 1 gives an example of quantised faces generated on the computer display. The original versions of the stimuli faces of six Caucasian males aged between 40 and 50 years, and unknown to the subjects, were depicted in full face. The outlines of the faces were fitted together in the context of the slide frames. The persons depicted had no beards, conspicuous haircuts, spectacles or other distinctive features,

[1]The author would like to thank Jüri Allik and Tiit Mogom for providing computer facilities (both software and hardware), which enabled generation of the quantised images and their photography.

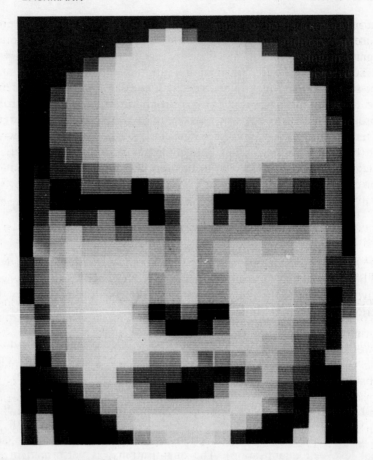

FIG. 1.   An example of the spatially quantised images of human faces used as stimuli in the experiments.

which can be subsumed under the so-called "easy cues" for identification. The photographic prints of the original versions of the stimuli (A, B, C, D, E, F) were mounted in two rows of three pictures on a notice board in the room in which the experiment took place. They were effectively visible to the students only if they turned their heads away from the screen, which was necessary in the training session and allowed during leisure breaks in the main experimental session. In the main session, after sufficient training, the students were able to perform the task without turning to the notice board, and hence our task could readily be termed *identification*.

The stimulus images, as projected on the screen, subtended about 8° of visual angle in the horizontal dimension (at the students' viewing position) and had an average luminance of about 20 cd/m^2. (We deliberately avoided any computations of spatial frequencies on the *absolute* spatial scale, because existing data convincingly show that contrast changes *per face* – i.e. changes in the relative spatial scale – are decisive in face recognition: cf. Bruce, 1988; Kalmus & Bachmann, 1980.)

The main task for the students consisted of six-alternative identification of the quantised tachistoscopic images of stimulus faces as projected on the screen. The students were instructed to respond by writing down one of the six alternative letters (A, B, C, D, E, F) according to their impression of which had been exposed (they were to guess if they were unsure). A supplementary task necessary for the control of the adequacy of accommodation consisted of the classical visual acuity task using Landoldt rings. The students had to write down the rings specifying their orientation.

Apparatus. The stimulus slides were exposed on the white screen by means of an "Alpha" slide projector with a fast shutter covering the objective, which enabled exposure durations in the necessary range of 1–200 msec.

Procedure. The students were seated in a dimly illuminated room in front of the screen. Each exposure trial was preceded by an aural warning requiring fixation at the centre of the screen. Exposure of the stimulus slide followed after 1 sec.

The training session consisted of 60 exposures of the non-quantised original versions of the stimulus faces. Each face was exposed 10 times for 200 msec each and at random in the sequence of 60 exposures. This session turned out to be sufficient for forming an effective requisite memory of which symbols belonged to which faces. At the end of this session, the students identified the faces with over 90% accuracy.

The main session was as follows. Each student received a quasi-randomised sequence with counterbalanced order of six different durations (1, 4, 8, 20, 40 and 100 msec), such that each alternative at each of the spatial quantisation levels was exposed four times (6 faces × 4 times × 8 quantisation levels × 6 exposure durations = 1152 exposures per student in the main condition). After each 48 exposures of the main stimuli, the students were allowed to rest for 3–4 min without changing the lighting conditions. As the supplementary condition, 384 exposures of the Landoldt stimuli for the acuity control task were randomly intermixed with the main stimulus exposures, thus yielding 1536 exposures in total per student. Each daily session consisted of 384 exposures.

Results

The results were expressed as a percentage of correct responses as a function of exposure duration, with spatial quantisation level as the para-

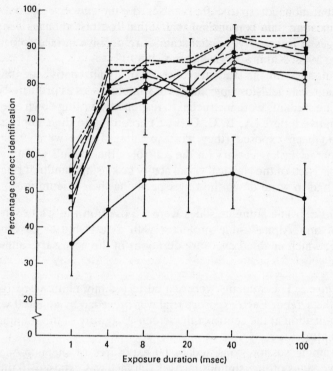

FIG. 2. Percentage correct identification of the quantised images of faces as a function of duration of exposure and the level of spatial quantisation. ——●——, 15 pixels per face; ——○——, 18 pixels per face; ——■——, 21 pixels per face; — — ● — —, 24 pixels per face; — — ○ — —, 27 pixels per face; — — ■ — — —, 32 pixels per face; —·—·—, 44 pixels per face; ·····, 74 pixels per face. The confidence limits are drawn for the 15 pixels per face condition and the lowermost and uppermost points of the rest of the quantisation conditions at the 95% confidence level.

meter (see Fig. 2). Simple inspection of Fig. 2 and the respective 95% confidence limits (calculated according to the arcsin transform: cf. Gubler, 1978) indicate that:

1. In general, the identification of quantised images of human faces improves with an increase in the length of exposure.
2. There is not any substantial dependence of identification efficiency on the level of spatial quantisation within the range of 18–74 pixels per face.
3. There is an abrupt decrease in identification when moving from 18 or more pixels per face to 15 pixels per face.

Hence the operational defining spatial level of identity within the constraints provided by the variables of this experiment and expressed as the maximum local square-shaped space-average luminance region sufficient for identification, can be equalled to 1/18, or 0.06 of the facial horizontal diameter. The fact that 94% of the Landoldt acuity control trials yielded correct responses indicates that facial identity was not perceived due to visual blur (i.e. not by virtue of the *spatial* filtering out of the high-frequency "noise" in the shape of the pixels' edges and right-angle structure).

Discussion

The results clearly show that within the constraints set by our variables (six versions of similar faces invariant with regard to race, general age, sex, etc.), some decisive perturbation in the face processing routine takes place when moving from 18 to 15 pixels per face. That this is not an artefact of a limited temporal exposure condition (cf. the notions of successive micro-genetic scanning of different spatial scales of an image over cumulative temporal epochs: Bachmann, 1987; Sergent, 1986; Watt, 1988) is evidenced by the fact that at all exposure durations, the stimuli with 18 or more pixels per face behaved analogously and their efficiency significantly exceeded that of 15 pixels per face. The value of this break-up border in terms of local change of the spatial quantisation level obviously precludes any sensible theoretical interpretation in terms of disintegration of the identity cues of local facial component features. For example, when moving from 18 to 15 pixels per face quantisation, the pixel size is changed from an average 0.056 to 0.067 of the inter-auricular horizontal dimension. This means that, if we calculate averages for the horizontal and vertical dimensions of the component features, we get approximately 4 pixels per nose, 2 pixels per eye, 3.8 pixels per mouth, 3 pixels per eyebrow and 1.2 pixels per visible part of the iris.[2] It is hard to believe that these poor pixel structures are sufficient to carry enough information for the components to be recognised as the individual features pertaining to a given face. Rather, we may conclude that the local feature processing models fail to explain this result and that more Gestalt-oriented global configuration-sensitive processing models seem more plausible. But the abrupt reduction in the identification efficiency with such a minor spatial change of the elementary pixel structure suggests the existence of some critical value of some important measure within the complex integrative metrics of the configurational interrelationships of the distribution of the gradients of spatial contrast (or their local maxima and/or local minima).

---

[2]Whether this fact of the diameter of the iris being the most close dimension to the elementary facial pixel-component is a mere coincidence or whether it points to the iris as a crucial face-recognition unit (cf. the possibility to precisely localise it within the context of the facial configuration) deserves special attention in the future.

It is clear that the reader may not be happy with the confound in our experimental method: with the exposure durations employed, Bloch's Law states that an increase in exposure duration or luminance has equivalent effects on subjective brightness. The visual system integrates luminous energy over short temporal intervals and, consequently, it is hard to tell whether the increase in identification efficiency is mainly due to the increased energy content of the display, or the increased temporal representation of the stimulus image. To test the impact of these factors, we performed Experiment 2.

EXPERIMENT 2

In an earlier unpublished study, we obtained the average brightness functions of 10 observers for the exposure conditions analogous to those of Experiment 1, but randomly using different neutral density filters to alter exposure luminance. As an outcome, we obtained a number of exposure duration *vs* brightness functions. Then, by drawing suitable isobrightness lines (a y = constant type of function) and by projecting the intersections of the isobrightness lines and individual brightness functions onto the temporal axis, we produced a table of correspondences between definite filters and values of exposure duration, which define the necessary combinations for isobrightness. In Experiment 2, all exposures were in accordance with the said table.

Method

The method was as for Experiment 1, except that at each exposure duration condition the suitable neutral density filter was placed before the objective of the projector. This meant that in terms of brightness, all exposures were equal to a 2-msec exposure with the filter NS-6. The respective luminance equalled 4 cd/m^2. There was also a slight difference with regard to the exposure durations used: 2, 4, 8, 100 and 200 msec. This was motivated by the need to obtain adequate isobrightness with the filters at hand.

Results and Discussion

The results were analogous to those of Experiment 1, except that the difference in identification efficiency between the 15 pixels per face condition and the bulk of other quantisation conditions was a little bit smaller (see Fig. 3). But comparison of the means (based on Fisher's ρ-method: cf. Gubler, 1978) revealed that with a 2-msec exposure, this difference was significant at the $P < 0.018$ level (at 4 msec exposure, $P < 0.013$; at 100

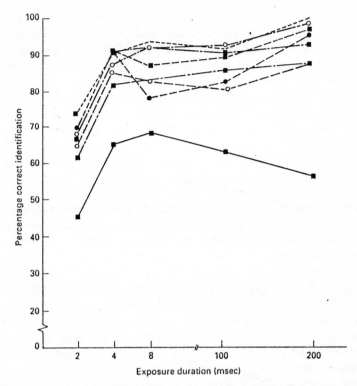

FIG. 3. Percentage correct identification of the quantised images of faces exposed in the isobrightness regime as a function of the duration of exposure and the level of spatial quantisation. The lowermost continuous line = 15 pixels per face.

msec exposure, $P < 0.005$; at 200 msec exposure, $P < 0.001$). Only at 8 msec exposure did the percentage correct with 15 pixels per face (69%) not significantly differ from the nearest higher efficiency level (76% with 24 pixels per face quantisation).

Also, the general shape of the identification function (46, 67, 69, 62 and 57% respectively for 2, 4, 8, 100 and 200 msec) in this experimental condition was rather similar to the non-monotonic recognition functions of the quantised images in the most-coarse quantisation condition of our earlier studies (Bachmann, 1987; Bachmann & Kahusk, 1987). The significance of the difference between the maximum of 69% with 8 msec exposure and 57% with 200 msec exposure ($P < 0.04$) of the non-monotonic function of this experiment points to the possibility that in identification we also may speak of the attention-dependent microgenetic process of moving from coarse to fine spatial scales of analysis of the inner representation (see General Discussion). The reason why in Experiment 1 this regularity is expressed only as a slight trend ($P < 0.1$ for the difference of 55.6 and 48.6% of the 15 pixels per face function in Fig. 2) may be related to the fact that the higher energetic regime could provide conditions in which the operation of microgenetic attentional scanning mechanism(s) is partly supplemented by the operation of some more primitive lower-level mechanism of brightness distribution matching in the longer-lasting sensory register. The energy-invariant/time-variant conditions and the addition of one longer exposure time in Experiment 2 may have enforced the successive global-to-local scanning or microgenesis (Bachmann, 1987; 1989; Navon, 1977; Sergent, 1986; Watt, 1988) to take its fuller effect. But this also means that we should be cautious when comparing experiments on identification (and matching with standards) which enable the elaboration of the lower-level, sensory-dependent mechanisms of brightness distribution comparisons, with experiments of recognition accomplished as the classification of unpredictable objects (as in the study by Bachmann, 1987).

GENERAL DISCUSSION

What can be said concerning alternative approaches to the processing of information contained in images of human faces and what directions of future research can be outlined as based on the present study? First of all, let us make some remarks about processing models of face recognition. As it was argued above, local feature processing (feature listing or integrating) models seem invalid in the light of the present results.

The local "dissolving" of features and replacing them with a pattern of few pixels, e.g. in the rather efficient 18 pixels per face condition, supports this conclusion, as well as the fact that images of 18 and 74 pixels per face were almost equally effective in providing information for facial identity (despite the fact that the outlines of the original faces were similar and that "easy cues" for discrimination were absent). The spatial-frequency filtering model does not provide a good explanation either, because (1) the temporal factor did not have any decisive effect on the relative effectiveness of the 15 pixels per face vs 18 pixels per face identification in Experiment 1, and (2) the optical blurring of these images as an equivalent of low-pass filtering did not show any decisive differences in the effective appearance of these faces. Template matching as the absolutely uneconomical mechanism for pattern recognition (identification) has received sound criticism by Uttal (1988), with which we readily agree. But what then are the models which are at least consistent with our results? First of all, prototype models (e.g. Valentine's, 1988, multidimensional vector model) seem not to be at odds with the present data, if it were possible to find a way to explain how it is that a small shift in the coarseness of the pixels' spatial "stratification" yields such a dramatic decline in performance. Commonsense thinking predicts that there should be some immanent relational metrics along which the prototypes and "deviant" individual faces can differ and that if – by virtue of using spatial contrast distribution, which is characteristic of certain quantised images – this difference reaches a certain critical value, then a "catastrophic" break-up (cf. Thom, 1975) in face-processing routines could occur. However, it is impossible to answer on the basis of the experimental design employed in the present study, what this metric could be.

Secondly, we could also consider some cross-correlational or autocorrelational models in the context of face identification (e.g. Uttal's, 1975, approach). It is not too hard to imagine how, with increasing coarseness of quantisation, the spatial (spatio-temporal) autocorrelator gives consistent results, signifying identity, but at a certain point, with further increasing coarseness, the determination of the pixel structure as noise or as signal becomes equivocal. Moreover, the pixel size characteristic of the quantisation level where the break-up of identification commences may well be a proper measure of the standard spatial shift of two different samples of the same input pattern which is used by the natural perceptual "autocorrelator" in the nervous system. Or, to use Uttal's terms, a spatial range of lateral connections, can be determined by the procedure of systematic change in the coarseness of quantisation. (Of course, to develop Uttal's autocorrelational *detection* model to the *identification* model, we need some implementation in terms of stored prototype patterns to correlate with and, consequently, multiple alternative autocorrelational procedures with the highest correlation value with a given memory-stored prototype being the basis for identification. Here we notice some similarities between the autocorrelational and prototype-based approaches.)

It is interesting to note that the conditions for transforming test images that lead to a decrease in Uttal's autocorrelator efficiency include deformation of straight lines into curves and angles, which is of course introduced into the coherent facial structure by the increase in the size of pixels, not to speak of the opposite effect of an increase in autocorrelation of the spurious masking structure. Anyway, the distributed processing imperative, necessary in order to corroborate our configuration-sensitive experimental results, is explicitly acknowledged by Uttal (1988). One more consistency with the correlational approach which we notice in our data is related to the effect of exposure duration: Increasing the duration of exposure may provide an increasing number of the actual data samples for the autocorrelator (including correlation of the actual pattern with memory representations) and yield an increase in processing efficiency. It is not without interest to mention that in a fairly close approach to simulated three-dimensional perception, Lappin, Doner and Kottas (1980) found a dramatic decrease in the percentage correct discrimination when moving from one level of (perfect) correlation between the contents of successive input frames to another level of slightly smaller correlation. The further decrease in correlation, however, did not lead to the expected decrease in discrimination. The formal similarity of this "critical zone" of change in the value of independent variables as leading to a dramatic decline in performance in both Lappin et al. and our own results may not be a mere coincidence, but may point to the very general law of critical relational measures which defines the range of permissible perturbations in the geometry of input patterns, beyond which the processing routines for performing a given perceptual task are left helpless. The importance of some energetic variable for the working of these routines can be deduced from the differences between the results of Experiments 1 and 2 (compare Figs 2 and 3).

In recent years, the microgenetic approach to pattern recognition has become quite popular (Bachmann, 1987; Sergent, 1986; Watt, 1988). The main idea behind this approach is that different levels or aspects of the image become perceptually available at different moments of real time while this accumulative process of percept development is going on. It is agreed that a stimulus image can be "used" by the perceptual system in alternative ways by building up and/or matching with multiple representations derived from the same stimulus object and that this multiple coding procedure progresses through a lawful, ordered set of operations.

The approach offered by Sergent (1986) seems consistent with the results of the present study, with some minor reservations. Because our students knew beforehand that all of the stimuli were human faces, then the early processing stages which rely upon the coarse spatial information and signal the mere presence of some face, were operationally redundant. Only beginning with a certain quantisation level will information which is precise enough to signal identity be scanned out. But the seeming lack of interaction of exposure duration and quantisation level in Experiment 1 casts some doubts about the straightforwardness of the successive development of the perceptual *representations* with gradual integrating luminous energy over time (cf. Sergent, 1986). Even if Sergent (1986) allows for the iterative nature of this representation build-up, she still seems to consider that *early-level* visual *availability* develops through the microgenetic phases. But why, then, in our Experiment 2 and in the recognition functions of Bachmann (1987) with coarse quantisation did an increase in exposure duration lead to a *decrease* in identification (recognition)? The availability of coarse-scale information which was sufficient for better performance at shorter exposures should still be there. The point, it seems, is that the coarse-scale representations have been built up, but they are no longer *used*; instead, the perceptual system has become tuned to analyse fine-scale representations, which leads, in the case of the presence of pixels masking structure, to a decrease in performance efficiency. On the other hand, the fine-scale detailed information should also be represented beginning from the early stages of microgenesis, though not used at these early stages. Otherwise, we cannot understand why there is a clear advantage for the images with fine-scale quantisation over the most-coarse ones even at the shortest exposure durations (and both in variable brightness and isobrightness regimes). Thus the microgenetic conceptions with one more additional degree of freedom in the operation of inner mechanisms have more flexibility in order to deal with the above-mentioned regularities in our data: Specifically, we would outline conceptions in which the early-level representation build-up is relatively independent of the higher-level perceptual utilisation of these representations (see Bachmann, 1987; Watt, 1988). The microgenetic nature of perception is thought to manifest just in these second-order operations. As Bachmann (1987) has pointed out, what matters is attention, but not merely perceptual representation. The different spatial scales of the image are present in the processing system earlier than some consciousness-generating (retouch-) mechanism makes use of them, but "making use of them" follows the microgenetic rule according to which the actualisation progresses from large-scale, coarse information to fine-scale, detailed information.

In the theory by Watt (1988), it is also allowed that the finest spatial scales are available at all times, but only for the texture-type of discriminations. In the case of perceptual objects, the basic algorithm of Watt's theory provides the basis for a progressive, spatial scale, a hierarchical computation of spatial position for all levels of detail. It is required that the filters of different spatial resolution be switched out of the summation stage of the procedure, starting with the largest and moving through to the smallest. We would stress the term *switch out*, by virtue of which the microgenetic process appears more like decomposition. Watt (1988) has put forward some informal ideas concerning the possibilities of flexible higher-level control over the perceptual tuning of different spatial levels of analysis. This theory seems very capable of predicting the results of our experiments.

Consider the case with fine-scale quantisation. With ever-increasing exposure duration, the filter system has more and more time and energy to complete a fuller analysis of the stimulus and the probabilities of recognition/identification according to large-scale and fine-scale distinctive information summate to give ever greater efficiency estimates. Consider the situation with coarse quantisation. Initially, the increase in exposure duration could help to build up a more adequate large-scale perceptual image, but afterwards the switch-out of large-scale filters altogether with the ongoing operation of progressively smaller filters leads to a predominance of fine-scale information in the perceptual image. Because the distinctive features of the facial image are "dissolved" within the square-shaped pixels, then perception will be dominated by the irrelevant structure of fine edges and right angles and the efficiency of the task will be low. The perceptual system will no longer benefit from the additional fine-scale information. The only problematic comment we would add is that the term *stimulus* be replaced by *initial stimulus representation* in Watt's conception in order to better satisfy the flexibility requirement discussed previously.

The pattern recognition algorithm, poetically labelled "Damn the Details" by its author (Guberman, 1984), also belongs to the family of global-to-local processing models and is very much in agreement with Watt's conception of scanning from coarse to fine spatial scales of an image, but the theoretical background of it is more close to Gestalt psychology.

According to Guberman (1984), the segregation of an object and its interpretation should be performed simultaneously for the whole image with regard to all potential objects. An object is defined as something which affords "sensible" interpretation; an interpretation is termed "sensible" given that it is congruous with interpretation of all other objects within the image. A crucial capacity of vision is to be prepared to ignore the detailed scrutiny of an image. If applied to image analysis, the previously mentioned algorithm starts by giving values to x according to the $y = 0$ value of the function $y(x)$, which defines zero-crossings of an image luminance distribution function. Then we have intervals between the values of x satisfying $y = 0$. As a next step, the shortest interval is found (e.g. $/x_k, x_{k+1}/$ with length l_1). Then with systematic erasure of the shortest intervals, a hierarchy of intervals is built up. This hierarchy is described by its own function $n(l)/N$ where $n(l)$ equals the number of intervals left after erasure of the interval with length equal to l. It is easy to understand how this basic idea as described in the case of unidimensional brightness distribution can be generalised to two dimensions. Applying his algorithm to real images, Guberman inverses the order of analysis and starts with the most-coarse level of description.

The shape of the function $n(l)/N$ which is built up for the brightness distribution function $y(x)$ can be regarded as a generalised description of an image. The exact position of the steps of the general function defines the characteristic size of the details of the image; an interval with the lack of details with size less than l_0 segregates characteristic objects. The more the stepness of the function $n(l)/N$ is expressed, the more the brightness distribution function can be characterised as highly organised. (According to Gelfand and Tsetlin (1966), a well-organised function is a function of many variables which can be described with a small number of parameters.) Guberman's algorithm for object segregation and description belongs to the family of non-local algorithms, because the question about if a given interval can be specified as an object is answered depending on the size of all other segregated objects. Here we meet a feature which may turn out to be very useful in the light of the well-established scale-invariance and state-invariance of facial identity (cf. Bruce, 1988).

If we now return to our paradigm – the paradigm of spatially quantised images introduced into the microgenetic, space–time analysis of perceptual processing – then we may notice several appealing features of Guberman's approach. Guberman's requirement that description of any part of the image should be performed in such terms that can also be applied to all other parts is satisfied by the virtue of using the procedure of generating homologous pixel structure over the whole image. In Guberman's approach, decompositions of images are performed not by a full listing of the elements, but by the ordered analysis of severely restricted classes of decompositions. Compare this with the impossibility of listing all of the meaningful elements with a more or less coarse quantisation condition in our paradigm. And the definition of Gestalt as the meaningfully (sensibly) coarsened description of an image echoes the very idea of the quantisation procedure. It is sufficient to have some 15–18 pixels, hence to have a coarsened description, but still have the information sufficient to carry identity within the constraints provided by the stimulus alternatives.

What are the potential problems that can be approached by the present research strategy? First of all, we could mention the key problem: What really happens in the communicated contents of the original stimulus image when we replace the 18 pixels per image quantisation with 15 pixels? What is the critical factor hidden behind the simple and seemingly non-substantial increase in the pixel size? When answering this question, we may approach the understanding of some substantial factor or measure for faces to be identifiable. Secondly, in order to develop some more penetrating analyses, one has to include the phase-shift of the quantisation within the spatial window which defines the original stimulus. In other words, via this procedure, which is in general a spatial-frequency-invariant operation, we can discover what is optimal for recognition (identification) – either the eye-centred quantisation, nose-centred quantisation, mouth-centred quantisation or facial outline-centred quantisation, if any. It is possible that the absence of systematic improvement of identification with ever-finer quantisation above 18 pixels per face (cf. Fig. 2) has something to do with the above-mentioned factors. Whereas quantisation in our experiment was performed with spatial reference (centration) to the whole image, then by changing the quantisation level we also changed the relative centration of the local spatial quanta with regard to the facial components and thus the finer quantisation in certain conditions may have been less favourable than the coarser quantisation. The third prospective idea is that by using rectangular pixels we could study which dimension (vertical or horizontal) is more important in face recognition and identification. This can be done by leaving horizontal pixel size invariant and by varying only its vertical size and vice versa, and then finding out what are the respective effects on performance. Fourthly, turning our interest towards the problems of memory, we could ask, at what spatial quantisation level a priming effect for face recognition could originate? When using quantised images of different resolution as primes and original non-quantised images as the test stimuli, we are able to answer these questions.

The only strong conclusion though which we can draw from the present experimental results is that there exist at least some cases where for facial identity to be inferred by the perceptual system, it is sufficient to present a quantised version of the original, non-quantised image such that no more than 18 pixels per face in the horizontal dimension and 24 pixels per face in the vertical dimension are present. These constraints do not exclude faces without extraneous and/or "easy cues" for identification.

Manuscript received September 1989
Revised manuscript received March 1990

REFERENCES

Bachmann, T. (1987). Different trends in perceptual pattern microgenesis as a function of the spatial range of local brightness averaging. *Psychological Research*, *49*, 107–111.

Bachmann, T. (1989). Microgenesis as traced by the transient paired-forms paradigm. *Acta Psychologica*, *70*, 3–17.

Bachmann, T. & Kahusk, N. (1987). *Nonmonotonic microgenetic function for the perceptual representation of quantized visual images of objects*. Workshop on Knowledge Representation and Information Processing, Berlin (Abstract), p. 45.

Bruce, V. (1988). *Recognising faces*. London: Lawrence Erlbaum Associates Ltd.

Guberman, S. A. (1984). A theory of Gestalt and the systems approach [in Russian]. In *Systems research: Methodological problems 1, a yearbook 1984*. Moscow: "Nauka".

Gubler, E. V. (1978). *Computational methods of analysis and recognition of the pathological processes* [in Russian]. Moscow: "Meditsina".

Harmon, L. D. & Julesz, B. (1973). Masking in visual recognition: Effects of two-dimensional filtered noise. *Science*, *180*, 1194–1197.

Kalmus, M. & Bachmann, T. (1980). Perceptual microgenesis of complex visual pattern: Comparison of methods and possible implications for future studies. *Acta et Commentationes Universitatis Tartuensis*, *529*, 135–159.

Lappin, J. S., Doner, D. C. & Kottas, B. L. (1980). Minimal conditions for the visual detection of structure and motion in three dimensions. *Science*, *209*, 717–719.

Morrone, M. C., Burr, D. C. & Ross, J. (1983). Added noise restores recognizability of coarse quantized images. *Nature*, *305*, 226–228.

Navon, D. (1977). Forest before trees: The precedence of global features in visual perception. *Cognitive Psychology*, *9*, 353–383.

Sergent, J. (1986). Microgenesis of face perception. In H. D. Ellis, M. A. Jeeves, F. Newcombe & A. Young (Eds), *Aspects of face processing*. Dordecht: Martinus Nijhoff.

Thom, R. (1975). *Structural stability and morphogenesis: An outline of a general theory of models*. Reading, Mass.: Benjamin.

Uttal, W. R. (1975). *An autocorrelation theory of form detection*. Hillsdale, N.J.: Lawrence Erlbaum Associates Inc.

Uttal, W. R. (1988). *On seeing forms*. Hillsdale, N.J.: Lawrence Erlbaum Associates Inc.

Valentine, T. (1988). *A prototype model of face recognition*. Paper presented at the meeting of the European Society for Cognitive Psychology, Cambridge, September.

Watt, R. (1988). *Visual processing: Computational, psychophysical and cognitive research*. London: Lawrence Erlbaum Associates Ltd.

EUROPEAN JOURNAL OF COGNITIVE PSYCHOLOGY, 1991, *3* (1) 105–135

Perception and Recognition of Photographic Quality Facial Caricatures: Implications for the Recognition of Natural Images

Philip J. Benson and David I. Perrett

Psychological Laboratory, Department of Psychology, University of St Andrews, Fife, U.K.

The perception and recognition of photographic images of famous faces was compared with the same images transformed to produce caricatures of different degrees of exaggeration. Following Brennan (1982; 1985), caricatures were produced by first comparing the position of facial features in a frame-grabbed image with the average position for a series of faces; deviations from the average were then accentuated by a constant fraction (16, 32 or 48%). Photographic quality caricatures for seven famous faces were generated by distorting regions of the original images in accordance with the change in feature positions. Images reducing the distinctiveness of faces (anticaricatures) were produced by decreasing deviations from the norm. In Experiment 1, perceptual ratings of the degree to which images resembled the individuals depicted was found to vary with the degree of caricaturing (-32, -16, 0, $+16$, $+32\%$). Interpolation from the data indicated that the best likeness occurred for images with a small degree of positive exaggeration ($+4.4\%$ on average). The magnitude of this caricature advantage correlated with the familiarity with the target faces and with the quality of

---

Requests for reprints should be addressed to Philip J. Benson, Psychological Laboratory, Department of Psychology, University of St Andrews, Fife KY16 9JU, U.K.

This work forms part of a collaborative investigation into face recognition, funded by an ESRC programme award XC15250001 to Vicki Bruce (University of Nottingham), XC15250002 to Ian Craw (University of Aberdeen), XC15250003 to Hadyn Ellis (University of Wales, Cardiff), XC15250004 to Andrew Ellis (University of York) and Andrew Young (University of Durham) and XC15250005 to David Perrett (University of St Andrews). Phil Benson is funded by the ESRC St Andrews award. David Perrett is a Royal Society University Research Fellow. We thank D. Davis for his contribution to the development of caricature production software, Nicholas Parsons for providing photographs of himself and allowing us to publish his caricatures, two anonymous reviewers for their comments on an earlier draft of the manuscript, and Vicki Bruce as editor of this special issue for her useful criticism of the final manuscript. We are grateful to Andy Young for predicting caricature effects in non-matching trials, and the participants at the 7th ESRC Grange-over-Sands Workshop.

---

the caricaturing process as assessed independently by caricature artists. Experiment 2 examined the recognition of normal and caricatured images in a name/face matching task. Overall, the subjects' fastest reaction times occurred for images with positive caricaturing. The caricature advantage was primarily attributed to improved performance on trials where the name and face did not match. The results suggest that both the precise metric proportions of faces and the way faces deviate from average are represented in memory. The results also indicate that the "super-fidelity" of caricatures found (Rhodes, Brennan & Carey, 1987) is not restricted to line drawings and may, therefore, have implications for how we recognise natural facial images.

INTRODUCTION

Caricatures are often gross distortions of the faces they represent. Moreover, a cartoon caricature is usually depicted with a very few lines. Despite the impoverished and distorted nature of the information in caricatures, we are remarkably good at recognising the individuals that they represent. Indeed, recent findings (Rhodes et al., 1987; see below) indicate that line-drawn caricatures can be recognised more efficiently than veridical line drawings. It is likely, therefore, that an understanding of how caricatures "work" in activating representations of familiar individuals will help our understanding of how normal images of faces are stored in memory and recognised in everyday life. This paper compares the perception and recognition of caricatures and veridical images of familiar faces. We first describe techniques for producing caricatures automatically. These were originally devised for manipulating line drawings but we have extended them to continuous tone images. These techniques have allowed us to examine whether caricature effects found with line drawings have more general applicability to the processing of natural images. Secondly, they have allowed us to examine the bizarre possibility that an image of a face can be artificially transformed so that it looks more like the person than the original natural image.

How Caricatures Work

Perkins (1975) speculated on what parameters were necessary for caricaturing to work. He suggests that humour, "ugliness" and expression of personality are irrelevant to making caricatures recognisable, even though these are probably the most enjoyable aspects of cartoon art.

It is generally agreed that caricatures work by selectively accentuating particular details of a face (Brennan, 1985; Perkins, 1975). Presumably, the details which get accentuated in caricaturing are those which are characteristic of that individual. The skill of the caricature artist begins with realising which features are characteristic. There seems to be some consensus across artists as to which features should be caricatured for a given face. For example, Goldman and Hagen (1978) studied the caricaturing of Richard Nixon by 17 artists and found a high degree of concordance as to what was caricatured.

The features of an individual face that are characteristic are those which differentiate that person from the general population in which they live. This definition of characteristic features embodies a comparison between the features of the face in question and those which are normal or average for a population of faces. The degree to which a feature departs from the population average is a measure of how characteristic that feature is. It follows that not all faces are suitable for caricaturing. If a person has facial proportions close to average then there will be nothing deviant and nothing to caricature.

Choosing the Appropriate Norm for Comparison

Careful attention must be given to the definition of an average face against which an individual's face is compared. Chance, Goldstein and McBride (1975) and Shepherd (1981) showed that people recognise faces from their own race better than faces of others, and therefore cross-racial caricaturing is undesirable. Unless some humorous distortion was required, cross-sex caricaturing again would also be unsuitable because of configural differences between male and female faces.

Stereotypical influences are also critical to successful caricaturing; pop stars are often thought of and portrayed as having deviant appearances (bright clothing, long hair, excesses of jewellery, etc.), politicians tend to conform (normally clean imaged, suited, with well-groomed hair). The age parameter is important in the same context with many pop stars either depicted as very young and naive or aged hippies from the 1960s, and political leaders typically old and haggard. From these considerations, successful caricaturing of a face needs to be done with respect to an average derived from the same age range. Contrasting a face against an average face of younger age will be likely to enhance the age of the target (this may be desirable for generating amusing effects but is likely to impair recognition). Stereotypical influences of age and socioeconomic class are also important in the recognition of faces (see Cross, Cross & Daly, 1971; Dion, Berscheid & Walster, 1972; Klatzky, Martin & Kane, 1982a; 1982b; Klatzky & Forrest, 1984). In caricaturing and recognising a face, we may compare it to a norm for the appropriate age, sex, race, and perhaps perceived socioeconomic status or occupation.

Once the features of a face which are characteristic have been established, a decision must be made as to the degree to which the features are to be reduced or exaggerated in the caricature. This has been found to depend on a number of factors. Different artists use different degrees of exaggeration. For Nixon's face, artists varied in the degree of exaggeration from 12 to 86% of the veridical feature dimensions (Goldman & Hagen, 1978). The extent of exaggeration also increased with time and with the decline in Nixon's popularity.

Automated Caricature Synthesis

Brennan (1982; 1985) developed a computer model to generate line-drawn caricatures. Brennan's procedure utilised the idea of comparing a target face to the norm for a population of faces and then exaggerating deviations. Images of real faces were digitised and aligned so that interocular separation was constant across faces. For each face a fixed number of points around the main features (eyes, nose, mouth, ears, smile lines, hair, etc.) was manually recorded. Veridical line drawings of the original faces were generated by linking appropriate points using spline curves.

To caricature a given face the x-y co-ordinates of feature points were compared with those of the "facial norm" (produced by averaging the data sets for many faces), and the distance between the target face and the norm calculated. These values indicate the extent to which particular facial feature points deviate from the norm. Caricatures were produced by multiplying each deviation by a fixed percentage. (Amplifying differences by a constant % means that features are exaggerated in proportion to the difference from the norm, and thus features close to the norm are relatively unaffected.) For example, in a caricature exaggerating deviations by + 50%, a point on the end of the nose which was 20 units from the norm would be displaced a further 10 units to a position deviating from the norm by 30 units. Similarly, to produce a representation diminishing all deviations by 50% (a 50% anticaricature or −50% caricature), the nose point would be shifted to a final distance 10 units from the norm. Having calculated all the modified feature positions, line-drawn caricatures were produced by linking up appropriate points around each facial feature.

It should be noted that the caricature process exaggerates differences in feature positions relative to the interocular separation (which is standardised for all faces). Because the process is relative, all dimensions including interocular separation are evenly caricatured. For a face that is average in every dimension except an unusually narrow separation of the eyes, the outline of the face will be evenly expanded by caricaturing. Thus in the end-product the eyes will lie even closer together relative to the overall shape of the face. Other proportions of the face, such as the height/width ratio, will remain normal, though the face will appear magnified.

Advantages and Limitations of Automatic Caricaturing

This process has the advantage that it does not require the skills of a caricature artist. Because all deviations are amplified to the same extent, those deviations which are characteristic of a given individual should also be accentuated. Furthermore, all exaggerations can be controlled quantitatively.

Another advantage of the automated process is that the holistic cues such as the spatial configuration between features are also transformed. While it is clear that faces are recognised on the basis of information from individual features, it has also been established that the configuration of features has a profound impact on the facial appearance (Haig, 1984; 1986; Rhodes, 1988; Sergent, 1984; Shepherd, Ellis & Davies, 1977). The dimensions of faces which go to make up configuration cues are not well established (Yamane, Kaji & Komatsu, 1988); however, it is not necessary to know which features or configurational cues are perceptually important as the process automatically amplifies all deviations, and should therefore include all relevant cues.

The process is not without problems. Perhaps the least obvious limitation is the demarcation of the feature points on the original image of the face; this can be difficult and is subjective (particularly with cheek bones). Different operators will apply different subjective criteria to determine where smile lines finish, etc. As a result, lines will be differentially accentuated, because small differences in feature points get amplified in the caricature. Finally, while the process is good for exaggerating feature shape and configuration, it is not good for exaggerating hair texture or style. Indeed, it is the internal features rather than the external hairstyle, etc., which is important in the recognition of familiar faces (Ellis, Shepherd & Davies, 1979; Young et al., 1985). There is, however, a danger in removing the hair or other parts of the face in so far as a lack of contextual information may impair recognition.

A further limitation is that the input faces must all have roughly the same pose. This usually involves standardisation to the frontal view. Only details visible in the frontal view are therefore accentuated. Unfortunately, the nose profile so often caricatured in cartoons is not visible from this view. Furthermore, there are a number of psychological studies which indicate that the face turned half way to profile presents a perspective view which has advantages in certain recognition and face matching tasks (Bruce, Valentine & Baddeley, 1987; Thomas, Perrett, Davis & Harries, submitted). This effect is not entirely consistent as the half profile view does not seem to confer an advantage on the recognition of familiar faces (for a discussion, see Bruce et al., 1987; Harries, Perrett & Lavender, in press). In principle, using a standard ½ profile pose could circumvent the limitation, but such standardisation is even more difficult with pictures of famous faces.

Comparisons Between Caricatures and Veridical Images

We are adept at recognising caricatures despite the relative lack of information that they contain. Many authors have questioned whether caricatures are in any way better representations than natural images. Perhaps the caricature contains not only the essential minimum of information, but because the information is accentuated they may also be "super-fidelity" or "super-normal" stimuli. Such a concept derives from ethological studies in which accentuation of particular dimensions of natural stimuli can produce behaviour which is more marked than that produced by natural stimuli. For example, if a nesting herring gull is given a choice between two eggs, one a natural egg and one larger than life size, it will attempt to roll the large egg back to the nest in preference to the natural egg (Hinde, 1982).

Hagen and Perkins (1983) and Tversky and Baratz (1985) attempted to assess the validity of the super-fidelity concept of caricatures. They found no advantage for caricatures over veridical representations of faces when comparing recognition performance. The latter study also failed to find a result for name/face matching. In these experiments, however, comparisons were made across two different media. Photographs were used for veridical representations but caricatures were line drawn. Photographs clearly contain much more information than line drawings (Davies, Ellis & Shepherd, 1978). So any potential advantage which caricatures had as better representations could have been offset by the impoverished medium of display.

Rhodes et al. (1987) used Brennan's procedure to make a balanced comparison between recognition of veridical and caricature line drawings. They compared recognition of normal line drawings with caricatures which had been exaggerated 50% away from the average face and "anti-caricatures" where departures from average were attenuated 50%. For faces of familiar individuals (departmental students and staff), student subjects were significantly quicker to name caricatures than veridical line drawings or anticaricatures. The mean reaction times were 3.2, 6.4 and 12.3 sec for +50% caricatures, 0% veridical drawings and −50% anticaricatures respectively.

Although the caricatures were recognised more quickly than the veridical images, they were not identified more accurately. The proportion of correct identifications was 33, 38 and 27% (for caricature, veridical and anticaricature images), but the differences were not significant. Thus there would appear to be a caricature advantage from the reaction time data, but not from the accuracy data. Other studies of caricature recognition for famous faces have found a speed/accuracy trade-off with faster but less accurate recognition of 50% caricatures (Carey, 1989, pers. comm.).

Rhodes et al. also investigated how well subjects perceived the resemblance of the caricature images of familiar faces to the depicted individual. Subjects rated the goodness of likeness of seven randomly ordered pictures consisting of ±75, ±50, ±25 and 0% caricatures. The highest ratings were found for veridical images 0% and +25% caricatures (these images were rated approximately equally). The distribution of scores was not symmetrical about the 0% veridical image; positive caricatures (+25, +50 and + 75%) were rated higher than their counterpart anticaricatures (−25, −50 and −75%). Indeed, the distribution of scores was significantly shifted away from the veridical image towards images with positive caricaturing. Again the data suggested a caricature advantage. Interpolating from the data the peak of the rating distribution occurred at a caricature level of +16%. Because Rhodes et al. (1987) measured ratings for 0, ±25, ±50 and ±75% caricatures, actual ratings for a 16% caricature have yet to be obtained. Two possibilities exist. If the distribution of the ratings is sharply peaked, then the 16% caricature level might produce significantly higher ratings than the 0% veridical image. In this case, the +16% image could be considered *supernormal*. Alternatively, the distribution might be fairly "flat topped", in which case there would be no differences in ratings for 0, +16 and +25% caricatures.

In a recent series of studies, Rhodes and McLean (submitted) examined the recognition of familiar birds whose line-drawing representation had been enhanced using the caricature "algorithm". For expert ornithologists (but not for non-specialist subjects), some evidence was found for a caricature advantage with significantly faster reaction times to +50% caricatures than to veridical line drawings. However, the experts were significantly *less* accurate in recognising the +50% caricatures compared to the veridicals (and all other levels). This study, then, provides some evidence that the caricature advantage might not be restricted to faces.

EXPERIMENTAL STUDY OF PERCEPTION AND RECOGNITION: PHOTOGRAPHIC CARICATURES

The findings described above are important because they suggest that we might store in memory the way in which faces deviate from a norm, rather than storing a veridical structural description of particular features or feature configuration. The caricature advantage found by Rhodes et al. (1987) was based on line drawings. While the recognition advantage found may have implications for the nature of mental representations, it is necessary to entertain the possibility that the results rely on processes unique to line drawings. For example, cartoon conventions may apply only to simplified line-drawn illustrations. Independent of whether veridical line drawings and natural images access the same stored representations, the caricaturing process may yield different effects on the recognition of line drawings and natural images. It is important therefore to determine whether a caricature effect can be obtained with natural photographic stimuli. To this end, we have sought to extend the methods of Brennan (1985) and Rhodes et al. (1987) to compare the perception and recognition of normal images and caricatures with photographic detail.

Experiment 1

Rationale

The objective of Experiment 1 was to determine the possibility of manipulating images such that they looked more like the target faces than the original images. Evidence for facial caricatures being perceptually supernormal images was from interpolation only (Rhodes et al., 1987) and as noted is open to other interpretations. Furthermore, the perceptual advantage of caricatures detected so far is only small. It could be argued that the use of caricature photographs might enlarge the caricature advantage at the perceptual level.

Methods

Subjects.   A total of 30 voluntary members of staff, postgraduates and undergraduates from the Department of Psychology at St Andrews took part in the experiment. All of the subjects were familiar with the people depicted in the photographs.

Stimuli.   The stimuli were produced using the techniques of Brennan described above, but extended to allow pixel-based images to be transformed in accordance with the caricature distortions (Benson & Perrett, in press a, b; Benson, Perrett & Davies, in press). Full-colour (24-bit) or grey-scale (8-bit) images of faces (live, photographs or video-tape) were frame-grabbed using a Pluto 24i graphics system and a JVC BY-110 video camera and RS-110 remote control unit. Interpupilary distance for each face was standardised. Images were then transferred to a Silicon Graphics IRIS 3130 graphics computer for processing.

For each image, the *x* and *y* co-ordinates of 186 feature points are defined manually (see Appendix; see also Brennan, 1985). The feature points of the input face were compared to those of a facial norm. Appropriate norms were prepared for adult Caucasian male and female faces (using 14 faces for the male, and 11 for the female).

Differences between feature points and the average face were then accentuated or diminished by 16 or 32%, producing five data sets (-32, -16, 0, $+16$ and $+32$% caricatures). These degrees of distortion were chosen because Rhodes et al. indicated that a $+16$% caricature would produce the best likeness. Following Brennan's procedure, feature points were linked to form line drawings. Line drawings were not used further in image processing, but formed a useful tool to determine whether the face had been correctly delineated.

The face was divided up into a mesh of triangular tessellations, the vertices of each polygon formed by 3 adjacent feature points from the 186 originally delineated. One tessellation, for example, joins the innermost points of the left and right eyebrows and a point at the middle of the lower hairline. Sets of corresponding tessellations were produced for the veridical image and for each level of image caricaturing. The grey-scale pixel values from each tessellation of the veridical image were then remapped into the corresponding tessellation in the caricatured image (see Benson & Perrett, in press b, for details of this process). If the eyebrows become separated during caricaturing, the triangle between the eyebrows and forehead becomes wider at the base, and hence the pixel information within that space becomes "stretched".

Seven famous faces (television actors and personalities) were digitised and caricatured at the ±32, ±16 and 0% levels. The final versions of the veridical (0%) images used for study were constructed by back-transforming a $+16$% caricature; in effect, this used the pixels and the feature co-ordinates of the $+16$% caricature as the source and the feature co-ordinates of the original 0% image as the destination. This was done as a precaution to ensure that any anomalies (at pixel level) in the pixel remapping process required to produce ±16 and ±32% caricatures would also be present in the 0% caricature. Otherwise, the 0% caricature might be detectable as the only image without "glitches" and hence regarded as the best (most natural) representation. In fact, no obvious anomalies were visible in any of the processed images.

Continuous tone 5 × 7 inch black-and-white photographs were taken of each caricature displayed on the computer terminal (examples are given in Fig. 1). The pictures were mounted horizontally on card strips such that two sets of stimuli were produced. An anticaricature-biased set contained -32, -16, 0 and $+16$% distortions, while a caricature-biased set contained -16, 0, $+16$ and $+32$% distortions. Two partial sets were constructed rather than a complete set of five images to avoid the truest likeness or least distorted image (0%) always lying in the middle of a set.

−48% Caricature   0% Veridical   48% Caricature

FIG. 1.   Images of Nicholas Parsons exaggerating or diminishing the differences in position and dimensions of facial features from an average face. The −48% caricature (left) shows the target face as having a 48% less distinctive *feature configuration* than the veridical (0%). Conversely, those distinctive features found by the generator in the veridical have been accentuated by 48% giving a +48% caricature (right).

Procedure.   The subjects were presented with either four anti-caricature-biased sets and three caricature-biased sets or vice versa, varying equally for each of the seven faces amongst all 30 subjects. Thus no subject saw the entire range of five caricature levels for a given face. Each subject was required to give three verbal ratings: (a) familiarity of the person depicted (7 = highly familiar, 1 = don't know person), (b) best likeness of that person by selecting from the four images presented, the picture which looked most like the depicted person, and (c) goodness of likeness of photograph chosen (7 = very good, 1 = very bad).

Assessment of Image Transformations by Caricature Artists.   It is possible that mistakes could occur in the computer caricaturing process itself. For example, small inaccuracies in the manual placement of feature points in the veridical image, might lead to inappropriate distortions in the caricature production process. We were keen to obtain some independent measure of the quality of the caricature manufacturing process. We therefore consulted three artists familiar with portrait and caricature production. They were informed as to the nature of the image transformation (a comparison with a facial norm and accentuation of differences) and were then shown the 0, +16 and +32% caricature images. They were interviewed for any general comments and were asked to rate the images of the seven processed faces. Specifically, they were asked to compare the features distorted in the +16 and +32% images with the features they found characteristic for the depicted individual, and whether the distortions introduced were ones they would have expected for successful caricaturing. Their ratings were requested on a 7-point scale (7 = good caricature accentuating right details; 4 = no remarkable change to image; 1 = bad caricature with wrong details accentuated).

Results

A two-way repeated measures analysis of variance was carried out on the "best likeness" ratings with the seven target faces and two sets of stimuli (caricature- and anticaricature-biased sets) as main factors. There was a significant effect of the face subjected to caricaturing [$F(6, 196) = 3.021$, $P < 0.01$), which may indicate that only some of the faces caricatured well. There was no effect of stimulus set (anticaricature- vs caricature-biased sets) [$F(1, 196) = 0.186$, $P > 0.6$] and there was no interaction between target face and stimulus set [$F(6, 196) = 1.052$, $P > 0.3$]. Because there was no significant effect of the presentation set (-32 to $+16\%$ or -16 to $+32\%$) on ratings of best likeness, the data were pooled for further analysis. Figure 2 gives the overall frequency with which images at different levels of caricaturing were chosen as the best likeness. The mean of the distribution occurred at a caricature level of $+4.4\%$. A t-test was conducted to determine whether this sample mean departed from that expected from the null hypothesis that caricature distortions had no effect on the image perceived as the best likeness of a face. Under this hypothesis, subjects would be expected to rate the 0% caricature or veridical image as most like the target individual. The distribution of the level of caricatures (0, ±16, $\pm32\%$) chosen as best representation of the seven faces by the 30 subjects is significantly different from the 0% mean expected by the null hypothesis ($t = 2.18$, d.f. $= 29$, $P < 0.04$).

Because the subjects may have seen Margaret Thatcher's face in a caricatured state before the experiment, the overall effect of caricature manipulation was therefore assessed using the data for the six other faces. These data still showed a significant bias towards positive caricaturing for ratings of best likeness ($t = 2.09$, d.f. $= 29$, $P < 0.05$).

Further, it is noted that the subjects rated caricatures more like the target individuals than anticaricatures [matched-pairs t-test, pooled caricature ($+16\%$ and $+32\%$) vs anticaricature (-16% and -32%) data: $t = 3.021$, d.f. $= 6$, $P < 0.05$]. Thus images accentuating distinctiveness were rated higher than images decreasing distinctiveness.

Caricaturing of Individual Faces. Because the overall analysis indicated a significant effect of the face caricatured on ratings of likeness, the results for the different faces were analysed separately. Figure 3 gives the distribu-

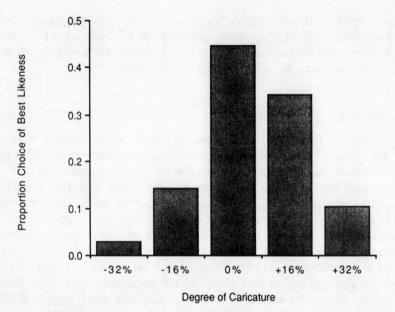

FIG. 2. Experiment 1: Overall ratings of perceived likeness for caricatures of seven familiar faces. Ordinate = proportion of subjects choosing an image as the best likeness of the target face. Preference for images is expressed as a proportion of the number of times the image was available for choice (thus correcting for the different number of subjects seeing ±32% than other levels of caricatures). Abscissa = distortion of image from the veridical image. The data show a preference for caricatures over anticaricatures, the mean of the distribution is shifted away from the 0% and lies at +4.4%.

tion of ratings for different caricature levels for each of the seven faces. For each face, the mean level of caricaturing for images chosen as the best likeness is given in Table 1. A positive percentage in column 1 indicates that more subjects chose images with +16 or +32% than images with the same degree of distortion but in the anticaricature domain (−16%, − 32%). The faces of Anita Dobson, Margaret Thatcher and Nicholas Parsons all have distributions significantly different than that expected by the null hypothesis ($t = 4.74$, d.f. = 29, $P < 0.001$; $t = 4.37$, d.f. = 29, $P < 0.001$; $t = 2.57$, d.f. = 29, $P < 0.02$). For each of these faces, it would seem that the image producing the best likeness was one with a small degree of positive caricaturing (+11.2, +7.5 and +5.3% respectively). For the other faces, the average percentage caricaturing for best likeness ratings were not significantly different from 0%.

Quality of Original Image. It might be expected that poor quality starting images would produce ineffective caricatures. Starting images could be poor in terms of photographic quality or because they were

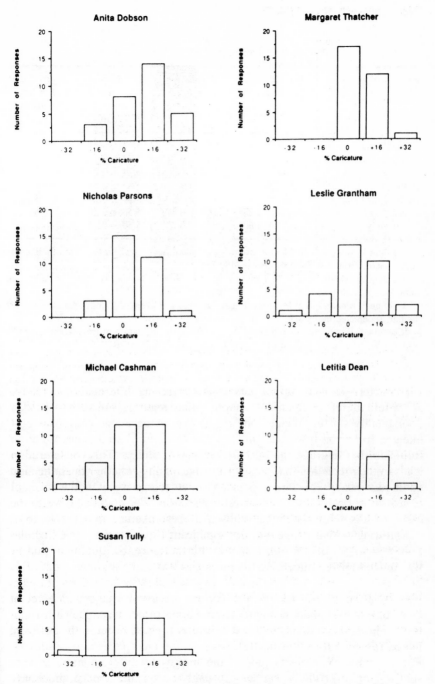

FIG. 3. Experiment 1: Ratings of perceived likeness of caricatures of seven familiar faces. Ordinate = number of subjects (out of 30) choosing an image as the best likeness of the target face. Abscissa = distortion of image from the veridical image.

TABLE 1
Ratings for Caricatures of Seven Famous Faces

Face	Best Likeness % Caricature[a]	Familiarity (1 = high, 7 = "who?")[b]	Goodness of Likeness (1 = good, 7 = bad)[c]	Expert Rating (1 = best, 7 = worst)[d]
Anita Dobson	11.20 ± 2.56	6.27 ± 0.26	5.67 ± 0.24	1
Margaret Thatcher	7.47 ± 1.67	6.77 ± 0.15	5.74 ± 0.22	1
Nicholas Parsons	5.34 ± 2.08	5.97 ± 0.35	5.74 ± 0.23	4
Leslie Grantham	3.73 ± 2.62	6.20 ± 0.20	5.87 ± 0.24	5
Michael Cashman	2.67 ± 2.44	6.14 ± 0.24	5.34 ± 0.34	3
Letitia Dean	0.53 ± 2.23	6.07 ± 0.31	5.50 ± 0.28	6
Susan Tully	−0.53 ± 2.60	6.27 ± 0.23	5.50 ± 0.23	7

[a]Column 1: Mean (± S.E.M.) for level of % caricaturing for image selected as best likeness (interpolated from distributions displayed in Fig. 3).

[b]Column 2: Mean (± S.E.M.) for ratings for subjects' familiarity with the individual depicted.

[c]Column 3: Mean (± S.E.M.) for ratings of goodness of likeness of image selected as most similar to depicted individual.

[d]Column 4: Rank order of ratings of the success of the caricature process (comparing 0% and +32% caricatures) judged by experts (caricature/portrait artists).

uncharacteristic of the target person. Accentuating differences from average would therefore accentuate inappropriate features. For such faces with poor quality starting images one might expect the image chosen as best likeness to be the 0% caricature, as any computer-based transformation would further degrade the initially inadequate image. This consideration leads to the prediction that ratings of image quality (whether the image is a good likeness of the target person) should correlate with the level of caricaturing chosen as the best representation. Correlation between the quality judged for the image chosen as best likeness and the level of caricaturing of that image was not significant (Spearman's Rank Correlation: $r_s = 0.025$, d.f. = 208, $P > 0.1$). Furthermore, the quality of images was judged fairly uniform across faces and was generally high (see Table 1).

Correlation of likeness ratings for the veridical image and level of caricature of best likeness might be more appropriate here. Such a correlation is, however, unlikely to yield a different result, because the veridical image turned out to be the best likeness for most faces and observers. Furthermore, all subjects judged the images to differ in likeness very subtly. Not surprisingly, ratings of quality of veridical image and image chosen as best likeness are very close.

Familiarity with Target Face.   The rating of familiarity with the target person correlated with the degree of caricaturing of the image chosen to best represent that person ($r_s = 0.251$, d.f. $= 208$, $P < 0.005$). That is, for more familiar faces, the caricaturing process was more successful and positive caricatures enhanced the likeness of the original image. For less familiar faces, the caricaturing was less successful. The effect was still significant when the results for Margaret Thatcher's face were excluded ($r_s = 0.228$, d.f. $= 178$, $P < 0.02$).

Ratings by Caricature Artists.   The assessments of the three caricature artists showed a high degree of concordance as to which faces they thought the caricature process had distortions in the correct direction and which faces the process had produced inappropriate results.

Of greater importance was the correspondence between their judgements of success of the computer caricaturing process and the extent of the caricature bias in the selection of images judged to be most like the target faces. The artists rated the caricatures of Margaret Thatcher and Anita Dobson as most successful. The distortions for the faces of Michael Cashman and Nicholas Parsons were also seen as in the right direction. For Leslie Grantham, there was little perceptible distortion, whereas the distortions for Letitia Dean and Susan Tully were seen as ineffectual or in the wrong direction. Overall, the magnitude of the caricature bias for subjects making perceptual judgements of the best likeness showed a significant correlation with the rank order of expert ratings of the quality of the caricaturing process ($r_s = 0.883$, d.f. $= 5$, $P < 0.01$).

Experiment 2

Rationale

Experiment 1 revealed a small but significant bias in subjects' perceptual ratings of manipulated images. Interpolating from the results, images judged to look most like a target figure would have a small degree of positive caricaturing.

Rhodes et al. (1987) found that the effects of caricaturing on recognition of familiar faces were stronger than the effects on perceptual ratings of how like an individual a line drawing was judged. With line drawings, Rhodes et al. found $+50\%$ caricatures were named faster than veridical line drawings. Despite this, $+50\%$ caricatures were perceptually judged to be less like the target individuals than veridical drawings. Thus the effects of caricaturing on speed of recognition appear more likely to benefit from caricaturing than perceptual judgements of the goodness of likeness.

Experiment 2, therefore, set out to determine whether a more marked caricature effect could be found with caricatured photographs using a recognition task. Unfortunately, the small number of stimulus faces used in Experiment 1 meant that this material was not suited to the naming recognition task used by Rhodes et al. (1987). We therefore employed a name–face matching task following a similar design to Rhodes and McLean (submitted) and Tversky and Baratz (1985).

Methods

Subjects.   A total of 11 subjects participated in the experiment, which lasted approximately 1 hour and for which they were paid £3. None of the subjects in Experiment 2 had taken part in Experiment 1.

Stimuli.   The images used were identical to those used in Experiment 1 with the addition of ±48% caricatures for each of the famous faces. The grey-scale pictures were stored in on-line disk files on the IRIS workstation to be recalled individually for display on the monitor. A black cardboard mask was made to cover the monitor display leaving only an elliptical viewing aperture through which the seven faces would appear. This was used so as to remove extraneous background details and limit subjects' use of hair outline as a recognition cue. In this way, the subjects' attention was focused on internal facial features.

Procedure.   The subjects were seated approximately 80 cm from the 19-inch IRIS display. One of the seven names appeared in the centre of the screen (through the aperture) for 1 sec followed by a blank display for 1 sec. This was followed by one of the seven faces, which remained visible until a response was made. The subjects were requested to press the "yes" key if the name matched the face, "no" otherwise; lateralisation of response keys was alternated between subjects. The stimuli were allocated to four experimental blocks. Each block contained each of the seven faces caricatured at each of the seven levels (0, ±16, ±32 and ±48%) with two trials in which the name and subsequent face matched and two trials in which the name and face did not match. The order of faces, caricature level, and match/non-match trials were randomised within each block. Thus, overall, each subject made 16 decisions about each face at each caricature level. For each level of caricature, it was arranged that on non-match trials each face was paired with all possible non-matching names. No practice session was administered in case any caricature recognition advantage persisted only for the first block of trials.

Results

Level of Caricature Producing Subjects' Most Efficient Responses. Figure 4a gives the distribution of caricature levels producing the fastest overall reaction time for each of the 11 subjects. For this analysis, correct match and non-match trials for all of the seven target faces were averaged together. The averaging was performed separately for each of the seven levels of caricaturing (±16, ±32, ±48 and 0%) for each subject. The caricature level producing the fastest reaction time for each subject was then evident by comparing the means for the seven levels.

If all image manipulations away from the original image affect reaction times adversely, one would predict a peaked distribution with most of the subjects having fastest reaction times for the veridical image (0% level). (It is also possible that image manipulations have no effect on processing efficiency, in which case the mean level of caricaturing producing the fastest reaction time would again be 0%, but the distribution of reaction times across level of caricature would be flat.) As can be seen from Fig. 4a, the majority of subjects had their fastest reaction times when the image was positively caricatured 16 or 32%. The mean of the distribution was significantly shifted from the 0% level of image manipulation [$F(1,10) = 5.2, P = 0.01$]. In this way, caricaturing can be seen to enhance recognition. (Interpolating from the distribution, optimal speed of processing would occur for +19% caricatures.)

The effect does not reflect any kind of speed–accuracy trade-off, because the distribution of caricature levels producing the most accurate performance for each subject showed a similar trend for better performance with images that were positively caricatured (Fig. 4b). The mean of the distribution of highest accuracies was, however, not significantly different from the 0% caricature level [$F(1,10) = 1.78, P = 0.1$].

Reaction Times. To assess the evidence of the effects of distinctiveness of features on reaction time, planned comparisons were used to contrast different levels of positive caricaturing (accentuating distinctiveness) with matched levels of negative caricaturing (diminishing distinctiveness). Planned comparisons indicated a distinctiveness effect with caricatures being processed faster than anticaricatures at both the 16 and 32% levels [$F(1,10) = 8.7, P = 0.014; F(1,10) = 7.24, P = 0.023$, respectively). There was no distinctiveness effect at the ±48% levels of caricature ($P = 0.9$).

To assess the evidence for a caricature advantage, the mean reaction time for each level of caricaturing was compared to the mean reaction time for the veridical image. The veridical image was processed significantly faster than both the +48 and −48% caricature levels [$F(1,10) = 5.06, P = 0.048; F(1,10) = 9.55, P = 0.011$], but was not significantly different from other levels of caricature.

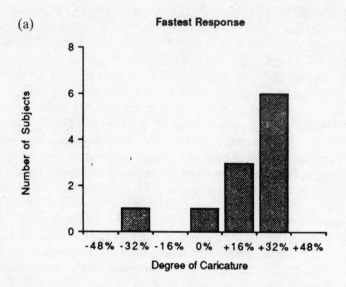

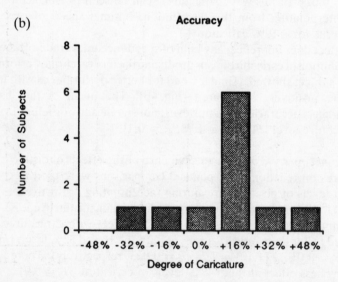

FIG. 4.   Experiment 2: (a) Distribution of conditions producing the fastest reaction times for 11 subjects across different levels of caricaturing. (b) Distribution of conditions producing the highest accuracy of response for 11 subjects across different levels of face caricaturing.

Match Trials

To facilitate interpretation of the results, two separate one-way analyses of variance were performed on the match and non-match trials (Fig. 5). For congruous (match) trials, analysis indicated a significant overall effect of caricaturing on reaction times [$F(6,60) = 2.66$, $P = 0.024$].

Planned comparisons indicated no significant advantage for caricatures over anticaricatures (distinctiveness) or over the veridical image (caricature advantage). Indeed, the only emergent differences were that the veridical image led to faster reaction times than both the +48 and −48% caricatures [$F(1,10) = 7.51$, $P = 0.021$; $F(1,10) = 8.7$, $P = 0.014$].

Non-match Trials

With non-match trials, a different picture emerged. One-way ANOVA revealed a significant overall effect of caricature level on reaction time to correctly reject a face not matching a preceding name [$F(6,60) = 3.73$, $P = 0.003$].

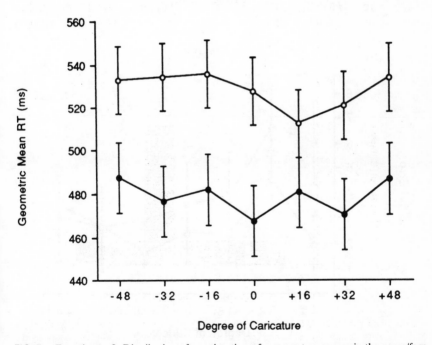

FIG. 5.   Experiment 2: Distribution of reaction times for correct responses in the name/face matching task with match and non-match trials plotted separately. Positive caricatures significantly improve subjects' accuracy in rejecting non-match trials. Error bars denote the 95% confidence interval of mean reaction times. ●, Match; ○, non-match.

Distinctiveness.   Planned comparisons indicated a distinctiveness effect with caricatures being processed faster than anticaricatures at both the +16 and +32% levels [$F(1,10) = 13.4$, $P = 0.004$; $F(1,10) = 5.57$, $P = 0.04$, respectively]. There was no distinctiveness effect at the ±48% levels of caricature ($P = 0.96$).

Caricature Advantage.   Planned comparisons between performance with veridical images and that with different levels of caricature revealed that reaction times were significantly faster for +16% caricatures than for veridical images [$F(6,60) = 7.02$, $P = 0.024$]. No other differences were evident.

Accuracy.   An analysis of the number of errors using two-way ANOVA revealed a significant main effect of the degree of caricature [$F(6,60) = 3.47$, $P = 0.005$]. Figure 6 shows the overall accuracy of subjects. The effect of trial type (match/non-match) showed a trend for more accurate performance with incongruous trials which did not reach significance [$F(1,10) = 4.60$, $P = 0.058$]. There was no significant interaction between these factors [$F(6,60) = 1.58$, $P = 0.17$]. Planned contrasts revealed an increase in accuracy with 0 and +32% over the −32% anticaricature

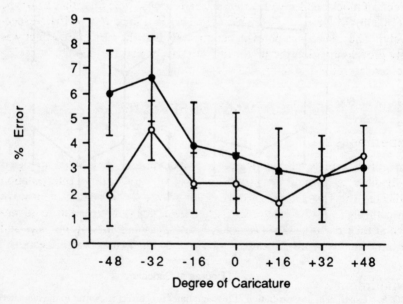

FIG. 6.   Experiment 2: Effect of level of facial caricaturing on accuracy of subjects' judgements for match or non-match between a name and subsequently presented face image. Error bars denote the 95% confidence interval. ●, Match; ○, non-match.

$[F(1,10) = 5.52, P = 0.041; F(1,10) = 8.07, P = 0.018$, respectively), but no other differences.

Separate one-way ANOVA for caricature level effects on accuracy data revealed accuracy differences for the match trials $[F(6,60) = 2.69, P = 0.023]$ but not for the non-match trials $[F(6,60) = 2.2, P = 0.055]$. For match trials, planned contrasts showed improved accuracy in favour of caricatures at +32 and +48% over the respective anticaricature levels $[F(1,10) = 7.45, P = 0.021; F(1,10) = 5.2, P = 0.046$ respectively]. There was no evidence of a caricature advantage.

Effect of Novelty of Caricature on Recognition

A two-way ANOVA (four blocks of trials, seven caricature levels) was performed to assess whether caricature effects were affected by experience with stimuli within the task. There was no effect of trial block on reaction times $[F(3,40) = 0.728, P = 0.539]$, and block number did not interact with caricaturing effects on reaction times $[F(18,240) = 1.004, P = 0.457]$. As expected, the degree of image distortion affected performance $[F(6,240) = 5.277, P < 0.0001]$. Separate one-way ANOVAs showed no effect of trial block on either match $[F(3,40) = 0.795, P = 0.502)$ or non-match $[F(3,40) = 0.65, P = 0.587]$ responses, and there was no interaction between the effects of block and level of caricature on response time for either trial type $[F(18,240) = 1.136, P = 0.328; F(18,240) = 1.466, P = 0.104$, respectively]. Thus there was no evidence to show that the caricature effect was only prevalent within the first series of trials or that the novelty of seeing the caricatures led to improved recognition.

SUMMARY OF RESULTS

Experiment 1

Perceptual ratings of the degree to which images resembled depicted individuals was found to vary with level of caricaturing. Interpolation indicated the best likeness would occur with a small degree of positive caricaturing (+4.4% on average). The magnitude of the caricature advantage at the perceptual level correlated with the familiarity of the faces and with the quality of the caricaturing process as judged by caricature experts.

Experiment 2

Overall analysis of the degree of image manipulation producing the fastest reaction times for individual subjects revealed a caricature advantage. This increased speed of processing for caricatured images did not reflect any speed–accuracy trade-off. Caricaturing images can therefore produce more efficient processing in a task requiring matching of a person's face and name.

In the overall analysis of variance of reaction times (containing match and non-match trials), the caricature advantage did not achieve statistical significance. Three factors might have contributed to the lack of effect. First, the caricature advantage was relatively small in magnitude amounting to a 3% increase in speed. Secondly, the amount of caricaturing producing optimal speed of processing varied across subjects, some performing best with +16% caricatures, others with +32% caricatures. Finally, and of more theoretical interest, the effects of caricaturing appeared to depend on the type of trial. There was no caricature advantage on congruous trials when the name matched the subsequently presented face image. The caricature advantage was prevalent, however, on incongruous trials where the face and name did not match. With non-match trials, +16% caricatures were processed significantly faster than the veridical images. Again the increase in speed of processing was not an artefact produced by a speed–accuracy trade-off.

GENERAL DISCUSSION

Investigations using computer-generated caricatures have indicated that a systematic distortion of a facial line drawing improves recognition. Images with a slight degree of positive caricaturing were found to provide a better likeness of an individual than veridical images. The results obtained here thus supplement Rhodes et al.'s (1987) study. The present results indicate that the caricature advantage is not restricted to line drawings but also occurs for images containing photographic detail. The caricature advantage may therefore tell us about the processing of natural images and cannot be taken to reflect simply a series of artistic conventions used in line-drawn cartoons.

Explanations of the Caricature Advantage

These results have implications for the nature of representations stored in memory. Rhodes et al. (1987) suggested two explanations for a caricature advantage. The first explanation suggested that caricatured representations of faces are actually stored in memory rather than veridical representations. The details of feature configuration, shape, size and colouration stored in memory would be exaggerated by the way they differ from the norm or the prototypical face. It could be predicted from this hypothesis that caricatures would be more efficiently recognised because they are closer to the stored representations.

A second explanation is that representations stored in memory are veridical but that caricaturing aids the process of matching the input image to the veridical representations. This retrieval advantage can also be explained as follows. Rhodes et al. (1987) suggested that the attempt to match the caricature to stored veridical templates might lead to a greater relative activation of the target face compared to non-target (distractors), even though the absolute level of activation of the target might be reduced compared to that produced by the veridical line drawing. Searching for a potential match against the stored representations of all familiar faces is presumably an extensive task. The caricaturing process could "constrain" the search, because exaggerating the features would make it easier to realise qualitatively what kind of features the target face possesses. Thereafter, search could be restricted to only those faces with approximately the right feature dimensions, e.g. face X has a big nose, therefore do not attempt matches with representations of faces with small noses.

The second explanation would be appropriate if faces are stored as distances in multidimensional space at the centre of which is the norm for a particular face type (McClelland & Rumelhart, 1985; Rhodes, 1988; Valentine & Bruce, 1986). Thus, nose length might be one dimension, interocular separation another. When a caricature is presented for recognition, the exaggeration of particular feature deviations from the norm will increase the distances (in the multidimensional space) of the caricatured face from representations of other faces.

One potential problem with this interpretation is that a caricature image will also be further away from the position of the target face in multidimensional space as compared with the veridical image. The caricature advantage must come, therefore, from the fact that a small increase in distance from the representation of the target face is more than offset by the large increase in distance from the representations of non-target faces.

In summary, the advantage for caricatures could result from (1) mimicking the stored information or (2) optimising the retrieval process.

The first model can be taken to make the prediction that caricatured images should be perceived as being more like the face they represent than veridical images. From the study of Rhodes et al. (1987) and the present study, there is a small but significant trend in the data to support this claim. Interpolation from the data of both studies indicates that the highest rating for best likeness occurs for images with a small degree of positive caricaturing (4–16%). In the present study, the strength of the caricature advantage was found to vary across faces and the overall effect might well have been stronger if the quality of the processing had been uniformly good (see below).

The interpretation of perceptual ratings of different images is not, however, clear cut. The actual distribution of ratings could be flat between

0% and some level of positive caricaturing (+16% in our study and +25% in that of Rhodes et al., 1987). Thus, although the distribution of ratings might statistically peak at +4.4% caricature in the present study and at + 16% caricature in the study of Rhodes et al., the ratings for these slightly caricatured images might not be significantly higher than the veridical image. One could also say slightly positive caricatures are no better but also no worse than the veridical image as representations of individuals. On the other hand, anticaricatures are consistently perceived as poorer representations than veridical images.

The second model (where caricatures give faster access to veridical representations held in memory) is perhaps favoured by the dissociation between recognition and perception of likeness. Rhodes et al. (1987) found +50% caricatures were recognised faster than the veridical representations but were judged to be of inferior likeness compared to the veridical. Here, too, we found a significant caricature advantage in the recognition of + 16% caricatures, yet no differences in the perceptual ratings of 0 and 16% caricatures.

The Distinctiveness Hypothesis

A number of authors (Bartlett, Hurry & Thorley, 1984; Cohen & Carr, 1975; Going & Read, 1974; Light, Kayra-Stuart & Hollander, 1979; Winograd, 1981) note that when subjects concentrate upon the atypical features of a face, they are less likely to confuse that face with others. It is perhaps not surprising that more distinctive faces are easier to recognise.

An effect of distinctiveness can also be seen in the present study. Positive caricaturing accentuates deviations from the norm and hence should make a face more distinctive. Positive caricatures (+16 and +32%) were judged better likenesses than the anticaricatures of the same degree. Furthermore, in the name/face matching task, there was evidence to show that the +16 and +32% caricatures were processed more efficiently than anticaricatures. These distinctiveness effects, like those of Rhodes et al. (1987) and Rhodes and McLean (submitted), occur even though the magnitude of the image deformation from the veridical image is exactly matched for positive and negative caricatures.

Representing Relative and Metric Proportions of a Face

The caricature advantage is argued (above) to reflect the existence of an abstract configural representation for familiar faces. This representation stores the configural information about how faces differ from one another and hence how individual faces deviate from average.

Caricatures present the interpretational system with a conundrum. It is possible that at an abstract configurational level of representation the caricature forms a better match than a veridical image because a caricature *draws attention* to the way the face differs from the norm and therefore presents information in the same format as the abstract representation. Caricatures are, however, distortions of reality and observers are sensitive to the distortion. The fact that subjects can perceptually judge a caricature to be a distortion from reality implies that, at some level, representation(s) of each face must be veridical and maintain the metric proportions of the face.

It is of course possible that there are multiple representations for particular faces (for a discussion, see Bruce, 1982; Bruce & Young, 1986; Marr & Nishihara, 1978). One level might be concerned with representing pictorial or photographic details and would maintain an accurate metric account of the dimensions of the image. At a higher more abstract level concerned with differences between faces, representations might be more concerned with the selective storage of deviations of faces from prototypes. In this two-stage processing scheme, the metric or pictorial code would maintain veridical dimensions and the abstract code might stress the importance of configural deviations from the norm or prototype.

Caricature Advantage in Name/Face Matching

If one concedes that both the metric proportions of a face and the manner a face differs from the norm are stored in the brain, then it is possible to account for the greater benefits of caricaturing found with non-match trials in Experiment 2. These two types of information could be present in the same representational code, though it is easier to consider two separate codes.

On trials where the name and face stimulus are the same identity, a caricature may form a better match with the abstract representation of the target face than a veridical image. On the other hand, at the level of the metric code, the match between input image and representation will be less good. Thus any advantage of the caricature at the abstract level will tend to be offset by the disadvantage at the metric level.

In the case of non-match trials, this conflict is not present. For example, if the target name is Michael Cashman and the stimulus face subsequently presented is a veridical image of Nicholas Parsons, then the image will not match the abstract representation of Cashman's face, nor will it match the metric representation of Cashman's face. A "no" or "doesn't match" response can be given as soon as sufficient evidence is amassed indicating the unacceptable nature of the match between input to representations of the target face.

If we now consider the case where a positive caricature of Parson's face follows Cashman's name, it is evident that the evidence for mismatch can be accumulated more rapidly. The caricature of Nicholas Parsons will form a very bad match to the abstract representation of Cashman's face and a poor (possibly very poor) match to the metric representation of Cashman's face. For the non-match trials, caricaturing can be seen to aid recognition because it increases the discrepancy between input image and the stored representation(s) of the target face.

This explanation predicts an increasing advantage for more exaggerated caricatures. Alternatively, on non-match trials the advantage may come because a caricatured image of Nicholas Parsons may be recognised as Nicholas Parsons quicker than a veridical image. Matching the abstract representation of Parsons is quick and performed in parallel without reference to the matching to the veridical representation of Parsons. Any evidence that the face is not Cashman is a signal to stop the recognition search.

Photographic and Line-drawn Representations

The magnitude of the caricature advantage was small in the present study (see Figs 2 and 3). With photographic images, interpolation from the data indicates that a caricature level of +4.4% would on average be chosen as best likeness, whereas with line drawings Rhodes et al. (1987) found a value of +16%. Likewise in the recognition task with photographic caricatures we found a caricature advantage with +16% caricatures but a disadvantage with much larger caricatures (+48%), whereas Rhodes et al. reported a significant advantage for +50% caricatures of line drawings.

Simple line-drawn faces are impoverished stimuli containing no texture, colour, shadows, etc. At the level of the metric code for facial attributes, line drawings will match stored representations less well than real photographs. Line drawings may, however, maintain all the configurational information necessary to access abstract codes of the relative proportions of facial features. Thus line-drawn caricatures can reap the benefits of improved matching to representations at the abstract configurational level without suffering such a disadvantage at the metric level. In this sense, greater advantages would be expected for caricaturing impoverished representations of faces.

Quality of Starting Image

The amount of caricaturing present in the image chosen as best likeness was affected by the identity of the face portrayed. Because faces differ in the amount that they deviate from the norm, different levels of caricaturing might be required for efficient matching of the input to the stored representation. If a face has a highly deviant nose and lips, then these may not need further exaggeration in caricatures. The difference found here between the level of caricaturing required for best likeness may thus reflect the feature dimensions of the target face chosen.

Alternatively, this result may arise from limitations of the processing technique or from the poor quality of starting images. In the present study, the subjects rated all the images they chose as best likenesses as being good representations of the target individuals. Thus we can assume that the starting images for each of the faces was at least adequate. A photograph may be of good quality in terms of contrast, focus, pose and lighting image. In this sense, it may be a good likeness of an individual; however, it is often the case that nuances such as expressions, gestures, facial asymmetry and posture that are typical of a person are absent from a given photograph. One only has to inspect family snapshots to appreciate this; often someone we know very well, while still recognisable in a snapshot, is none the less caught with an atypical posture or expression. Leslie Grantham smiled for the BBC portrait photograph that we used as a starting image, but how frequently did he smile as "Dirty Den" in the TV series *East Enders*? Perhaps the subjects were more familiar with stern, cynical or even morose expressions that were more typical of his TV role. In attempting to assess the quality of our original images, it is possible that the subjects rated the goodness of likeness more with reference to photographic quality than with reference to the visibility of characteristic features and expressions.

Caricature artists noted that when preparing a caricature, they have the opportunity to experience many instances and views of a target's face before constructing a portrait, and can therefore spot the appearance of facial features, expressions, mannerisms, etc., which are characteristic of the individual. The automated process has access only to one starting image and no matter how good the photographic quality is, if important idiosyncratic features or expressions are absent in that starting image they will not be accentuated in the final caricature.

Expert Assessment of Caricature Processing

For some of the faces, particular feature transformations such as raising the forehead, were considered distortions rather than accentuations typical of a caricature of the face in question. While individual artists may pick on slightly different features to accentuate, the three artists interviewed were in agreement as to which images had been caricatured successfully and which had not. The ratings of artists with experience in caricaturing faces thus provided an independent measure of the quality of the computerised image transformations. Of great interest was the finding that the ratings of the experts as to the quality of the caricature processing correlated with a tendency by the subjects to choose caricatured images as those most like the target faces. This provides evidence for thinking that the magnitude of the potential caricature advantage was underestimated in the present study. It might have been larger if the computer processing or selection of starting images was improved.

It is important to note that this argument is not circular, and artificially produced by both the artists and the other subjects judging the same dimension. The two ratings were qualitatively different; caricature experts had to determine the extent deviations introduced by the computer were those that they would have introduced. The subjects, on the other hand, were simply choosing which out of a set of images they thought looked most like a target face. They were aware that images had been deformed to differing extents but were attempting to choose an image most similar to how the person looked in real life.

Familiarity and Caricaturing

Rhodes et al. (1987) found a caricature advantage for the recognition of familiar faces but no advantage for unfamiliar faces. Rhodes and McLean (submitted) also found a caricature advantage for line drawings of birds, but only with subjects who were highly familiar with the targets. The results of the present study also show an effect of face familiarity. The caricature advantage at the perceptual level was greater for faces that were more familiar to the subjects. That is, images with a greater degree of positive caricaturing were judged to be more like the target face when the face was highly familiar.

The relation of the caricaturing success to face familiarity is expected from both explanations of the caricature advantage (in terms of mimicking stored representation or optimising retrieval), because there would be no long-term representation for unfamiliar faces. Under the first explanation, caricatures would fail because there would be no caricatured representation in memory. Under the second explanation, caricatures would also fail because there would be no veridical representation in memory to match the caricatured input image.

It is true that to recognise an unfamiliar face, even after a short interval, some representation must be stored, but evidently the type of representation and/or matching process used for unfamiliar faces is qualitatively different from that for familiar faces and is not affected by caricaturing. Familiarity is known to produce qualitative differences in the processing of faces. For familiar faces, more attention is paid to the internal facial features, whereas for unfamiliar faces, more attention is paid to the external detail of the hair. Future work on caricaturing might show stronger effects if the hair of target faces was masked out during perceptual and recognition tasks.

The results suggest that to achieve the biggest caricature advantage, highly familiar or famous faces should be chosen as target images. There are problems, however, with using the faces of some highly famous politicians and media stars because they may already have been subjected to caricaturing. In our present study, this confound of familiarity and previous caricaturing was present only for Thatcher's face. Data from the other faces not known to have been subjected to caricaturing before the experiment still revealed a significant correlation between familiarity and degree of positive caricaturing accepted as providing the best likeness.

Applications: Reducing False Positives in Identification

The present study has demonstrated advantages in recognising caricatures generated automatically from photographs of faces. The effect of caricaturing did not appear to improve recognition performance by enhancing the hit rate or speed, perhaps because of the conflict between the different ways information about individual faces is represented in the brain. Nevertheless, the study does suggest that the caricaturing process could have practical applications, because they may aid recognition by decreasing the number of false positives. The evidence presented here suggests that false targets are eliminated from consideration with greater efficiency when the image under scrutiny is a caricature than when it is a veridical image. In other words, with caricatures, subjects may not be any more able to identify the target face but may be more sure of who it is not ("I don't know who it is but I'm certain its not X, or Y").

Manuscript received September 1989
Revised manuscript received May 1990

REFERENCES

Bartlett, J. C., Hurry, S. & Thorley, W. (1984). Typicality and familiarity of faces. *Memory and Cognition*, *12*, 219–228.

Benson, P. J. & Perrett, D. I. (in press a). Gregorian physiognomy. *Perception*.

Benson, P. J. & Perrett, D. I. (in press b). Synthesising continuous-tone caricatures. *Image and Vision Computing*.

Benson, P. J., Perrett, D. I. & Davies, D. N. (in press). Towards a quantitative understanding of facial caricatures. In V. Bruce & M. Burton (Eds), *Processing images of faces*. Norwood, N.J.: Ablex.

Brennan, S. E. (1982). *Caricature generator*. Unpublished thesis, MIT.

Brennan, S. E. (1985). Caricature generator: Dynamic exaggeration of faces by computer. *Leonardo*, *18*, 170–178.

Bruce, V. (1982). Changing faces: Visual and non-visual coding processes in face recognition. *British Journal of Psychology*, *73*, 105–116.

Bruce, V. & Young, A. (1986). Understanding face recognition. *British Journal of Psychology*, *77*, 305–327.

Bruce, V., Valentine, T. & Baddeley, A. (1987). The basis of the 3/4 view advantage in face recognition. *Applied Cognitive Psychology*, *1*, 109–120.

Carey, S. (1989). Personal communication at the 6th ESRC-funded Grange-over-Sands Workshop on Face Processing.

Chance, J., Goldstein, A. G. & McBride, L. (1975). Differential experience and recognition memory for faces. *Journal of Social Psychology*, *97*, 243–253.

Cohen, M. E. & Carr, W. J. (1975). Facial recognition and the von Restorff effect. *Bulletin of the Psychonomic Society*, *6*, 383–384.

Cross, J. F., Cross, J. & Daly, J. (1971). Sex, race, age and beauty as factors in recognition of faces. *Perception and Psychophysics*, *10*, 393–396.

Davies, G. M., Ellis, H. D. & Shepherd, J. W. (1978). Face recognition accuracy as a function of mode of representation. *Journal of Applied Psychology*, *63*, 180–187.

Dion, K. K., Berscheid, E. & Walster, E. (1972). What is beautiful is good. *Journal of Personality and Social Psychology*, *24*, 285–290.

Ellis, H. D., Shepherd, J. W. & Davies, G. M. (1979). Identification of familiar and unfamiliar faces from internal and external features: Some implications for theories of face recognition. *Perception*, *8*, 431–439.

Going, M. & Read, J. D. (1974). Effects of uniqueness, sex of subject, and sex of photograph on facial recognition. *Perceptual and Motor Skills*, *39*, 109–110.

Goldman, M. & Hagen, M. A. (1978). The forms of caricature: Physiognomy and political bias. *Studies in the Anthropology of Visual Communication*, *5*, 30–36.

Hagen, M. A. & Perkins, D. (1983). A refutation of the hypothesis of the superfidelity of caricatures relative to photographs. *Perception*, *12*, 55–61.

Haig, N. D. (1984). The effect of feature displacement on face recognition. *Perception*, *13*, 505–512.

Haig, N. D. (1986). Exploring recognition with interchanged facial features. *Perception*, *15*, 235–247.

Harries, M. H., Perrett, D. I. & Lavender, A. (in press). Preferential inspection of views of 3-D model heads. *Perception*.

Hinde, R. A. (1982). *Ethology: Its nature and relations with other sciences*. Glasgow: Collins/Fontana.

Klatzky, R. L. & Forrest, F. H. (1984). Recognising familiar and unfamiliar faces. *Memory and Cognition*, *12*, 60–70.

Klatzky, R. L., Martin, G. L. & Kane, R. A. (1982a). Influence of social-category activation on processing of visual information. *Social Cognition*, *1*, 95–109.

Klatzky, R. L., Martin, G. L. & Kane, R. A. (1982b). Semantic interpretation effects on memory for faces. *Memory and Cognition*, *10*, 195–206.

Light, L. L., Kayra-Stuart, F. & Hollander, S. (1979). Recognition memory for typical and unusual faces. *Journal of Experimental Psychology: Human Learning and Memory*, *5*, 212–228.

McClelland, J. L. & Rumelhart, D. E. (1985). Distributed memory and the representation of general and specific information. *Journal of Experimental Psychology: General*, *114*, 159–217.

Marr, D. & Nishihara, H. K. (1978). Representation and recognition of the spatial organisation of three-dimensional shapes. *Proceedings of the Royal Society of London*, *B200*, 269–294.

Perkins, D. (1975). A definition of caricature, and caricature and recognition. *Studies in the Anthropology of Visual Communication*, *2*, 1–24.

Rhodes, G. (1988). Looking at faces: First-order and second-order features as determinants of facial appearance. *Perception*, *17*, 43–63.

Rhodes, G. & McLean, I. (submitted). Distinctiveness and expertise effects with homogeneous stimuli: Towards a model of configural coding.

Rhodes, G., Brennan, S. & Carey, S. (1987). Identification and ratings of caricatures: Implications for mental representations of faces. *Cognitive Psychology*, *19*, 473–497.

Sergent, J. (1984). Configural processing of faces in the left and right cerebral hemispheres. *Journal of Experimental Psychology: Human Perception and Performance*, *10*, 554–572.

Shepherd, J. W. (1981). Social factors in face recognition. In G. M. Davies, H. D. Ellis & J. W. Shepherd (Eds), *Perceiving and remembering faces*, pp. 55–78. London: Academic Press.

Shepherd, J. W., Ellis, H. D. & Davies, G. M. (1977). Perceiving and remembering faces. *Report to the Home Office POL/73/1675/2411*.

Thomas, S., Perrett, D. I., Davis, D. N. & Harries, M. H. (submitted). Effect of perspective view on recognition of faces.

Tversky, B. & Baratz, D. (1985). Memory for faces: Are caricatures better than photographs? *Memory and Cognition*, *13*, 45–49.

Valentine, T. & Bruce, V. (1986). The effects of distinctiveness in recognising and classifying faces. *Perception*, *15*, 525–535.

Winograd, E. (1981). Elaboration and distinctiveness in memory for faces. *Journal of Experimental Psychology: Human Learning and Memory*, *7*, 181–190.

Yamane, S., Kaji, S. & Komatsu, H. (1988). What facial features activate face neurons in the inferotemporal cortex of the monkey? *Experimental Brain Research*, *73*, 209–214.

Young, A. W., Hay, D. C., McWeeny, K. H., Flude, B. M. & Ellis, A. W. (1985). Matching familiar and unfamiliar faces on internal and external features. *Perception*, *14*, 737–746.

APPENDIX 1

List of the 186 feature points logged on the digitised facial image. Each feature has a fixed number of points describing it (#), from left to right and top to bottom in order:

#	feature	#	feature
1	left pupil	7	top of upper lip
1	right pupil	7	bottom of upper lip
5	left iris	7	top of lower lip
5	right iris	7	bottom of lower lip
3	bottom of left eyelid	3	left side of face (ear area)
3	bottom of right eyelid	3	right side of face (ear area)
3	bottom of left eye	7	left ear
3	bottom of right eye	7	right ear
3	top of left eye	11	jaw line
3	top of right eye	13	hair line (forehead)
3	left eye line	13	top of head (hair)
3	right eye line	3	left smile line
6	left side of nose	3	right smile line
6	right side of nose	3	left cheekbone
6	left nostril	3	right cheekbone
6	right nostril	2	left upper lip line
6	top of left eyebrow	2	right upper lip line
6	top of right eyebrow	2	chin cleft
4	bottom of left eyebrow	3	chin line
4	bottom of right eyebrow		

EUROPEAN JOURNAL OF COGNITIVE PSYCHOLOGY, 1991, 3 (1) 137–145

The Effects of Distinctiveness, Presentation Time and Delay on Face Recognition

J. W. Shepherd

Department of Psychology, University of Aberdeen, Aberdeen, U.K.

F. Gibling

Metropolitan Police, London, U.K.

H. D. Ellis

School of Psychology, University of Wales College Cardiff, Cardiff, U.K.

The distinctiveness of a face has been found to be an important factor in face recognition. We investigated the effect of the distinctiveness of a face upon subjects' speed and accuracy of recognition following different presentation times and retention intervals. It was found that (1) hits decreased with increasing delay; (2) false alarms increased and d primes decreased with a presentation time of 1 sec compared with 5 sec; (3) distinctive faces received more hits and higher d primes than non-distinctive faces; and (4) response latencies were shorter for distinctive targets than for distinctive distractors or non-distinctive targets or distractors. These results were discussed in terms of the literature on the distinctiveness effect in face recognition.

INTRODUCTION

The distinctiveness of a face has been found to be an important factor influencing the recognition of faces (Bartlett, Hurry & Thorley, 1984; Cohen & Carr, 1975; Winograd, 1981). This is true for the recognition of previously presented unfamiliar faces (Light, Kayra-Stuart & Hollander, 1979), for reaction times for recognising familiar faces (Valentine & Bruce, 1986a) as well as for reaction times to the familiarity of celebrities' faces (Valentine & Bruce, 1986b). Furthermore, the ease of recognising distinc-

Requests for reprints should be addressed to John Shepherd, Department of Psychology, University of Aberdeen, Aberdeen AB9 2UB, U.K.

This research was supported by an ESRC grant (COO232260). We are grateful to Eddie Stephen for his technical expertise in writing the computer software for the experiment.

tive faces applies not only to more correct identifications of faces, but to a lower incidence of false positive responses (Bartlett et al., 1984).

One reason for the interest in the distinctiveness effect is that it has implications for models of how faces are represented in memory. Both Light et al. (1979) and Valentine and Bruce (1986a; 1986b) interpret these effects as providing evidence for a prototype theory of face recognition. According to this theory, a prototype face is extracted from all the faces an individual encounters in daily life, and each new exemplar is encoded by reference to this prototype. The attributes on which faces vary are conceived as axes or vectors extending in all directions from the prototype. A typical face, which will have a close resemblance to the prototype, will be located in a conceptual space close to the origin, and because typical faces are assumed to be more common than distinctive faces, will have a high density located in the vicinity of the prototype. In contrast, distinctive or atypical faces will be located at some distance from the prototype on at least one axis, and are less likely than typical faces to have similar faces in close proximity.

If the advantage in memory of distinctive faces is based upon their being encoded on distinctive features, it may be predicted, as Light et al. (1979) have, that reduction of the inspection time for target faces should reduce the advantage found for distinctive faces, because this should reduce the opportunity for the subject to identify distinctive features and encode them. In a test of this prediction, they found that reducing inspection time from about 7 sec to about 2 sec did not significantly reduce the difference in recognition performance between distinctive and typical faces.

In reporting this result, however, Light et al. (1979) did acknowledge that an inspection time of 2 sec might have been long enough for subjects to encode the maximally informative areas of the face. Accordingly, in the present experiment, the effect of differences in inspection time on the distinctiveness effect are tested for inspection times shorter than those used by Light et al.

A second factor which may be expected to interact with distinctiveness is the delay between presentation and testing. This was investigated by Courtois and Mueller (1981), who tested subjects immediately, 2 days or 28 days after presentation. They found no interaction between distinctiveness and delay for correct identifications, but reported a greater increase in false positives for typical than for atypical faces over the longer delay interval. These results would be consistent with a prototype theory in which representations of typical faces, as they lose information over time, become more readily confused with representations of other faces, than do distinctive faces. Light et al. (1979) report that typical faces had a greater inter-item similarity than did distinctive faces, and hence it should be more difficult to discriminate old from new faces as information about faces is lost over an increasing delay period. In contrast, distinctive faces should remain absolutely and relatively more discriminable, because even if their representations lose information, there are fewer similar faces with which to be confused.

A third objective in the present study was to compare a recognition measure based on hits and false alarms with that of response latencies, in the light of Chance and Goldstein's (1987) contention that the latter measure may be a more sensitive measure of retention. They reported an increase in latencies with increasing retention period without a corresponding drop in hit rate. Bartlett et al. (1984) also found that reaction times for hits and for correct rejections were lower for distinctive faces than for typical faces. It was predicted that these results would be replicated here, and that the increase in latencies for non-distinctive targets would be greater than that for distinctive targets over the retention period.

METHOD

Subjects

A total of 96 postgraduate and undergraduate students (55 females and 41 males) took part in the experiment and were paid for their services.

Material

The stimuli used were colour transparencies selected from an original pool of 1000 male faces. A sample of slides of 240 clean shaven men, under 30 years of age and not wearing spectacles was drawn, which was then separated into three sets of 80. These were presented to different groups of subjects who were asked to rate each face on three personality traits. Two hours later, a surprise recognition test was administered in which the same 80 faces were presented, but in a different pose. A recognition score was computed for each face based on the proportion of subjects who recognised it. From these, the 30 with the highest recognition score and the 30 with the lowest recognition score were selected. To check that this procedure had succeeded in discriminating "distinctive" from typical faces, all 60 faces were than rated.

Prints of the 60 faces were presented to a separate group of 12 subjects, who were asked to sort them into nine categories, running from 1 = "least distinctive" to 9 = "most distinctive". No constraints were placed on the distribution of the prints among the nine categories. From this, a "distinctiveness" score was computed for each face. The mean distinctiveness rating for the least memorable 30 faces was 3.47, and the mean for the most memorable was 5.99. A test of the difference between the two sets of faces gave a t-value of 6.69 (d.f. = 58, $P < 0.001$).

Apparatus

The slides were back-projected from a Kodak Carousel S-RA projector onto a screen which formed the window into a separate room in which the subject sat. The presentation of slides was controlled and responses collected by an Apple IIe microcomputer, which timed responses to the nearest 5 msec. The subject had two horizontally arranged response keys labelled "Yes" and "No" with which to make a response.

Design

The design of the experiment was a $2 \times 3 \times 2$ factorial design in which the between-subjects variables were presentation time (1 and 5 sec) and delay (immediate, 1 day and 1 month), and the within-subjects variable was distinctiveness of the faces (high and low). Thirty target faces, 15 distinctive and 15 non-distinctive, were presented to the subjects either for 1 or 5 sec. The subjects were required to recognise the 30 target faces mixed with 30 distractors (15 distinctive and 15 non-distinctive) either immediately or after delays of 1 day or 1 month. Within each condition, those faces which had been shown as targets and those shown as distractors were reversed for half of the subjects. In addition, the pose of the target faces was altered between presentation and test; half the faces were presented in full-face and tested in three-quarter profile and the other half of the faces were presented in three-quarter profile and tested in full-face.

Procedure

In the presentation phase of the experiment, the 30 target faces were presented to the subjects for either 1 or 5 sec. The subjects were told to look at the faces carefully as they would be required to try to recognise them later. Following presentation of the faces, the subjects in the immediate test condition received the recognition test, whereas those subjects in the two delay conditions were asked to return after the requisite delay period.

The procedure was identical following each delay. Different poses of the 30 target faces (half in full-face and half in three-quarter profile) were mixed with the 30 distractors (again half full-face and half three-quarter profile) and the subjects were required to recognise those faces they had seen earlier. The subjects responded by pressing one of the two response keys. Left and right positions for the two keys were counterbalanced across subjects in each condition. The need to be as quick but as accurate as possible was emphasised and reaction times and responses were recorded by the computer.

RESULTS

Hits, false alarms, d primes and median reaction times were calculated for the distinctive and non-distinctive faces. Four analyses of variance (ANOVA) were performed on these data in which the between-subjects variables were (1) delay (immediate, 1 day and 1 month), (2) presentation time (1 and 5 sec), (3) target-distractor faces (set I/set II) and (4) pose (full-face to three-quarter profile/vice versa); the within-subjects variable was distinctiveness of the faces.

Hits

The overall hit rate in the experiment was 55.4%. An analysis of the subjects' hits revealed just two significant main effects and no significant interactions. There was an effect for delay [$F(2,72) = 3.28$, $P < 0.05$], which showed that mean hits decreased with increasing delay from 8.96 in the immediate condition to 8.44 with a 1-day delay and 7.56 with a 1-month delay. In addition, there was a highly significant effect for distinctiveness [$F(1,72) = 84.37$, $P < 0.0001$], with distinctive faces receiving more hits ($\bar{x} = 9.62$) than the non-distinctive faces ($\bar{x} = 6.98$). The effect of presentation time just failed to reach significance [$F(1,72) = 3.49$, $P = 0.066$], and this showed a trend for the 5-sec presentation time to result in more hits ($\bar{x} = 8.71$) than the 1-sec presentation time ($\bar{x} = 7.89$).

False Alarms

An analysis of the false alarm data revealed just one significant effect for presentation time [$F(1,72) = 5.24$, $P < 0.05$]. This showed that the 1-sec presentation time resulted in more false alarms ($\bar{x} = 4.48$) than the 5-sec presentation time ($\bar{x} = 3.49$). Delay and distinctiveness had no significant effect upon false alarms.

d Primes

The analysis of d primes showed significant effects for distinctiveness [$F(1,72) = 13.57$, $P < 0.0001$] and for presentation time [$F(1,72) = 13.38$, $P < 0.0005$]. This revealed higher d primes to the distinctive faces ($\bar{x} = 1.16$) compared to the non-distinctive faces ($\bar{x} = 0.77$) and following the 5-

TABLE 1
Subjects' Median Reaction Times to Distinctive and Non-distinctive Targets and Foils as a Function of Retention Interval and Presentation Time

Delay:	Immediate		1 Day		1 Month		
Presentation Time:	1 sec	5 sec	1 sec	5 sec	1 sec	5 sec	Mean
Distinctive targets	1139.7	1089.5	1150.5	1033.7	1019.7	1165.9	1099.8
Distinctive foils	1460.4	1494.7	1402.6	1070.0	1207.8	1276.6	1318.7
Non-distinctive targets	1255.8	1542.9	1350.0	1117.7	1185.8	1378.9	1305.2
Non-distinctive foils	1483.5	1553.4	1461.6	1179.7	1187.1	1272.4	1356.3
Mean	1377.5		1220.7		1211.8		
	1 sec: 1275.4						
	5 sec: 1264.6						

sec presentation time ($\bar{x}$ = 1.24) compared to the 1-sec presentation time ($\bar{x}$ = 0.69). As with the false alarm data, there was no effect for delay.

Reaction Times

Table 1 shows the subjects' median reaction times, in milliseconds, for correct responses only, to the distinctive and non-distinctive targets and distractors as a function of presentation time and delay. An ANOVA was performed on these median reaction times, with the distinctive and non-distinctive targets and distractors as a within-subject variable. The ANOVA revealed just one significant effect for the targets/distractors [$F(3,270)$ = 15.61, $P < 0.0001$], showing that more rapid responding occurred to the distinctive targets than to any of the other faces.

DISCUSSION

The results replicate and extend previous findings. First, distinctive faces were more readily recognised than non-distinctive faces. Secondly, the distinctiveness effect held across presentation times and across retention intervals of up to 4 weeks. Thirdly, the distinctiveness effect was found on measures of hits, d prime and latency to correct response, but not for false alarms. It was found that distinctive faces were recognised more accurately and more rapidly than non-distinctive faces. The distinctive targets were recognised over 17% more accurately and 200 msec more quickly than the non-distinctive faces.

Although the distinctive faces were better recognised overall than the non-distinctive faces, there was no evidence of distinctiveness interacting with presentation time on any of the measures. This indicates that there was no specific enhancement in the recognition of the non-distinctive faces under the more favourable conditions.

This replicated the findings of Light et al. (1979, experiment 2), who used presentation times of 2 and 7 sec, in contrast to the 1- and 5-sec exposures used here. Light et al. predicted that the reduced exposure time would diminish the advantage shown by the distinctive faces by reducing the opportunity of the subject to encode the distinctive attribute of the distinctive faces. They speculated that their failure to find the effect might be due to the 2-sec exposure not being sufficiently short. However, even with the exposure time reduced to 1 sec, the distinctive faces were still more easily recognised than the non-distinctive faces.

If the advantage enjoyed by the distinctive faces had been the result of processes operating during storage/retrieval, we predicted that the recognition of the distinctive faces would be less affected by long retention intervals than the non-distinctive faces. Once again, this was not found to be the case. As with presentation time, hit rate decreased with increasing delay and this decrement was the same for both types of faces. In this case, it is difficult to explain the effect in terms of the experimental conditions, because 4 weeks is a relatively long retention interval. If the effect were going to occur at all, then it should have been evident at such a retention interval. However, it is not exactly clear what is the influence of delay upon face recognition and the literature is equivocal as to its effect. A number of studies have found that accuracy declines following delays of up to 2 months (e.g. Brigham, Maass, Snyder & Spaulding, 1982; Courtois & Mueller, 1981; Davies, Ellis & Shepherd, 1978; Deffenbacher, Carr & Leu, 1981; Krouse, 1981). In contrast, a number of other studies have found face recognition to be remarkably robust over delays of up to 6 months with single targets (Goldstein & Chance, 1971; Laughery, Fessler, Lenorovitz & Yoblick, 1974; Laughery & Fowler, 1980; Shepherd, Ellis & Davies, 1982).

As in the study by Valentine and Bruce (1986b), the latencies for recognising distinctive targets were lower than those for non-distinctive targets, or for distinctive distractors. This is a pattern which might have been expected given a significant effect for distinctiveness on hit rate, but not on false alarms. It differs from that reported by Bartlett et al. (1984), who found that distinctive targets were recognised and distinctive distractors rejected faster than their non-distinctive counterparts. Valentine and Bruce (1986b) suggested that the difference between their results and the results of Bartlett et al. may be explained by differences in task demand, one being a familiarity judgement for known faces, and the other a recognition memory task. It is possible that differences in task requirement between the present study and that of Bartlett et al. may account for differences in the pattern of latencies. Indeed, even within the latter experiment, the nature of the input task affected latencies. Where subjects rated the stimulus item on friendliness, the typicality effects for latencies did not occur; where subjects wrote a verbal description of each target immediately after presentation, typicality effects were strong, but latencies were generally longer. The presentation rate was more rapid in the present study than in Bartlett et al.'s, which may have enhanced any differential encoding advantage for distinctive faces without necessarily affecting the response to distractors at the recognition phase. In any case, it appears that latency data are sensitive to input instructions, though not to delay.

In sum, although distinctiveness, presentation time and delay before testing were each found to affect at least one measure of recognition performance, these effects were independent of each other.

Manuscript received October 1989
Revised manuscript received May 1990

REFERENCES

Bartlett, J. C., Hurry, S. & Thorley, W. (1984). Typicality and familiarity of faces. *Memory and Cognition*, *12*, 219–228.

Brigham, J. C., Maass, A., Snyder, L. D. & Spaulding, K. (1982). Accuracy of eyewitness identification in a field setting. *Journal of Personality and Social Psychology*, *42*, 673–681.

Chance, J. E. & Goldstein, A. G. (1987). Retention interval and face recognition: Response latency measures. *Bulletin of the Psychonomic Society*, *25*, 415–418.

Cohen, H. E. & Carr, W. J. (1975). Facial recognition and the von Restorff effect. *Bulletin of the Psychonomic Society*, *66*, 383–384.

Courtois, M. R. & Mueller, J. H. (1981). Target and distractor typicality in facial recognition. *Journal of Applied Psychology*, *66*, 639–645.

Davies, G., Ellis, H. & Shepherd, J. (1978). Face identification: The influence of delay upon accuracy of Photofit construction. *Journal of Police Science and Administration*, *6*, 35–42.

Deffenbacher, K., Carr, T. H. & Leu, J. R. (1981). Memory for words, pictures and faces: Retroactive interference, forgetting and reminiscence. *Journal of Experimental Psychology: Human Memory and Learning*, *7*, 299–305.

Goldstein, A. G. & Chance, J. E. (1971). Visual recognition memory for complex configurations. *Perception and Psychophysics*, *9*, 237–241.

Krouse, F. L. (1981). Effects of pose, pose change and delay on face recognition performance. *Journal of Applied Psychology*, *6*, 651–654.

Laughery, K. R. & Fowler, R. H. (1980). Sketch artist and Identi-kit procedures for recalling faces. *Journal of Applied Psychology*, *65*, 307–316.

Laughery, K. R., Fessler, P. K., Lenorovitz, D. R. & Yoblick, D. A. (1974). Time delay and similarity effects in facial recognition. *Journal of Applied Psychology*, *59*, 490–496.

Light, L. L., Kayra-Stuart, F. & Hollander, S. (1979). Recognition memory for typical and unusual faces. *Journal of Experimental Psychology: Human Learning and Memory*, *5*, 212–228.

Shepherd, J. W., Ellis, H. D. & Davies, G. M. (1982). *Identification evidence: A psychological evaluation*. Aberdeen: Aberdeen University Press.

Valentine, T. & Bruce, V. (1986a). Recognising familiar faces: The role of distinctiveness and familiarity. *Canadian Journal of Psychology*, *40*, 300–305.

Valentine, T. & Bruce, V. (1986b). The effect of distinctiveness in recognising and classifying faces. *Perception*, *15*, 525–535.

Winograd, E. (1981). Elaboration and distinctiveness in memory for faces. *Journal of Experimental Psychology: Human Learning and Memory*, *7*, 181–190.

EUROPEAN JOURNAL OF COGNITIVE PSYCHOLOGY, 1991, 3 (1), 147–176

What's in a Name? Access to Information from People's Names

Tim Valentine
Department of Psychology, University of Manchester, Manchester, U.K.

Serge Bredart
Faculté de Psychologie, Université de Liege, Liege, Belgium

Rebecca Lawson ànd Geoff Ward
Department of Experimental Psychology, University of Cambridge, Cambridge, U.K.

The processing of people's names is contrasted with face recognition and word recognition. The effects of the familiarity of initial and surnames and frequency of surnames (the number of people with the same surname) were investigated in several tasks. It was found that the effects of name familiarity and surname frequency were analogous to the effects of word frequency in tasks which did not require access to memory for individuals (a nationality decision and naming latency). In tasks which do require access to memory for individuals (familiarity decision and a semantic classification), the effect of surname frequency was analogous to the effect of distinctiveness in face recognition. The results are discussed in terms of a functional model of name processing in which name recognition units mediate between the output of word recognition units and access to identity-specific semantics.

Requests for reprints should be addressed to Tim Valentine, Department of Psychology, University of Manchester, Manchester, M13 9PL, U.K.

The experiments reported here were carried out while the first author was employed by the Medical Research Council at the MRC Applied Psychology Unit, Cambridge. This research was a direct result of conversations between the first two authors during the first summer school organised by the European Society for Cognitive Psychology at Bernried, Germany. We thank the Society and the Volkswagen Foundation, who sponsored the summer school, for making our collaboration possible. We would also like to thank Andy Young and Vicki Bruce for helpful comments on an earlier draft of the manuscript.

INTRODUCTION

Much of the recent theoretical development in the face recognition literature has resulted from an analogy drawn between recognition of familiar
faces and words (Bruce, 1979; 1981, 1983). The most influential theoretical
development that has resulted from this analogy has been the emergence of
information-processing models of face recognition, based on the concept of
face recognition units (Bruce & Young, 1986; Ellis, 1986; Hay & Young,
1982). The original conception of a face recognition unit (FRU) was as a
threshold device (Hay & Young, 1982), directly analogous to a logogen in
Morton's (1969; 1979) model of word recognition. Each face recognition
unit is assumed to contain a stored structural description of a familiar face.
Thus there is an FRU for every known face, which will be activated by all
occurrences of a particular individual's face. In later models, FRUs are
seen as signalling resemblance rather than as operating in a binary fashion
(see Bruce & Young, 1986). The level of the output of an FRU will depend
upon the resemblance between the stored representation of a familiar face
and the current input from earlier visual processing. The FRUs mediate
between structural encoding processes and the access of semantic information about individuals (identity-specific semantic information; see Fig. 1).
An activated FRU enables the semantic information about the appropriate
individual to be accessed.

Bruce and Young (1986) note that there is a sequence of functional
components which is common to the recognition and naming of objects,
faces and words. Briefly, the sequence comprises formation of an input
code; activation of a recognition unit; access to semantic information; and,
finally, access to a name code. Word recognition differs in that it is
assumed that name codes can be activated directly from the word recognition units (see Fig. 1). This framework has been successful in accounting
for similarities and differences between face, word and object recognition
in a range of experimental paradigms including priming (Bruce, 1986a;
Bruce & Valentine, 1985; 1986; Ellis, Young, Flude & Hay, 1987),
semantic categorisation and naming (Young, McWeeny, Ellis & Hay,
1986b; Young, McWeeny, Hay & Ellis, 1986c) and interference studies
(Bredart, 1989; Young et al., 1986a: See Bruce & Young, 1986 and Young
& Ellis, 1989, for reviews).

Most of the experiments cited above, which were inspired by comparisons between faces and words, have in fact involved comparisons between
faces and people's names. Thus the analogy implies that names are
arbitrary verbal labels associated with faces and are represented and
processed in the same way as words. This begs the question of whether a
distinction between words and names should be made in the analogy with
face recognition.

Frequency of occurrence of stimuli is one factor that has received comparatively little attention in the analogy between faces and words, despite the ubiquitous effects of word frequency in the word recognition literature. There are at least two reasons why this factor may have been overlooked. First, there is some theoretical debate in the word recognition literature about the locus of word frequency effects (see Monsell, Doyle & Haggard, 1989, for a brief review). Traditional models of word recognition have attributed word frequency effects to the identification process being frequency sensitive. For example, in a recognition unit model, the recognition units for high-frequency words could either have a lower threshold or a higher resting level of activation than the recognition units for low-frequency words. Recently, it has been argued that the identification of visually presented words is not frequency sensitive but the major effects of frequency arise from later task-specific processes (Balota & Chumbley, 1984; 1985). However, Monsell et al. (1989) present evidence that unique identification rather than later processes is the primary locus of frequency effects.

A second problem in using the analogy between words and faces to explore the effects of frequency is that the appropriate analogy is not clear. A possible analogy exists between the degree of familiarity of a face and the frequency of a word. Initially, this analogy appears promising. Familiarity has been found to facilitate RT in a familiarity decision task (Valentine & Bruce, 1986a). Bruce (1983) argues that a familiarity decision (i.e. deciding whether a face is familiar) is analogous to a lexical decision between words and pronounceable nonwords (i.e. deciding whether a letter string is familiar). Therefore, the effect of familiarity of a face in a familiarity decision task is analogous to the advantage found for high-frequency words in a lexical decision task. However, there is a sense in which the familiarity of a face differs from the frequency of a word. A high-frequency word is usually used to refer to any occurrence of a concept (e.g. the word "dog" will be used to refer to a particular dog or to any dog). In contrast, the familiarity of a face is always associated with the same individual. A full name or initial and surname may be familiar because it is the name of a familiar individual, in the same way that an individual's face can be familiar. This will be referred to as the *familiarity* of a name. However, it is important to note that the familiarity of an individual's face and the familiarity of an individual's name are not equivalent. For example, a film actor's face may be more familiar than his name. (It is possible to recognise that an actor has appeared in a previous film without knowing his name.) It is also possible for a name to be more familiar than a face. For example, a newspaper columnist's name might be familiar but her face entirely unfamiliar.

A name (either a first name or surname alone) may also be familiar because it is shared by many people. For example, the surname "Moore" might refer to Roger Moore (actor), Patrick Moore (astronomer), Dudley Moore (actor) or many other individuals who share the same surname. A measure of the number of people who have the same name will be referred to as the *frequency* of a name. Thus, familiarity of names and faces is a property related to the individual person. The number of times a name is encountered will depend on the frequency of the name and the degree of familiarity of people who have the name. Word frequency is an estimate of the relative number of times a word will be encountered, and therefore is analogous to the combined effects of the familiarity and frequency of a name. It should be noted that the familiarity of a name can only be assessed for a name unique to an individual (e.g. an initial and surname or full name), but frequency can refer to either a first or surname alone.

Names are a sub-class of words and must obviously share some early processing in common with word recognition. However, names have some properties in common with words and some properties in common with faces. Like words, names can access all occurrences of the name or word. For example, the word "Moore" can apply to all individuals who have the surname Moore. Like faces, names can also access semantic information specific to individuals. For example, reading the name Roger Moore accesses information about the actor who is best known for playing James Bond in films.

We propose that name recognition units, the logical equivalent of face recognition units, mediate between the word recognition system and access to identity-specific semantic information about individuals (see Fig. 1). The output of word recognition units which represent names connect to name recognition units. The input to name recognition units could be first or surnames alone, initial and surname or full names. There is a word recognition unit for every familiar word (or name) and there is a name recognition unit for every familiar individual. Phonological output codes can be accessed directly from name recognition units. This route is analogous to the direct route from word recognition units to phonological output codes. Young et al. (1986b) and Young, Ellis and Flude (1988) report evidence that phonological output codes (name codes) can be accessed in parallel to identity-specific semantics from written names but that phonological output codes can only be accessed from faces via identity-specific semantics.

The experiments reported here are intended as an exploratory study of the effects of familiarity and frequency in processing names. Research concerning the processes involved in recognising names has been rather neglected compared to the amount of research on recognising faces, though there has been quite a lot of recent research on name *recall*. McWeeny, Young, Hay & Ellis (1987) showed that names are particularly

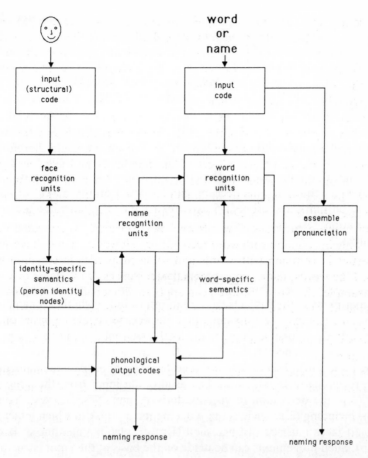

FIG. 1.   A functional model of face, name and word recognition. The routes for face and word recognition are standard models adapted from Bruce and Young (1986), except that a route for naming unfamiliar words is shown. It is proposed that name recognition proceeds via name recognition units which mediate between word recognition units and identity-specific semantics.

difficult to recall in a laboratory task. Indeed, naming famous faces has been found to be an effective way of eliciting a tip-of-the-tongue state in the laboratory (Hanley & Cowell, 1988; Yarmey, 1973). Difficulty in remembering names is often reported in everyday life (Young, Hay & Ellis, 1985), particularly among the elderly (Cohen & Faulkner, 1986; Martin, 1986). Flude, Ellis & Kay (1989) described an anomic aphasic patient who could not name many familiar faces but had full access to semantic information about familiar people. Semenza and Zettin (1988; 1989) report cases of a selective anomia for proper names. Therefore, a systematic study of the processes involved in recognising and recalling names is of some practical as well as theoretical significance.

Experiments 1 and 2 are intended to examine the effects of frequency and familiarity in tasks which do not require access to information relating to specific individuals. Experiment 1 involves a decision concerning the probable national origin of names (Belgian *vs* British). It is assumed that the task only demands analysis at the level of an input code but can be facilitated by the activation of a word recognition unit (see below). In Experiment 2, the effect of familiarty and frequency on pronunciation latency for names is examined. This task is assumed to require access to phonological output codes. In Experiments 3 and 4, a familiarity decision to names is required. This decision can be based on the output of name recognition units. Experiment 5 explores frequency effects in a semantic classification task and is assumed to require access to identity-specific semantics.

EXPERIMENT 1

In Experiment 1, the subjects were required to judge whether a name was British or Belgian. It was assumed that this decision could be based on the input code. It is possible to judge the likely nationality of a name even if it has never been encountered before (i.e. there is no appropriate word recognition unit). This task is designed to be an approximate analogue of face processing tasks which can be based on an input from the structural code (e.g. the derivation of visually derived semantics: Bruce & Young, 1986), including tasks such as sex judgements or a task in which intact and jumbled faces must be distinguished (Bruce, 1986b; Valentine & Bruce, 1986b). Such judgements can be made on the basis of the input (structural) code for faces, but Bruce (1986b) found that both sex judgements and face classification can be made more rapidly to familiar faces than to unfamiliar faces, presumably due to a top-down influence from FRUs for familiar faces. An appropriate analogue from word recognition to the nationality decision task used in Experiment 1, might be one which requires subjects to classify letter strings as similar to words of their own language or a foreign language. However, we know of no studies in which the effect of word frequency has been examined in such a task.

A nationality judgement could be based upon the degree to which the input code resembles an English orthography. However, if there is a word recognition unit for the name, the activation of a word recognition unit could also provide an input to the nationality decision process (cf. Bruce, 1986b; see Fig. 1). A "British" response made on the basis of activation of a word recognition unit would be almost certainly correct, as all Belgian names in Experiment 1 were unfamiliar to the subjects. Word recognition units would only exist for names which had been encountered before. Therefore, low-frequency, unfamiliar names are the only class of British names for which word recognition units are unlikely to exist. If it is assumed that the nationality decision process accumulates evidence from the input code and top-down influence from the word recognition units until some criterion is reached, the classification of low-frequency, unfamiliar British names would be slower than the other names because the input from word recognition units would be unavailable.

An effect of frequency on classification of familiar British names was not predicted because the nationality decision task does not require unique identification at the word recognition unit level. The input to this decision could be based on a measure of overall activity among word recognition units without the need to identify one particular unit as activated. Monsell et al. (1989) point out that there is no reason to suppose that such use of the lexicon should be frequency sensitive.

Method

Subjects.   A total of 24 students from the University of Cambridge acted as subjects, of whom 21 were males and 3 females.

Stimuli.   Eighty names served as the stimuli for Experiment 1: 40 were British names and 40 were Belgian names. Each name consisted of an initial and surname. The names were selected according to the frequency of occurrence of the surname and the rated familiarity of the initial and surname using the criteria stated below. The 40 names of each nationality consisted of: 10 familiar, high-frequency names; 10 familiar, low-frequency names; 10 unfamiliar, high-frequency names; and 10 unfamiliar, low-frequency names. The British names were selected on the following criteria. The frequency of a surname was estimated by counting the number of occurrences in the Cambridge and district telephone directory. The high-frequency surnames had a minimum of 1 occurrence per 5000 entries. The low-frequency surnames had a maximum of 1 occurrence per 50,000 entries and had at least 1 entry in the directory. A set of "familiar" and "unfamiliar" names was generated by pairing surnames of famous people with the appropriate initial, and names for which the experimenters could not think of a famous person with an initial from the set used for famous names chosen at random. Twenty students, who did not take part in any of the subsequent experiments, rated each name (initial and surname) for familiarity on a 7-point scale (1 = unfamiliar, 7 = highly familiar). These ratings were used to select the set of British names used in Experiments 1–3. Each of the four sets of ten items were matched on the length of the surname. As far as possible, surnames with unusual spelling

TABLE 1
Mean Familiarity Ratings, Frequency (Occurrences per 100,000 Entries)
and Number of Letters in Surname of the British Names Used in Experiments 1–3
(standard deviations are shown in parentheses)

	Familiar Names		Unfamiliar Names	
	High-frequency	Low-frequency	High-frequency	Low-frequency
Familiarity	6.23 (0.35)	6.27 (0.49)	1.51 (0.35)	1.32 (0.21)
Frequency	128.10 (108.0)	1.23 (0.54)	128.03 (124.6)	1.43 (0.50)
Number of letters	6.2 (1.62)	5.6 (1.26)	5.7 (1.06)	5.9 (0.87)

patterns, or surnames which are also English words, were avoided. The mean familiarity, frequency and word length of each of the four classes of names are shown in Table 1. The stimuli are listed in the Appendix.

The set of 40 Belgian names used in this experiment were selected in a similar manner from the Liege and district telephone directory. Familiarity ratings were obtained from Belgian students. Belgian names that also occurred in the Cambridge telephone directory were excluded, with the exception of one name which had one occurrence only. These stimuli were also used in Experiments 4 and 5. Full details of the selection criteria are given in the description of the method of Experiment 4 and the stimuli are listed in the Appendix. Although the Belgian names were divided into the same four categories used for the British names, this categorisation was based on the ratings of Belgian students. All of the Belgian names were unfamiliar to the British subjects in this experiment.

Apparatus.   A BBC microcomputer was used to present the stimuli and log responses and reaction times from two response buttons.

Design.   The design included three within-subjects factors: the nationality, familiarity and frequency of the names. Ten stimuli in each cell of the design were presented. The task was to classify the names according to their nationality as quickly as possible. The Belgian names were included to generate the task demand. The results of primary interest were the effects of familiarity and frequency upon classification of the British names. The dependent variable was reaction time.

Procedure.   The experiment was preceded by a block of 20 practice trials. The items used in these trials were not used in the experimental trials, 10 were British names, 10 were Belgian names. Each name was presented in upper case in the centre of the screen until a response was made. The inter-stimulus interval was 2 sec. Four different random orders were used, and six subjects were tested with each order. The stimuli were presented in blocks of 20 items. The first block consisted of the practice items followed by four experimental blocks. The response buttons were labelled "British" and "Belgian". The subjects were told that they would see a series of names, half of which were British surnames and half of which were Belgian surnames. They were asked to judge whether each name was likely to be of British or Belgian origin as quickly but as accurately as possible. The subject held one response button in each hand. The assignment of buttons to the preferred or non-preferred hand was counterbalanced across subjects. Reaction times less than 200 msec or over 2 sec were treated as missing data.

Results

Separate analyses of British and Belgian names were carried out. The analysis of responses to British names will be discussed first. The mean error rate for British names was 14.4% (the analysis of errors is discussed below). The mean reaction times of correct responses to British names are plotted in Fig. 2. These data were subjected to an ANOVA with familiarity and frequency as within-subjects factors. There was a main effect of familiarity [$F(1,23) = 16.10$, $P < 0.001$]. Names of famous people were classified as British more quickly than unfamiliar names. There was a main effect of frequency [$F(1,23) = 28.82$, $P < 0.001$]. High-frequency names were classified more quickly than low-frequency names. There was also a significant interaction between these factors [$F(1,23) = 17.09$, $P < 0.001$]. Tukey HSD tests were used to analyse significant interactions in all of the experiments reported. Where critical differences (HSD) are quoted, unless stated otherwise, a statistical significance level of 0.05 was used. The main effect of familiarity was significant for low-frequency names ($P < 0.01$), but was not significant for high-frequency names (HSD = 51.5 msec). The main effect of frequency was significant for unfamiliar names ($P < 0.01$), but was not significant for familiar names (HSD = 55.2 msec). An items analysis of the RT data was also carried out, with frequency and familiarity as between-items factors. The results supported those obtained in the subjects analysis. There was a significant main effect of familiarity [$F(1,36) = 11.22$, $P < 0.005$] and frequency [$F(1,36) = 12.93$, $P < 0.001$]. The interaction was also significant [$F(1,36) = 5.94$, $P < 0.05$]. Tukey HSD tests showed that the effect of frequency was significant for unfamiliar names ($P < 0.01$), but was not significant for familiar names. The effect of familiarity was significant for low-frequency names ($P < 0.01$), but was not

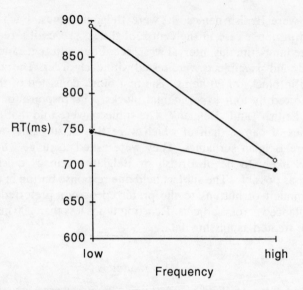

FIG. 2.   Mean reaction time to correctly classify names as "British" as a function of familiarity and frequency (Experiment 1). ●, Familiar; ○, unfamiliar.

significant for high-frequency names (HSD = 57.9 msec for all comparisons).

In view of the error rate being reasonably high (mean 14.4%), an ANOVA of errors made to British names was also carried out. The mean number of errors in each condition are plotted in Fig. 3. The main effect of familiarity was significant [$F(1,23) = 66.05, P < 0.001$]. More errors were made to unfamiliar names than to familiar names. The main effect of frequency was significant [$F(1,23) = 24.31, P < 0.001$]. More errors were made to low-frequency names than to high-frequency names. There was also a significant interaction between familiarity and frequency [$F(1,23 = 6.18, P < 0.05$]. Tukey HSD tests of the simple main effects showed that the interaction was due to a significant effect of frequency for unfamiliar names ($P < 0.01$), which was not found for familar names (HSD = 0.449). The simple main effect of familiarity was significant for both high-frequency names ($P < 0.01$) and for low-frequency names ($P < 0.01$; HSD = 0.535). The errors made to British names were also analysed by item. An ANOVA with familiarity and frequency as between-items factors revealed a main effect of familiarity [$F(1,36) = 12.98, P < 0.001$] and frequency [$F(1,36) = 4.11, P = 0.05$]. The interaction between familiarity and frequency was not significant in this analysis [$F(1,36) = 2.48, 0.10 < P < 0.15$].

The Belgian names were included to generate the necessary task de-

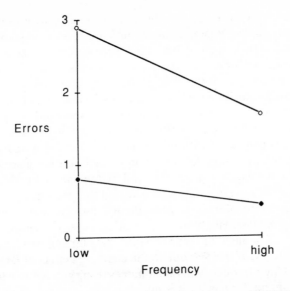

FIG. 3.   Mean number of errors (chance = 5) in classifying names as "British" as a function
of familiarity and frequency (Experiment 1). ●, Familiar; ○, unfamiliar.

mand, and were all unfamiliar and of low frequency to the subjects who
took part in this experiment. Therefore, it was expected that no effects of
frequency and familiarity would be found. The mean error rate for
Belgian names was 14.8%. An analysis of the error data is reported below.
An ANOVA of RT data revealed a significant main effect of frequency
$[F(1,23) = 12.00, P < 0.005]$. High-frequency names were correctly
classified as Belgian more quickly than low-frequency names. The interaction term was also significant $[F(1,23) = 4.47, P < 0.05]$. Tukey HSD tests
showed that the effect of frequency was significant for "unfamiliar" Belgian names $(P < 0.01)$, but not for "familiar" Belgian names. There were
no significant effects in an items analysis of the RT data.

   An ANOVA of errors made to Belgian names revealed only a main
effect of familiarity $[F(1,46) = 6.41, P < 0.05]$. Less errors were made to
"familiar" names than to "unfamiliar" names.

Discussion

The results of trials in which British names were presented, have clearly
shown that both the familiarity of a name and its frequency in the
population can affect the RT taken to classify a name as British. The
effects have been found to be interactive rather than additive. The analyses
by subjects and by items both show that frequency only affects the RT to

accept unfamiliar names and that the effect of familiarity is only found for low-frequency names. Reaction time to unfamiliar, low-frequency names is slower than reaction times to the other three classes of names, which do not differ from each other. This pattern of results is broadly consistent with the input code and activation of the word recognition units providing input to the nationality decision process. Decisions to low-frequency, unfamiliar names are slower because there is no input from the word recognition units for these names. There was no effect of frequency on decisions to familiar names. This is consistent with the assumption that the primary source of frequency effects is at the level of unique identification among the word recognition units which was not required by the nationality decision task.

An analysis of the error data also revealed that the effects of familiarity and frequency were interactive. As in the RT data, frequency only affected the accuracy of classifying unfamiliar names. However, in the error data, there was an advantage for familiar names over unfamiliar names independent of frequency. If this was due to the combined effect of familiarity and frequency of high-frequency, familiar names being greater than that of high-frequency, unfamiliar names, it is not clear why an effect of familiarity on RT to high-frequency names was not found. An alternative *post-hoc* explanation would be top-down influence from activity in the name recognition units providing an input to the nationality decision process. As there will only be name recognition units for familiar individuals, an input from name recognition units would contribute to an effect of familiarity for high- and low-frequency names. If recognition of a high-frequency name as a familiar individual is slow compared to nationality decision (see Experiment 3), the name recognition units could only influence the accuracy of slow nationality decisions. Therefore, the effect of activity in name recognition units would be expected to affect accuracy but not RT of nationality decisions to high-frequency names. This suggestion is supported by an informal between-subjects comparison between the mean RT for nationality decision to high-frequency familiar names in Experiment 1 (694 msec) and RT for familiarity decisions to the same names in Experiment 3 (789 msec). The equivalent comparison for low-frequency names is 746 and 748 msec respectively.

No effects had been predicted for the classification of Belgian names. However, it was found that high-frequency Belgian names were classified faster than low-frequency Belgian names. An examination of the stimuli suggested that the subjects may have been using spelling patterns in some names which were more common in French than in English (e.g. names ending in -et, -ez). The fact that the effect was not reliable across items suggests that there were a few items contributing to the effect. As no effect had been predicted, the sets of items were not well suited to examining it. However, the effect is consistent with the assumption that the nationality decision could be based on the input code. Spelling patterns which are unusual in British names could be rapidly rejected as British. An experiment designed to examine this point may be able to demonstrate that the subjects were sensitive to the orthography of names.

EXPERIMENT 2

The aim of Experiment 2 was to explore further the comparison between words and names by examining the effect of familiarity and frequency of names in a naming task. The task required the surname only of an initial and surname to be read aloud. In a naming task it is assumed that phonological output codes can be accessed directly from word recognition units for names as for words (see Fig. 1). There is some debate in the word recognition literature about the magnitude of the effect of frequency on naming latency. However, there is good evidence that high-frequency words can be pronounced faster than low-frequency words, although the effect is larger for irregular than regular words (Monsell et al., 1989; Seidenberg, Waters, Barnes & Tannenhaus, 1984). It should be noted that as far as possible irregular names were avoided in the stimulus set used in Experiment 2. The word recognition literature suggests that this would reduce the magnitude of the frequency effect to be expected. Notwithstanding the use of regular names, it was predicted that high-frequency names would be pronounced faster than low-frequency names. It was also predicted that low-frequency, unfamiliar names would be pronounced more slowly than either familiar names or high-frequency, unfamiliar names because a recognition unit is less likely to exist for low-frequency, unfamiliar names. If no recognition unit exists for a name because it has not been seen previously, the name must be read using grapheme–phoneme conversion rules or by analogy to other words.[1] Because subjects are likely to have encountered high-frequency names before, even if they are not names of famous people, it is only low-frequency, unfamiliar names for which the direct route from recognition units to phonological output codes is unlikely to be available. Therefore, it is predicted that high-frequency, unfamiliar names will be named faster than low-frequency, unfamiliar names.

---

[1]In drawing an analogy between names, words and faces it is assumed that the locus of the effect of frequency and familiarity is at the stage of identification of a familiar stimulus (i.e. activation of a recognition unit). Monsell et al. (1989) make the point that if a word is read by assembling pronunciation, the source of frequency sensitivity in identification is by-passed. The processes by which pronunciation of an unfamiliar word is assembled may also be frequency sensitive, but this is a different locus of an effect of frequency.

Accessing a phonological output code via the recognition unit route requires unique identification of the name. Because unique identification is believed to be frequency sensitive, it was predicted that high-frequency, familiar names would be named faster than low-frequency, familiar names. The relative magnitude of the effect of frequency on naming familiar and unfamiliar names is not easily predictable, because in the former case it arises from the frequency sensitivity of the direct route from recognition units and in the latter case it arises from the use of different routes.

Method

Subjects. A total of 24 students from the University of Cambridge acted as subjects, 3 of whom were female and 21 of whom were male. None had taken part in any of the other experiments reported here.

Stimuli. The 40 British names used in Experiment 1 served as the stimuli in this experiment.

Apparatus. The appartus was the same as used in Experiment 1, except that reaction time was determined by use of a voice key. The data logged on any trial could be "cancelled" by a push button operated by the experimenter. This was used to cancel trials on which the subject either read the name incorrectly or the voice key was triggered by some other sound.

Design. There were two within-subjects factors, familiarity and frequency of the names. There were 10 stimuli in each of the four cells of the design. The dependent variable was the reaction time. The stimuli were presented in a random order. Four different random orders were used. Six subjects were tested with each order of stimuli.

Procedure. The procedure was the same as for Experiment 1 except for the following details. The subjects' task was to read aloud the surname only as quickly as possible. There were 20 practice trials at the start of the session. Ten of the stimuli in the practice trials were famous names, ten were unfamiliar names. There was a 10-sec pause after the practice trials before the 40 experimental trials were presented in a single block.

Results

Errors were recorded on 5.2% of trials, either because the name was pronounced incorrectly, misread or because the voice key was triggered before the subject read the name. Accuracy data were not analysed

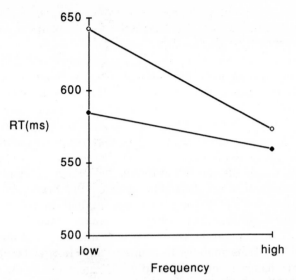

FIG. 4. Mean naming latency for names as a function of familiarity and frequency (Experiment 2). ●, Familiar; ○, unfamiliar.

further. Mean naming latencies are shown in Fig. 4. The naming latencies were subjected to an ANOVA with familiarity and frequency as within-subjects factors. There was a main effect of familiarity [$F(1,23)$ = 30.51, $P < 0.001$]: names of famous people were named faster than unfamiliar names. There was also a significant main effect of frequency [$F(1,23)$ = 80.20, $P < 0.001$], i.e. high-frequency names were named faster than low-frequency names. The interaction between frequency and familiarity was significant [$F(1,23)$ = 10.06, $P < 0.005$]. The simple main effects of this interaction were analysed using Tukey HSD tests. There was an effect of familiarity on naming of low-frequency names ($P < 0.01$), but not on high-frequency names (HSD = 19.4 msec). There was an effect of frequency on both familiar names ($P < 0.01$) and unfamiliar names ($P < 0.01$; HSD = 17.9 msec).

An items analysis of the naming latency data was also carried out. A main effect of familiarity [$F(1,36)$ = 4.64, $P < 0.05$] and a main effect of frequency [$F(1,36)$ = 5.51, $P < 0.05$] were found. The interaction term was not significant in the items analysis (F = 1.07).

Discussion

The results of Experiment 2 are consistent with the predictions based on names being represented within the lexicon of a recognition unit model of word recognition. High-frequency, familiar names were named faster than

low-frequency, familiar names. This effect is consistent with unique identification of words being frequency-sensitive. An effect of frequency was
also found on RT to name unfamiliar names. This is assumed to reflect the
likely need to assemble pronunciation for low-frequency, unfamiliar names
but not for high-frequency, unfamiliar names. The analysis by subjects
provided some evidence that the use of different routes for naming
unfamiliar names produced a greater effect of frequency than did the
frequency sensitivity of unique identification of word recognition units for
naming familiar names. However, this interaction was not supported by an
analysis by items.

No effect of familiarity was found for naming latency of high-frequency
names. An effect would be expected to the extent that the combined effect
of frequency and familiarity would be greater for high-frequency, familiar
names than for high-frequency, unfamiliar names. However, it is again
important to point out that the familiarity × frequency interaction was not
supported by the items analysis. In addition, any effect of familiarity for
high-frequency names is more likely to be contaminated by the names of
people personally familiar to individual subjects. It is possible that the
failure to find an interaction in the items analysis was due to the low power
of the items analysis in which the factors are between-items and there are
only 10 items per cell.

EXPERIMENT 3

Introduction

In Experiment 3, the effect of frequency on a name familiarity decision
task was explored. The task requires a subject to decide whether or not a
name is that of a familiar (i.e. famous) person. It should be noted that in
this task, unlike the tasks used in Experiments 1 and 2, a different response
is required to familiar and unfamiliar names. Therefore, the effect of name
familiarity *per se* cannot be investigated independently of any factors
affecting the different response types. The name familiarity decision task is
directly analogous to the face familiarity decision task which has been used
extensively in the face recognition literature. The face familiarity decision
task was developed as a task analogous to the lexical decision task in the
word recognition literature (Bruce, 1983).

A major difference between the name familiarity decision task and the
nationality decision and naming tasks, is that the familiarity decision task
requires the subject to access memory for familiar individuals. The nationality task and naming task required a response that was independent of

familiarity. Therefore, effects of familiarity were incidental to the task demands. The familiarity decision requires subjects to decide whether a name is of a familiar person and so the decision is assumed to be based on the output of name recognition units, and to require unique identification.

Reaction time in a lexical decision task is faster to high-frequency words than to low-frequency words. If name frequency is directly analogous to word frequency, it would be expected that high-frequency names would be accepted as familiar faster than low-frequency names. However, if it is assumed that there is a name recognition unit for every familiar individual, a high-frequency name will lead to activation of many recognition units. In contrast, a low-frequency name will cause activation restricted to a few recognition units. Therefore, when a low-frequency name is presented, it will be easier to detect that the stimulus matches the stored representation of a familiar individual name because there will be less "noise" from the units representing other individuals with the same name. Young and Ellis (1989) propose an analogous account of the effect of distinctiveness on face familiarity decision (Valentine & Bruce, 1986a; 1986b).

Method

Subjects.   A total of 24 students acted as subjects, 6 of whom were female and 18 of whom were male.

Stimuli.   The 40 British names used in Experiments 1 and 2 served as stimuli.

Apparatus.   This was the same as Experiment 1.

Design.   The design had two within-subjects factors, familiarity and frequency of the names. There were ten stimuli in each of the four cells of a 2 × 2 design. The subject's task was to decide whether each name was that of somebody familiar to him/her. The dependent variable was RT in a "yes/no" decision.

Procedure.   The procedure was the same as Experiment 1, except for the following details. There were 20 practice trials followed, after a break, by the 40 experimental trials. The subjects were informed that some of the names they would see were celebrities' names and some would be unfamiliar. They were instructed to press the "yes" button if the name was familiar, and the "no" button if it was not. They were also instructed to respond as quickly and as accurately as possible. As in Experiments 1 and 2, initial and surnames were presented.

164   VALENTINE ET AL.

Results

It is impossible to discuss the "error rate", because it is possible that a subject responded "no" to a name rated as familiar because the name was genuinely unfamiliar. However, "disagreements" only occurred on 8.9% of trials. Accuracy data were not analysed further. The mean correct RTs are plotted in Fig. 5. Separate analyses of "yes" and "no" responses were carried out. A single factor ANOVA of correct "yes" responses revealed a significant effect of frequency [$F(1,23) = 7.45, P < 0.05$]. Low-frequency, familiar names were accepted faster than high-frequency, familiar names. An ANOVA of correct "no" responses also revealed a significant main effect of frequency [$F(1,23) = 12.25, P < 0.01$]. Low-frequency, unfamiliar names were rejected faster than high-frequency, unfamiliar names. An ANOVA of all the RT data, taking familiarity as a factor, was also carried out. There was a significant main effect of frequency [$F(1,23) = 18.59, P < 0.001$] and a significant main effect of familiarity [$F(1,23) = 21.92, P < 0.001$]. "Yes" responses were faster than "no" responses. The frequency × familiarity interaction was not significant [$F(1,23) = 2.00, P > 0.15$].

An analysis by items was also carried out. A 2 × 2 ANOVA with familiarity and frequency as between-items factors, gave a significant main effect of familiarity [$F(1,36) = 23.2, P < 0.001$], but the main effect of

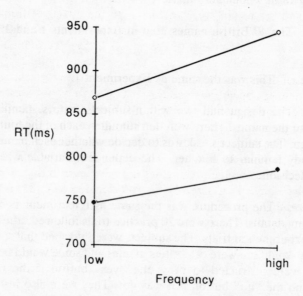

FIG. 5. Mean reaction time of correct responses in a name familiarity decision task as a function of familiarity (yes *vs* no responses) and frequency (Experiment 3). ●, Familiar; ○, unfamiliar.

frequency just failed to reach statistical significance [$F(1,36) = 3.70$, $P = 0.06$]. The interaction between familiarity and frequency was not significant ($F < 1$).

Discussion

The results from Experiment 3 have demonstrated that a name familiarity decision can be made more rapidly to a low-frequency name than to a high-frequency name. This effect of frequency was found for the RT to accept familiar names and for the RT to reject unfamiliar names. The main effect of frequency did not quite achieve statistical significance in the items analysis, but it is possible that this is due to the low statistical power of the items analysis. Frequency is a between-items factor, with only 10 observations per cell in the items analysis.

The effect of name frequency found in the familiarity decision task is the reverse of the effect of name frequency on the nationality and naming latency tasks. There was an advantage for high-frequency names in the nationality decision and naming tasks, but there was an advantage for low-frequency names in the familiarity decision task. The critical aspect of the familiarity decision task is that it requires access to memory for specific individuals, whereas the other tasks do not. Performance in the nationality and naming tasks depended on the combined effects of familiarity and frequency, and the results were analogous to the effects of frequency on word recognition. In the familiarity decision task, the specificity of a name to a familiar individual appears to be critical, giving rise to an advantage for low-frequency names. This result is consistent with familiarity decision being based on the output of name recognition units. In this task, the effect of name frequency appears analogous to the effect of distinctiveness in face familiarity decision (Valentine & Bruce, 1986a; 1986b). Distinctiveness of faces and frequency of names both determine the "spread" of activation across recognition units representing different individuals' faces or names.

The name recognition unit account of the effect of name frequency implies that it is the ambiguity of names that gives rise to the advantage of low-frequency names in a name familiarity decision task. Therefore, the use of less ambiguous stimuli, for example first and surnames, should reduce or remove the effect of frequency in name familiarity decision. This prediction was tested in Experiment 4.

EXPERIMENT 4

The aim of Experiment 4 was to investigate further the effect of name frequency in the familiarity decision used in Experiment 3. There were two experimental conditions in Experiment 4: in one condition the stimuli consisted of a first and surname (condition 1), and for a different group of subjects, the stimuli were an initial and surname (condition 2). It was predicted that the effect of frequency would be reduced for full names.

Method

Subjects.   A total of 32 undergraduate students (18 females and 14 males) participated. All were native French-speaking Belgians. Sixteen subjects were randomly assigned to each experimental condition.

Stimuli.   Twenty full names of famous people and 20 invented (unfamiliar) names were used. In each of these two categories of names, there were 10 high-frequency surnames and 10 low-frequency surnames. Familiarity ratings (for the familiar names) were obtained from an independent sample of 40 subjects who rated the names using a 7-point scale (1 = unfamiliar, 7 = highly familiar). Other real surnames and the same first names as those of the celebrities were used to construct the unfamiliar names used in condition 1. The unfamiliar names consisted of a first and surname combined in such a way that the full name was not that of a famous person (at least from the experimenter's viewpoint). A surname was judged to be of high frequency if it appeared at least once in 5000 entries, and to be of low frequency if it appeared less than once in 45,000 entries in the Liege area telephone directory. Details of familiarity, frequency and the number of letters in the names in each cell of the design are given in Table 2. The same stimuli were used in condition 2, except that each first name was replaced by the appropriate initial.

Apparatus.   A COPAM PC88C microcomputer was used to control stimulus presentation, random order generation and to log responses and RTs.

Design.   The format of the names presented was a between-subjects factor. The frequency (high/low) and familiarity (famous/unfamiliar) of the names formed two within-subjects factors. Response latency was the dependent variable.

Procedure.   The stimuli were presented on the computer screen in a different random order for each subject. The experiment was preceded by a short practice session using eight names that did not appear later in the experiment. The response keys were located on the keyboard. The left and right position of the "yes" and "no" response keys was counterbalanced across subjects. Other aspects of the procedure were the same as for Experiment 3.

TABLE 2

Mean Familiarity Ratings, Frequency (Occurrences per 100,000 Entries) and Number of Letters in Full and Surname of the Belgian Names Used in Experiment 4 (standard deviations are shown in parentheses)

	Familiar Names		Unfamiliar Names	
	High-frequency	Low-frequency	High-frequency	Low-frequency
Familiarity	5.26 (0.43)	5.33 (0.76)	—	—
Frequency	56.81 (27.09)	0.98 (0.83)	56.44 (24.49)	0.83 (0.23)
No. of letters, full names	13.00 (2.41)	13.80 (2.64)	13.50 (1.28)	13.80 (1.47)
No of letters, surnames	6.30 (1.19)	6.50 (2.01)	6.70 (1.62)	6.50 (1.21)

Results

Separate analyses were carried out on RTs to accept names of famous persons and on RTs to reject unfamiliar names. The number of "no" responses to famous names was low (5.6% in condition 1 and 6.9% in condition 2). These "incorrect" RTs and two correct RTs over 2 sec were treated as missing data. The mean correct RTs to the high- and low-frequency, familiar names were calculated for each subject. The data are shown in Fig. 6.

A 2 (condition) × 2 (frequency) ANOVA with repeated measures on the last factor was carried out on the mean RT to accept famous names. The main effect of condition was not significant ($F < 1$), nor was the main effect of frequency [$F(1,30) = 2.22$, $P > 0.1$]. However, there was a significant interaction between the two factors [$F(1,30) = 7.99$, $P < 0.01$]. Tukey HSD tests revealed that frequency had no significant effect when full names were presented, but RTs to high-frequency names were slower than RTs to low-frequency names in the initial and surname condition [$P < 0.01$, HSD (0.01) = 66 msec].

An analysis by items was also carried out. A 2 × 2 ANOVA with condition and frequency as between-items factors showed no main effect of condition or frequency (both F ratios < 1) and only a tendency for an interaction [$F(1,36) = 3.20$, $P < 0.08$].

The number of unfamiliar names incorrectly accepted as familiar was small (5.3% in condition 1 and 6.9% in condition 2). These "yes" responses and 13 correct RTs over 2 sec were treated as missing data. The mean correct RTs to unfamiliar names are plotted in Fig. 7. These data

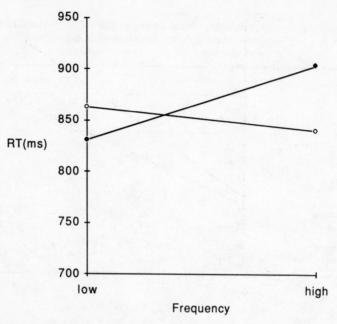

FIG. 6. Mean reaction time of correct responses to familiar faces in a familiarity decision task as function of format of name and frequency (Experiment 4). ●, Initial + surname; ○, full name.

were subjected to a 2 (condition) × 2 (frequency) ANOVA. The analysis revealed no main effect of condition ($F < 1$), a significant main effect of frequency [$F(1,30) = 60.87, P < 0.001$] and no interaction [$F(1,30) = 2.71, P > 0.1$]. RT to reject unfamiliar names was longer for high-frequency names (mean 1045 msec) than for low-frequency names (mean 922 msec). Mean correct RTs to reject unfamiliar faces were also analysed by item. The only significant effect was the main effect of frequency [$F(1,36) = 21.061, P < 0.001$]. Other F ratios were less than 1.3.

Discusssion

Experiment 4 replicated the results of Experiment 3, using an entirely different set of stimuli which were drawn from a different linguistic community. In both Experiments 3 and 4, familiarity decisions to familiar and unfamiliar initial and surname combinations were faster for low-frequency names than they were for high-frequency names. In Experiment 4, presentation of first and surnames was found to remove the effect of surname frequency on RT to accept familiar names but not on RT to reject unfamiliar names.

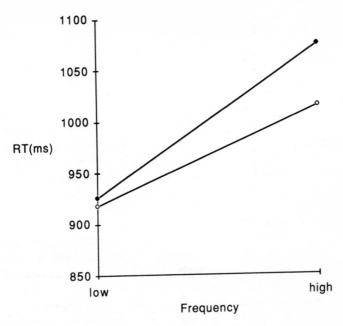

FIG. 7.   Mean reaction time of correct responses to unfamiliar faces in a familiarity decision task as function of format of name and frequency (Experiment 4). ●, Initial + surname; ○, full name.

The results of familiarity decisions to full names are consistent with the interpretation of frequency effects in terms of "noise" from competing name recognition units. A first and surname provides a much less ambiguous cue to an individual than an initial and surname. When coupled with a first name, the appropriate name recognition unit will be more highly activated, and name recognition units for individuals who share the same surname will be less highly activated than they would be following presentation of an initial and surname. Therefore, including first names reduces the "noise" from competing units and so removes the effect of frequency of the surname. It is interesting to note that there is an effect of frequency on rejection latency for unfamiliar first and surname combinations. In this case, there is not a single recognition unit that will be strongly activated by the particular first and surname combination, but for the high-frequency surnames there are likely to be more name recognition units for individuals who share the same surname which will be activated to some extent. In the absence of one very strongly activated unit, the greater amount of activity in these other units induced by a high-frequency surname is sufficient to slow down the rejection of a high-frequency name compared to the RT to reject a low-frequency name.

The account of the effect of frequency on familiarty decision discussed so far assumes that familiarity decision requires unique identification of an individual. The RT in a familiarity decision is assumed to depend upon a ratio or a relative threshold of activity of a particular unit above that of competing units. The familiarity decision task does not logically require unique identification, although the interpretation of frequency effects described assumes that in practice name familiarity decisions are based on unique identification. However, logically, it could be possible to perform the task on some level of a familiarity signal, without the need to identify a particular unit as the source of the activity. If such a familiarity signal – which was not specific to an individual – was the basis of familiarity decisions, an advantage for high-frequency names would be expected, as found in the nationality decision task (Experiment 1) and naming task (Experiment 2). Experiment 5 was run as a check on our interpretation of the frequency effects on familiarity decision. A semantic classification task was used in which familiar names have to be classified as politicians or TV personalities (Young et al., 1986b; 1986c). This task requires unique identification of an individual and access to identity-specific semantic information in order to classify the individual according to their occupation (Bruce & Young, 1986). We have argued that the locus of frequency effects in processing names is at the stage of unique identification at the level of name recognition units. Therefore, it is predicted that a semantic classification will show the same effect of frequency as familiarity decision. There is no *a priori* reason to suppose there would be any additional effect of frequency on the access to identity-specific semantic information.

EXPERIMENT 5

Method

Subjects.   A total of 12 French-speaking Belgian undergraduates participated in the experiment.

Stimuli.   Sixteen of the 20 famous names used in Experiment 4 served as stimuli. Initial and surnames were used. Eight high-frequency and eight low-frequency names were selected such that there were four politicians and four TV personalities in each frequency category. The mean familiarity scores were 5.35 for the high-frequency names and 5.45 for the low-frequency names. The mean frequencies (per 100,000 entries) were 61.27 and 0.95 respectively.

Apparatus.   This was the same as for Experiment 4.

Design and Procedure. There were two within-subjects factors, frequency and occupational category. The subjects' task was to decide whether each name was that of a politician or a TV personality. The two response keys on the keyboard were labelled "TV" and "POL". Other aspects of the design and procedure were the same as for Experiment 4.

Results

The mean correct RTs for each set of four stimuli were calculated and are plotted in Fig. 8. The error rate was low (4.16%). The errors and five correct RTs over 2 sec were treated as missing data.

A 2 × 2 ANOVA with repeated measures on both factors was carried out. The analysis showed a main effect of frequency [$F(1,11) = 26.08$, $P < 0.01$], the high-frequency names being classified more slowly than the low-frequency names. No other effects were significant (both F ratios < 1.4). The same pattern of results was found in an analysis by items. There was a main effect of frequency [$F(1,12) = 30.15$, $P < 0.001$], but the main effect of occupation just failed to reach significance [$F(1,12) = 4.12$, $P < 0.07$]. The interaction was not significant ($F < 1$).

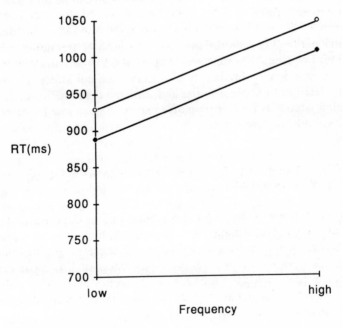

FIG. 8.   Mean reaction time in semantic classification of familiar names as a function of occupational category and frequency (Experiment 5). ●, Politicians; ○, TV personalities.

Discussion

Experiment 5 has shown that RT in a semantic classification is faster for low-frequency surnames than for high-frequency surnames. Thus the effect of frequency on semantic classification is similar to the effect of frequency on familiarity decision.

The model of face (and person) recognition in Fig. 1 predicts that semantic classifications would take longer than familiarity decisions because access to identity-specific semantics is required for semantic classification but not for familiarity decision. Young et al. (1986c) found that familiarity decisions to faces could be made faster than semantic classification of faces. Although a formal analysis of the data from the initial and surnames condition of Experiment 4 and Experiment 5 is not possible due to differences between the designs, an informal comparison of the RTs does support the theoretical prediction. The mean RT to correctly accept a name as familiar was faster than the mean RT to classify a familiar name according to the person's occupation (868 and 968 msec respectively).

GENERAL DISCUSSION

There are a number of empirical conclusions which can be drawn from the experiments reported:

1. RT in a nationality decision task was faster for high-frequency surnames than for low-frequency surnames if the initial and surnames were not of familiar individuals. Frequency of surname did not affect RT of nationality decision to familiar initial and surname combinations.
2. Naming latency is faster to high-frequency than to low-frequency surnames, both for familiar and unfamiliar initial and surname combinations.
3. RT to accept initial and surnames as familiar or reject them as unfamiliar is faster to low-frequency surnames than to high-frequency surnames. The effect of frequency on RT to accept familiar names is restricted to names presented as an initial and surname, but the effect of frequency on RT to reject unfamiliar names is found for full names and initial and surname stimuli.
4. Low-frequency, familiar initial and surname combinations are classified according to the person's occupation faster than high-frequency, familiar initial and surnames.

The experiments reported here provide evidence to support the proposed framework of processes involved in recognising people's names. The data are consistent with a framework in which it is assumed that names and words are represented by word recognition units, there being one unit for every familiar word or name. The output of word recognition units which represent names, connect to a set of name recognition units in which there is a unit for every familiar individual. Activation of name recognition units allows access to identity-specific semantics which can also be accessed through the face recognition system. In tasks which do not require identification of individuals, the combined effects of familiarity and frequency of names are analogous to word frequency effects in word recognition. In tasks which do require identification of individuals, the effect of name frequency is analogous to the effect of distinctiveness in face recognition. Although the effect of the degree of familiarity of names in a familiarity decision task has not been investigated here, it is predicted that the effect of familiarity of names would be analogous to the effect of familiarity of faces. RT in a face familiarity decision is faster for more familiar faces (Valentine & Bruce, 1986a). The analogous effect of familiarity of names in a name familiarity decision task would be predicted.

In Fig. 1, the phonological output codes for words and people's names are shown as sharing a common box because we know of no evidence which requires output codes for words and people's names to be separated. Young et al. (1986b) found that written familiar names could be read aloud faster than rearranged names. Subjects were faster to name "Jack Nicholson" and "Dean Martin" than they were to name "Dean Nicholson" and "Jack Martin". The advantage for familiar names could result from associative priming between word recognition units representing first and surnames (via the links to name recognition units). Alternatively, or in addition, there could be associative priming between phonological output codes. It is also possible that a similar (purely associative) effect could exist for words that often occur together in common phrases or expressions. Similarly, word recognition units for names and for words which are not used as names have not been distinguished in Fig. 1. We know of no evidence to force such a distinction to be made. Further research would be required to justify fractionation between names and words at the level of input units (word recognition units) or phonological output units.

The experiments reported here provide some initial evidence for a functional model of face, name and word recognition. Although the framework has been described in terms of a conventional information-processing model, we do not see any of the data presented as being inconsistent with an implementation in terms of a model based on cascade processes or parallel distributed processing.

Manuscript received August 1989
Revised manuscript received February 1990

REFERENCES

Balota, D. A. & Chumbley, J. I. (1984). Are lexical decisions a good measure of lexical access? The role of word frequency in the neglected decision stage. *Journal of Experimental Psychology: Human Perception and Performance, 10*, 340–357.

Balota, D. A. & Chumbley, J. I. (1985). The locus of word frequency effects in the pronunciation task: Lexical access and/or production. *Journal of Memory and Language, 24*, 89–106.

Bredart, S. (1989). Categorization of familiar persons from their names: A case of interference. *British Journal of Psychology, 80*, 273–283.

Bruce, V. (1979). Searching for politicians: An information-processing approach to face recognition. *Quarterly Journal of Experimental Psychology, 31*, 373–395.

Bruce, V. (1981). Visual and semantic effects in a serial word classification task. *Current Psychological Research, 1*, 153–162.

Bruce, V. (1983). Recognising faces. *Philosophical Transactions of the Royal Society of London, B302*, 423–436.

Bruce, V. (1986a). Recognising familiar faces. In H. D. Ellis, M. A. Jeeves, F. Newcombe & A. Young (Eds), *Aspects of face processing*, pp. 107–117. Dordrecht: Martinus Nijhoff.

Bruce, V. (1986b). Influences of familiarity on the processing of faces. *Perception, 15*, 387–397.

Bruce, V. & Valentine, T. (1985). Identity priming in the recognition of familiar faces. *British Journal of Psychology, 76*, 373–383.

Bruce, V. & Valentine, T. (1986). Semantic priming of familiar faces. *Quarterly Journal of Experimental Psychology, 38A*, 125–150.

Bruce, V. & Young, A. (1986). Understanding face recognition. *British Journal of Psychology, 77*, 305–327.

Cohen, G. & Faulkner, D. (1986). Memory for proper names: Age differences in retrieval. *British Journal of Developmental Psychology, 4*, 187–197.

Ellis, A. W., Young, A. W., Flude, B. & Hay, D. C. (1987). Repetition priming of face recognition. *Quarterly Journal of Experimental Psychology, 39A*, 193–210.

Ellis, H. D. (1986). Processes underlying face recognition. In R. Bruyer (Ed.), *The neuropsychology of face perception and facial expression*, pp. 1–27. Hillsdale, N.J.: Lawrence Erlbaum Associates Inc.

Flude, B. M., Ellis, A. W. & Kay, J. (1989). Face processing and name retrieval in an anomic aphasic: Names are stored separately from semantic information about people. *Brain and Cognition, 11*, 60–72.

Hanley, J. R. & Cowell, E. S. (1988). The effects of different types of retrieval cues on the recall of names of famous faces. *Memory and Cognition, 16*, 545–555.

Hay, D. C. & Young, A. W. (1982). The human face. In A. W. Ellis (Ed.), *Normality and pathology in cognitive functions*, pp. 173–202. London: Academic Press.

McWeeny, K. H., Young, A. W., Hay, D. C. & Ellis, A. W. (1987). Putting names to faces. *British Journal of Psychology, 78*, 143–149.

Martin, M. (1986). Ageing and patterns of change in everyday memory and cognition. *Human Learning, 5*, 63–74.

Monsell, S., Doyle, M. C. & Haggard, P. N. (1989). Effects of frequency on visual recognition tasks: Where are they? *Journal of Experimental Psychology: General, 118*, 43–71.

Morton, J. (1969). Interaction of information in word recognition. *Psychological Review, 76*, 165–178.

Morton, J. (1979). Facilitation in word recognition: Experiments causing a change in logogen model. In P. A. Kolers, M. Wrolstad & H. Bouma (Eds), *Processing of visible language*, pp. 259–268. New York: Plenum Press.

Seidenberg, M. S., Waters, G. S., Barnes, M. A. & Tannenhaus, M. K. (1984). When does irregular spelling or pronunciation influence word recognition? *Journal of Verbal Learning and Verbal Behavior*, *23*, 383–404.

Semenza, C. & Zettin, M. (1988). Generating proper names: A case of selective inability. *Cognitive Neuropsychology*, *5*, 711–721.

Semenza, C. & Zettin, M. (1989). Evidence from aphasia for the role of proper names as pure referring expressions. *Nature*, *342*, 678–679.

Valentine, T. & Bruce, V. (1986a). Recognising familiar faces: The role of distinctiveness and familiarity. *Canadian Journal of Psychology*, *40*, 300–305.

Valentine, T. & Bruce, V. (1986b). The effects of distinctiveness in recognising and classifying faces. *Perception*, *15*, 525–536.

Yarmey, A. D. (1973). I recognize your face but I can't remember your name: Further evidence on the tip-of-the-tongue phenomenon. *Memory and Cognition*, *1*, 287–290.

Young, A. W. & Ellis, H. D. (1989). Semantic processing. In A. W. Young & H. D. Ellis (Eds), *Handbook of research on face processing*, pp. 235–262. Amsterdam: Elsevier.

Young, A. W., Hay, D. C. & Ellis, A. W. (1985). The faces that launched a thousand slips: Everyday difficulties and errors in recognising people. *British Journal of Psychology*, *76*, 495–523.

Young, A. W., Ellis, A. W., Flude, B. M., McWeeny, K. H. & Hay, D. (1986a). Face–name interference. *Journal of Experimental Psychology: Human Perception and Performance*, *12*, 466–475.

Young, A. W., McWeeny, K. H., Ellis, A. W. & Hay, D. C. (1986b). Naming and categorising faces and written names. *Quarterly Journal of Experimental Psychology*, *38A*, 297–318.

Young, A. W., McWeeny, K. H., Hay, D. C. & Ellis, A. W. (1986c). Access to identity-specific semantic codes from familiar faces. *Quarterly Journal of Experimental Psychology*, *38A*, 271–295.

Young, A. W., Ellis, A. W. & Flude, B. M. (1988). Accessing stored information about familiar people. *Psychological Research*, *50*, 111–115.

APPENDIX

Stimuli Used in the "British" Condition of Experiment 1 and in Experiments 2 and 3

Familiar		Unfamiliar	
High-frequency	*Low-frequency*	*High-frequency*	*Low-frequency*
L. Piggott	A. Scargill	A. Murfitt	H. Otway
S. Coe	T. Wogan	R. Stock	G. Twigger
R. Burton	S. Cram	K. Swann	P. Rolt
P. Newman	R. Redford	D. Farrant	P. Solder
K. Everett	F. Bruno	G. Webster	A. Brunwin
M. Jackson	B. Sheen	M. Sharp	J. Oatham
J. Archer	G. Orwell	R. Morgan	B. Todman
K. Williams	R. Mayell	S. Hall	G. Keetch
B. Reynolds	M. Jagger	B. Simpson	R. Waycot
G. Howe	D. Hurd	K. Wright	K. Padbury

Stimuli Used in Experiment 4. Full Names were Presented in Condition 1 and Initial and Surnames were Presented in Condition 2. These Names (Initial and Surname) were also Used in Experiment 1 except that E. Close was Replaced by S. Rigot. The First Eight Names in the Lists of High- and Low-frequency, Familiar Names Served as Stimuli in Experiment 5

Familiar Names		Unfamiliar Names	
High-frequency	*Low-frequency*	*High-frequency*	*Low-frequency*
Dominique Wathelet	Georges Moucheron	Dominique Goffart	Geores Bedoret
Mamine Pirotte	Philippe Geluck	Mamine Compere	Philippe Latet
Michel Lecomte	Jacques Bredael	Michel Laval	Jacques Gomand
Theo Mathy	Joseph Buron	Anne-Marie Maes	Joseph Limelette
Ann-Marie Lizin	Phillipe Monfils	Theo Lempereur	Philippe Lehyme
Philippe Moureau	Antoinette Spaak	Philippe Delhez	Antoinette Rondis
Willy Claes	Jean Gol	Willy Boulanger	Jean Spelters
Gerard Deprez	Andre Bertouille	Gerard Melon	Andre Plumat
Edouard Close	Philippe Maystadt	Edouard Fontaine	Philippe Mouthuy
Michel Hansenne	Jean-Pierre Grafe	Michel Closset	Jean-Pierre Miron

EUROPEAN JOURNAL OF COGNITIVE PSYCHOLOGY, 1991, 3 (1) 177–198

Facenet: A Connectionist Model of Face Identification in Context

Anne-Caroline Schreiber, Stéphane Rousset and
Guy Tiberghien

*Laboratoire de Psychologie Expérimentale, U.A. CNRS 665, Grenoble,
France*

The role of contexts in face identification constitutes a weak point of existing cognitive models of face recognition. A connectionist system (Facenet) based on a layered network has been specified and implemented to investigate the processes underlying identification. The architecture of the Facenet system takes contextual information explicitly into account in the construction of identity representations, and is provided with a reinjection mechanism which gives it dynamic properties. The model proposes that three indicators are extracted in parallel in person identification from a face: familiarity feeling (feeling of *déjà-vu* of the face stimulus), identity feeling (feeling that we know the person) and identity content (information about the person resulting from the integration of the contexts). Facenet underwent an experimental procedure to study the structuring of identity representations in various learning conditions defined by the specificity and the variability of the encoding context. The simulation results showed a significant interaction in identification performance between the variability and specificity factors. Identification of faces learned in variable contexts was not affected by a contextual change during recognition, whereas non-variable faces were affected, and all the more so when their encoding contexts were non-specific. These results are discussed in terms of generalisation (through a "semantisation" process) and categorisation in a contextual distributed memory. Of course, this kind of result has no ecological validity, but the model offers new predictions for further experiments on real subjects.

INTRODUCTION

Connectionist models provide a new paradigm for the simulation of cognitive phenomena. The advanced formalisation of neural network

Requests for reprints should be addressed to Anne-Caroline Schreiber, Laboratoire de Psychologie Expérimentale, U.A. CNRS 665, B.P. 47X, 38040 Grenoble Cedex, France.

The mathematical expertise necessary for designing the connectionist system was provided by Shengrui Wang and François Robert, Laboratoire TIM3, Institut National Polytechnique de Grenoble, Grenoble, France. We are grateful to Tim Valentine for his helpful suggestions. Thanks are also due to Cecilia Carrière and Tim Brennen for help with translation.

dynamics, as well as the recent discovery of learning algorithms for complex networks (Grossberg, 1988; McClelland et al., 1986; Rumelhart et al., 1986b), make it now possible to consider real simulations of cognitive processes. Here, we will focus on the processes underlying person identification from faces. Identifying a person from a face requires not only the detection of the face familiarity, but it also means that the identity representations can be accessed from facial information. It is for this latter reason that the face can be considered as a universal identifier.

Our purpose is to propose a model of person identification from faces which integrates the role of the context during learning as well as during recognition. This kind of interaction between the specific processing of a focal stimulus (face) and the processing of the context of the encounter must be postulated in any successful face recognition model, to the extent that face recognition is very sensitive to contextual change. Thus, we aim to specify the functioning of two mechanisms by applying the encoding-specificity principle (Tulving & Thomson, 1973), which assumes that traces in memory are contextualised. These two mechanisms consist of the familiarity processing of the face stimulus and the construction and the access to that person's identity. It is from this perspective that we have designed a connectionist network, Facenet, in order to simulate face identification while integrating the dynamic role of context in the construction of identity representations.

Before presenting the simulation, we will outline the principal characteristics of the cognitive model of Bruce and Young (1986), which will serve as a theoretical reference for discussing Facenet's functioning. It is a model of the functional components involved in face recognition which is couched in information-processing terms. Three main components work towards a person identification from its face. The structural encoding component provides a perceptual description of the presented face. This perceptual description can match a previously stored representation, held in what Hay and Young (1982) defined as face recognition units (FRUs). This matching gives rise to the feeling of familiarity derived from a face. FRUs are described as localised abstract units responding by change in an overall activation level. Once a FRU is activated, it can then access person identity representations held in person identity nodes (PINs). These nodes are entry points to associative memory and contain the identity-specific semantic information (what a person does, where he lives . . .) that allows us to feel we have successfully identified the person. The sequential structure of module activation is partly based on the latency hierarchy classically found in face processing experiments. (e.g. Young, McWeeny, Hay & Ellis, 1986).

The broadest component of Bruce and Young's (1986) model, the "cognitive system", is responsible for all the aspects of processing not reflected in other modules. It can produce a feedback influence on the specific processing of other modules. The feedback of the cognitive system on PINs in fact denotes the role of contextual information (and subjects' expectancies) in identification judgements, and even in familiarity decisions, because PINs themselves influence FRUs. According to this functional model, it is through the cognitive system that the representational and situational recognition context interacts with the specific processing of the face stimulus. So, Bruce and Young's model hardly takes account of context effects involved in face recognition, except by invoking the cognitive system. Yet, as Davies (1988) underlines, there is an urgent need to take context explicitly into account in the core of face recognition models: This need is justified by the extent of context effects reported both in experimentation (Memon & Bruce, 1985; Tiberghien, 1986) and in everyday life (Young, Hay & Ellis, 1985). Besides, according to Bruce and Young, the role of context constitutes an unresolved issue in their model.

More generally, both in verbal and visual memory studies, it is accepted that encoding and retrieval processes are not merely determined by the characteristics of the stimulus itself, but also by the characteristics of the context in which it is presented. The encoding-specificity principle (Tulving & Thomson, 1973) fits well with context effects, by postulating that the retrieval probability depends on the degree of compatibility between encoding and retrieval context. This principle assumes that traces in memory are always contextualised because storing a stimulus results from the encoding of the complete episode in which the stimulus is perceived. Tulving (1983) draws a distinction between episodic memory (particular events), very sensitive to context effects, and semantic memory (concepts), which is much more independent of contextual fluctuations.

While the encoding specificity principle interprets context effects in terms of discriminability of memory traces, Baddeley and Woodhead (1982) stress that context effects could reflect a tendency for a familiar context to bias the subject towards claiming that the face is also familiar. The context effect could thus be nothing but a response bias. In order to dissociate the influence of context on the discrminability of the memory trace from its effect on response bias, Baddeley and Woodhead set up a cross-over recognition condition, by presenting "old" faces in "old" contexts which are re-paired and so do not correspond to the original learned association. Their results show a clear effect of context on performance. In three out of four cases, this effect appears to be entirely due to the influence of context on the response criterion. However, in one case, the results suggest that context may have been influencing discriminability in a way that might be expected on the basis of the encoding specificity principle. The authors conclude that "it would be unwise to argue that context effects in face recognition are entirely due to bias" (Baddeley &

Woodhead, 1982, p. 162). Likewise, more recently, Davies and Thomson (1988) dismiss response bias as the sole explanation of context effects. These authors provide an exhaustive review of the literature both in verbal and facial memory, which concluded that the existence of context effects in face recognition is now solidly established. Bruce and Young (1986) indicate that contextual effects found in laboratory studies and everyday life are not surprising when we consider the relationship between PINs and context. Indeed, as Thomson, Robertson and Vogt (1982, p. 148) underline, "the context defines the person", or in other words, identity representations result from the integration of contextual information, during the repeated presentations of a face (or a person) in context.

Laboratory studies (Davies & Milne, 1982; Thomson et al., 1982) show that the recognition of unfamiliar faces is strongly affected by a contextual change occurring between study and test, whereas recognition of familiar faces never seems to be affected. Bruce and Young interpret this discrepancy by reference to the existence of previously stored representations in long-term memory for familiar faces (FRUs and PINs, of course, do not exist for unfamiliar faces). This interpretation should be qualified, since faces that have been experimentally pre-familiarised remain very sensitive to contextual change (Seamon, 1982; Thomson et al., 1982, experiment 6); and in everyday life (Young et al., 1985) some faces, though familiar, are difficult to recognise when encountered in an unusual context (for instance, a very familiar face – your baker – is hard to identify at a football match!). One must therefore study in a more precise way the nature of these previously stored representations. If the content of identity representations results from a contextual integration, then the contextual learning conditions associated with a face must be a determining factor in explaining the slips of recognition.

Recently, several researchers (Bruce & Young, 1986; Tiberghien, 1989; Young & Ellis, 1989) have proposed that a connectionist simulation could constitute a useful approach to understanding and modelling the processes involved in face recognition. Concerning FRUs, repetition priming experiments (Ellis, Young, Flude & Hay, 1987) indicate that Bruce and Young's conception cannot account for the results obtained, because the same picture produces more priming compared with a different picture of the same face. This finding is incompatible with FRUs conceived as localised abstract units that respond to any view of a particular face. Ellis et al. (1987) underline that it is necessary to modify the idea of FRUs into a more instance-based conception and thus argue that a distributed model of FRUs may be more adequate. Concerning context effects, we have already pointed out that it would be pertinent to study the nature of PINs, because they are progressively constructed by integrating contextual information. In Bruce and Young's (1986) model, we do not know how these identity nodes are constructed. They consider that the context enters the model through the cognitive system at recognition, but the problem is that to understand the dynamic role of context in the access to identity, we must consider its role during the progressive creation of identity representations. Bruce and Young's functional model is a recognition model which does not take into account the way identity nodes are actually constructed, i.e. it does not model the learning stage. Accordingly, we have chosen a connectionist model because it enables us to model explicitly interactive processing between several different sources of information, and allows the simulation of a dynamic learning stage. In this way, we have been able to study how identity representations may be constructed.

FACENET ARCHITECTURE

Facenet is a multilayer network. This network comprises the minimum number of layers necessary to model only the memory processes which lead to familiarity estimation and identification. The coding of perceptual information as well as face naming are subjects of ongoing research. As learning in Facenet is guided by the output constraints, it is important to note that each layer is determined not only by its inputs but also by the output constraints which guide its structuring.

The First Layer

This input layer is divided into two parts: one representing face input and the other context input, each containing 25 cells. The face input section is coded by a vector with 25 components, and this vector is composed of five blocks. In order to simplify, we propose that each block codes a part of the face, or a macro-feature. To simplify matters further, we decided to code the contexts with a vector structure similar to the one used for the faces. Both vectors are at present arbitrary, because up to now we have been more interested in the study of the interaction between two pieces of information – facial and contextual – which creates identity representation, than in the system's perceptual plausibility. To enable Facenet to function directly from digitised faces, its forthcoming extension will demand a considerable increase in terms of the number of connections (and time of computation) compared with this first prototype.

Facenet takes contextual information explicitly into account, because both the creation and the access to identity depend on contextual input. In fact, as discussed in the introduction, identity is nothing but the integration of contextual information. For familiar people, part of their meaning is "where they live, what they do", and so on. For unfamiliar people, their identity is even more bound up in the contexts with which they are associated.

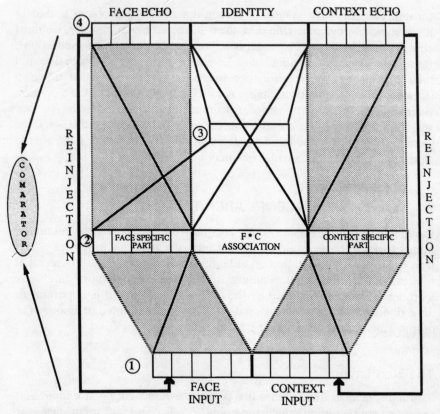

FIG. 1.   Facenet architecture is composed of four layers linked by a particular pattern of interconnectivity. The two lateral "beams" (shaded) make a specific processing of the inputs. All the other "beams" (delimited by continuous black lines) represent complete connections that make the interactive processing of the face and the context. The two lateral arrows indicate that face and context outputs can be reinjected into the inputs. The inputs/echoes comparator is involved at the learning stage (error measures for self-association) as well as at recognition (familiarity measure). The implemented system comprises 230 cells and 3950 connections.

The Second Layer

This is a hidden layer with 80 cells which is divided into three parts. The two lateral parts have 25 cells each, one of which is used exclusively for facial information, and the other which is used exclusively for contextual information. We assume, therefore, that for humans there is a specific face-processing structure separate from that for context (and other things). In the model, face- and context-specific processings are each shown by the two lateral patterns of interconnectivity (the shaded areas in Fig. 1). These lateral parts, due to a system of specific connections, are used to process the input by instituting a hierarchy between the five blocks of the face (and between the five blocks of the context): each block can be completely connected to 1, 2, 3, 4 and 5 blocks of the previous layer. These "beams" of specific connections are a first rough attempt[1] to introduce a feature hierarchy into the memory processes (by differentially weighting the influence of the input blocks upon the output blocks). Experimental results have shown indeed that some facial features are more important than others (Shepherd, Davies & Ellis, 1981).

The central part, which is called face–context association, is composed of 30 cells which are used to create the interaction between a face and its context. As we have already said, this association part is crucial for the construction of identity representations. It is wholly connected to the input layer. This central part should allow the construction of episodic associations between faces and contexts consistent with the encoding specificity principle: It thus models a memory structure that enables the dynamic emergence of contextualised episodic representations.

The Third Layer

This is composed of only 20 cells wholly connected to the face–context association and to the face-specific part in layer 2 and not to the context-specific part. This asymmetry in connectivity between layers 3 and 2 captures the focal status of facial information for person identification. Because the Facenet system simulates person identification from a face stimulus, it is obvious that the face has to be the privileged access key to identity. This third layer, because of its small size, would have to generalise and find common points in its inputs. Moreover, because it is the only one which is connected to the identity outputs, it enables the network to abstract its own identity representations in order to satisfy the constraint imposed in layer 4. From a computational point of view, even without this third layer, the network would be able to learn all the exemplars perfectly. However, we did want the constraints imposed in the identification output layer to act directly on the face–context association of layer 2. It will be only throughout the structuring of layer 3 that the identity constraint will organise layer 2 during learning. Given its upstream and downstream patterns of interconnectivity, layer 3 is a convergence zone which is

---

[1] In agreement with Tim Valentine, this hierarchy could result from the self-adaptation of the network to the probability of feature change in the exemplars database. The feature saliency reported in the literature could have been simulated with real digitised faces by studying the ontogenetic specification of a network with complete connections on the face-specific part before learning starts.

necessary because it gives the network the sole level of processing (of the inputs) which is only dedicated to the identity constraint.

With layers 2 and 3, Facenet has two hidden (and autonomous) layers, which enable it to structure its own representations. The progressive reduction of cells between the inputs, the face–context association part in layers 2 and 3 ensures a genuine interactive processing of the face and the context. As autonomous layers, the second and third layers allow the network to build its episodic and semantic memory concerning person identity by itself. It is in fact the connections between layers 2 and 3, and between layers 3 and 4, that actually encode the structure of identity representations in memory.

The Fourth Layer

The network's outputs are the emergent memory representations of the system and can be seen as equivalent to ecphoric information which, according to Tulving (1983), results from a synergistic process of interaction between memory structures and retrieval cues. Indeed, we can consider that retrieval cues are the exemplars presented to the network, that the structure of memory is the configuration of the network's weights and that the synergistic process is the computation within each cell. This output layer is divided into three parts. The middle one processes the central constraint of the network, which is identification. In this implementation, there is one cell for each identity to learn. In some way, each cell performs the same function as a PIN, because each node represents the place where a particular configuration of activation (produced by the ecphoric process) converges, in order to specify that the face presented in input has a particular identity. The value of an identity node is here only the strength of activation of this identity revealed by the ecphory.

The two lateral outputs are composed of 25 cells each (the same number as the input vectors) and are called "face-echo" and "context-echo". These echoes contain, in fact, the ecphoric representations that are the memory products (reminiscence) of the search; which means that they contain "the mental image" of the face (or contextual information) emerging during the search in memory. These echoes depend on both the specific processing of the inputs, and the face–context association part in layer 2. Obviously, each echo does not depend on the specific processing of the other input because there is no reason for the context to act directly on the face (and vice versa). Layer 3 also cannot be connected to the echoes because the constraints imposed on the echoes would have influenced layer 3 and the latter would no more have been solely dedicated to the identity constraint. On the other hand, the crossed "beams" of connections between face–context association and echoes are necessary to give the face–context association part its capacity to reconstruct an association at recognition by co-occurrence of the content of the face and the context echoes. Moreover, this gives the network its recall competency because the remaining connections between face–context association and the echoes enable it to recall a face from a context input (and vice versa).

FACENET FUNCTIONING

The system learns according to the algorithm of "gradient back propagation" discovered by Rumelhart, Hinton and Williams (1986a). During the identification stage, Facenet can reinject face-echo and context-echo into its input. The reinjection (feedback) is very important, as it creates a dynamic system. It enables the dynamic simulation of the search process in memory which occurs during person identification from a face. Of course, the feedback could also be introduced in the learning stage as in Jordan's (1986) model. This enables the network efficiently to learn time-dependent sequences. It is expected to be useful in dealing with the temporal variations (succession in pose or expression), which are important in the creation of face representations in memory. Thus feedback in the learning stage will be used when we study the specific face representation in addition to the identification processes.

The face and context inputs are represented by two vectors of 25 components (5×5 blocks). Each block contains only one 1 and four −1s to simplify the scanning of the data. During learning, a simple self-association of the outputs with their respective inputs is performed. This constraint forces the network to have its echoes equal to its inputs. By this self-association, the system *has* to learn the face and the context. Figure 1 indicates the presence of a comparator in the Facenet system. This comparator, by computing the different inputs/echoes (Euclidian distances), gives the error measures which are necessary during learning for the network to adapt its weights. This constraint of self-association may be linked to the theory proposed by Sayre (1986), according to which the human system's adaptation to its environment requires that the system constantly adjusts its internal representations to those resulting from perceptual processing. At the recognition level, it is the similarity between the reminiscence emerging on the face-echo and the information present in the output of the perceptual system (Facenet's input) that enables an immediate familiarity estimation of the face.[2] Indeed, a well-learned face will (by definition)

---

[2]This view echoes Tulving's proposition: "Familiarity reflects the similarity between the information provided by the retrieval cue, or the test item, on the one hand, and the information contained in the actualised emsemble of ecphoric information, on the other" (1982, p. 143).

have an echo equal to the inputs, so that if the similarity percept/echo is at a maximum, then the familiarity will be very high. Just as the learning stage (and thus familiarity acquisition) consisted of an adjustment constrained by the input/output similarity, the percept/echo discrepancy is intrinsically a familiarity indicator during recognition, and therefore performs the same functions as the FRUs in Bruce and Young's (1986) model. More precisely, the automatic mechanism (comparator) that during learning computed the distance input/output (to back-propagate the errors) is also during recognition, the mechanism which estimates, exactly in the same way, the familiarity of the inputs. This type of modelling unifies the learning and the recognition stages; the familiarity mechanism embodied by the comparator being fundamental at these two stages.

The central part of identification is a hetero-association. During the learning stage, the cell corresponding to the identity of the face presented would ideally be 1 and the others −1. This form of coding is an easy way to represent the various configuration states of a co-variation detector, which ensures the *constancy of identity*. Consistent with de Schonen and Mathivet (1989), such a co-variation detector (between sensorial inputs) might specify that the subject is faced with a constant stimulus in contextual fluctuations. This constraint imposed in layer 4 explicitly ensures the *constancy of identity* for the network.

To summarise, Facenet has three outputs which in fact constitute in themselves the emergent representations of the network in front of inputs: face-echo, identity output and context-echo. These three indicators are reconstructed by the interaction memory structure/retrieval cues and emerge in parallel for the identification process. The face-echo contains the mental image of the face and allows the "familiarity estimation" of the *face* stimulus (feeling of *déjà-vu* of the face). The identity output gives rise to "the feeling of identity", which indicates directly that the subject is faced with a *person* that has already been specified as an unique and constant object. The context-echo contains contextual information that *emerges* from memory and that constitutes "the content of the identity"[3] of the person. It also allows the estimation of the familiarity of the context, but this is of course not central to person identification from a face. This model

---

[3]We put forward the term "content of identity" because the memory structure takes part in the content of this emergence and because the context-echo is the sole place in the system where there is an emergence founded on contextual elements previously encoded. If a face was always encoded in the same context, then the content of identity emerging on the echo would be principally constituted of its previous encoding context elements (with low generalisation). For a person encountered in various contexts, the content of identity emerging on the echo during recognition will be constituted by an abstraction (higher generalisation) founded on the relations between the various contexts the system had learned.

thus predicts a dissociation between the feeling of identity and the content of identity. It also predicts the existence of a double dissociation between the feeling of familiarity and the feeling of identity. These hypotheses suggest obvious experimental studies to confirm or falsify Facenet.

A SIMULATION AND ITS RESULTS

The Facenet system underwent an experimental trial in order to study the interaction between facial and contextual information on the structuring of identity representations. The face–context relationship was manipulated through two experimental factors, the variability and the specificity of the encoding context.

Factors

Variability. A face can be learned several times in the same context (non-variable encoding condition) or several times in many different contexts (variable condition). According to Tulving (1983), presentation of episodes in different contexts progressively generates the creation of a semantic representation, thanks to a process of abstraction. Semantic representations are more independent of context effects than episodic representations. Conversely, presentation of episodes in an identical context preserves the contextual specificity of the episodes, which remain very dependent on context effects. Therefore, the factor of encoding variability could induce the transformation of episodic representations into semantic ones (through a hypothetical process of a "semantisation" of episodes). Experimental evidence of this hypothetical process is reported by Tiberghien (1986): The recognition of faces learned in four different contexts is less affected by a contextual change between studies and tests than recognition of faces learned four times in the same context. These kinds of results have been also found in word recognition (Hintzman & Stern, 1978; Smith, 1982). Tiberghien proposed a distinction between episodic and semantic familiarity, in order to take contextual factors into account during the acquisition of familiarity (i.e. during the learning stage).

Specificity. A context can always be associated with the same face (specific encoding), or a context can be shared by several faces (non-specific encoding). The factor of specificity is symmetrical to the factor of variability, because just as a variable face is encoded in several contexts, a non-specific context is encoded with several faces. The specificity factor is interesting because it links several faces together. So the learning list is structured like a semantic network, because a face is linked to a context, which is itself linked to another face, etc. According to Anderson (1983), long-term memory is a semantic network and spreading activation (diffusion of activation within a semantic network) is generally invoked to explain experimental results. Facenet is not a semantic network because, in themselves, its cells and connections have no meaning. But, it was interesting to study how a connectionist system was able to structure itself (in a distributed way) in order to learn a list of stimuli structured like a semantic network. It enabled us to study how the similarity structure contained in the corpus of examples could influence the structure of information in the Facenet system. It was thus interesting to see if a connectionist network is able to simulate these categorisation and spreading activation phenomena – classically found during retrieval – and this, of course, without supposing any semantic network organisation, but instead simply allowing it to arise out of the parallel and distributed processing of a base of examples with non-specific contexts.

Method

The Facenet system simulates one subject. Once its architecture is defined, it has to acquire a facial history, i.e. it must learn a list of patterns. The database used in this simulation contains 30 faces and 30 contexts. These inputs are in fact vectors of 25 components, composed of five blocks. These vectors can resemble each other on 0, 1 or 2 blocks. The learning list comprises 139 patterns (in a random order), one pattern being an association between one face and one context. The two experimental factors are crossed, and therefore there are four encoding conditions, as represented in Fig. 2. In each condition, there are four faces, two learned twice and two learned four times during one iteration of learning. The comparison between the faces learned twice and the faces learned four times will not be developed here because the experiment is aimed at studying the role of encoding contextual conditions and not the effect of the degree of learning. The 14 other faces of the database were included to give non-specific contexts their characteristic of non-specificity.

Before learning began, the weights were set at random between 0.5 and −0.5, and the parameter which characterises the sigmoidal function of each cell was also set at random between 0.5 and 1. Momentum was fixed at 0.01 and the learning rate at 0.3. The network was submitted to 1000 learning iterations, one iteration being composed of one presentation of the 139 patterns. At the end of the learning stage, all the testing patterns were very well learned. So, all the faces were very familiar to the network when presented in their context. Thus, the results of this simulation can be related to studies of familiar face recognition. The effects of both experimental factors on the learning speed were not studied because they depend on several random factors, such as the initial connection weights, the order

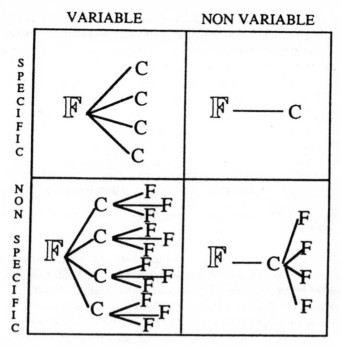

VARIABLE   NON VARIABLE

FIG. 2. The four encoding conditions obtained by crossing the two experimental factors.

of the list, etc. So, we studied the effect of factors at the recognition level. The recognition tests should reveal how the network has structured and integrated its knowledge during the learning stage.

Recognition Tests Concerning the Two Experimental Factors

First, the faces were presented in their encoding context. This test was carried out in order to ensure that all the faces to be compared had equivalent identity values (our dependent variable recorded on layer 4). This test showed that all the patterns were equivalent on identity strength. Thus, the learning degree could not interfere with the two manipulated factors. Therefore, the effect was tested by re-pairing old contexts with unassociated faces (cross-over recognition test).

For this second test, 15 old contexts which had never been associated with the four test faces (one for each encoding condition) were presented to Facenet, once with each of these faces. An analysis of variance was performed on the data of identity strength recorded after only one iteration of recognition (Fig. 3). During this test, we analysed only the identity

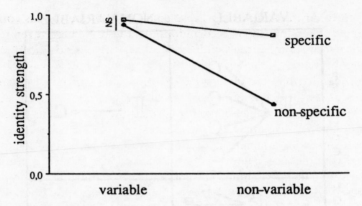

FIG. 3. Average of identity strengths recorded after the first iteration in the old re-paired contexts condition.

strength of the target face because all the others cells remained at -1. This phenomenon of high discriminability between identity values is due to the high level of learning in this experimental procedure.

The main effect of variability is significant, which means that the identification of faces encoded in variable contexts is less affected by a contextual change at recognition than the identification of non-variable faces $[F(1,56) = 10.6, P = 0.002]$. This is true whether the context is specific or not [for specific contexts: variable = 0.96, non-variable = 0.86, $t(28) = 2.83, P = 0.008$; for non-specific contexts: variable = 0.94, non-variable = 0.43, $t(28) = 2.77, P = 0.009$]. Thus, despite the maximal learning level, there is still a difference between faces encoded in variable and non-variable contexts.

In the same way, the identification of faces encoded with non-specific contexts is significantly lower than the identification of faces learned in specific contexts $[F(1,56) = 6.14, P = 0.015]$. But this latter conclusion must be qualified because of the significant interaction between variability and specificity factors $[F(1,56) = 4.77, P = 0.031]$. For non-variable faces, there is a specificity effect $[0.86 \ vs \ 0.43, t(28) = 2.35, P = 0.024]$. If a face was encoded in a specific context, its identification was better than if it was encoded in a non-specific one. On the other hand, there is no specificity effect for faces learned in variable contexts: the identification of such faces was very good, regardless of the specificity of their context $[0.96 \ vs \ 0.94, t(28) = 1.21, P = 0.23]$.

Discussion

Contextual variability during encoding seems to play an important role in the integration of information by the network. This variability enables the network to abstract an identity representation from the various contexts presented. Therefore, upon recognition, identity can emerge even if contextual information is irrelevant. The significant interaction corroborates this interpretation, because if variability really enables progressive abstraction of identity, one can understand that at such a high level of learning there is no longer a difference between specific and non-specific encoding contexts. At this level of learning, the positive effect of variability seems to override the negative effect of non-specificity.

Contextual non-variability induces an identity representation completely merged with the face–context pattern that had been learned. In order to have a strong identity output, this episodic face–context association must be preserved (or retrieved). Because the network has not been able to create an identity representation independent from that particular association, any contextual change will induce a weakening of the performance. This explanation can be applied to all of the non-variable faces.

But how should we explain the specificity effect concerning non-variable faces? When a face is encoded in a specific context, the network has learned to give an identity to this particular association, but the two components have never been learned with other identitites. So, the episodic trace is very distinctive for the network. Faces encoded with a non-specific context are even more affected by a contextual change on recognition. Non-specific contexts indeed have been learned many times with several faces. So, they have become attractive nodes, around which face–context associations are organised. Non-specific contexts have thus created categories, each category grouping together all the patterns sharing the same context. Therefore, because non-specific contexts are at the root of a categorisation process which organises information in the network, they play an important part in the creation of identity. And thus, identification of non-specific and non-variable faces is very sensitive to contextual change during recognition.

In order to find some corroboration for these interpretations, we studied the dynamic evolution of the network in a third recognition test. Faces were presented in completely new contexts, and we let the network reinject its echoes in input several times. A comparison of Figs 4 and 5 shows that the variability of effect found in the previous statistical analysis was replicated, because the identification of the faces encoded in the variable condition was not affected by a new context at recognition. There was great stability of identity during the reinjections and face familiarity was almost perfect (the similarity between the face initially presented and face-echoes is maximal). On the other hand, non-variable faces *were* affected by a new context. This is detectable by the evolution of identity as well as by the evolution of familiarity. However, Figs 4 and 5 show that they were affected in different ways.

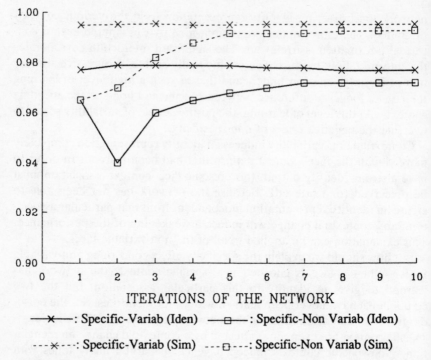

FIG. 4.   Study of the variability factor in a new recognition context, when encoding contexts were specific. Continuous lines represent identity values. Dotted lines represent the similarity between face-input and face-echo. These similarities (Euclidean distances) and identities (activation values) are superimposed on the same axis of co-ordinates only to compare visually the evolution patterns.

For a face encoded in a specific context (Fig. 4), identity dropped at the second iteration because the reinjected facial information was less pure (i.e. no longer composed of only 1s and −1s). Then, the appropriate context was progressively retrieved thanks to the reinjections and, therefore, identity strength increased. We note that the face familiarity indicator became better with each successive reinjection. In fact, the face-echo was never affected by the retrieval of the encoding context, and thus we can say that this face–context association is very distinctive in memory and is not likely to activate other associations.

For a face encoded in a non-specific context (Fig. 5), the second iteration is very interesting because there was an increase in identity strength which was not attributable to the face. Indeed, at the same time, face familiarity had diminished. It is in fact the reinjected context-echo that was responsible for this increase (because it allowed access to its category). But, during iterations 3 and 4, there was a simultaneous fall in identity and face

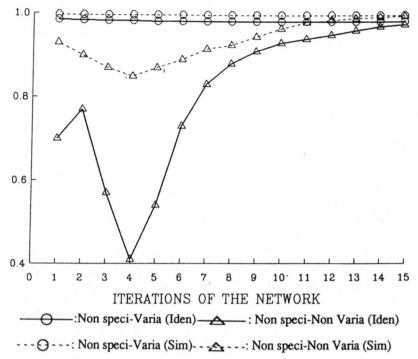

ITERATIONS OF THE NETWORK

——⊖——:Non speci-Varia (Iden)——△——: Non speci-Non Varia (Iden)

- - -⊖- - -: Non speci-Varia (Sim)- - -△- - -: Non speci-Non Varia (Sim)

FIG. 5.   Study of the variability factor in a new recognition context, when encoding contexts were non-specific. Continuous lines represent identity values. Dotted lines represent the similarity between face-input and face-echo. Similarity and identity are superimposed on the same axis of co-ordinates only to compare visually the evolution patterns.

familiarity. This fall symbolises spreading activation within an identity category: The face had activated its encoding context but, because this context was associated with other faces, the face-echo was more and more distorted because the network activated several faces at the same time (and other identities emerged weakly). From the fifth iteration, the network was finally able to choose, among all the activated associations, the one which corresponded to the face presented at input. Non-specific contexts have thus created categories. Once the category was retrieved, the network behaved as if the activation propagated to the other identities belonging to the same category. To make a successful identification, the network had to differentiate within the activated category, otherwise a false identification could have occurred.

The results of this simulation underline the fundamental role of the kind of relationship between face and context during the learning stage of the structuring of identity representations. The variability of encoding seems to induce an identity representation which is progressively abstracted from various contexts. So, identification can emerge even if the recognition context is irrelevant. The results of this simulation are thus compatible with the experimental results obtained by Tiberghien (1986), Hintzman and Stern (1978) and Smith (1982). Moreover, this result can be related to the technique proposed by Smith (1988) for overcoming the disturbing effects of environmental context-dependent memory. Consistent with this proposal, by varying the encoding context one can obtain an independence of memory from the contextual cues at recognition ("decontextualisation of knowledge").[4] For non-variable faces, their identity is completely linked to contextual information, and if contexts are non-specific, the network has created identity categories which can impair recognition. This result is compatible with those reported by Deffenbacher, Carr and Leu (1981), which show that faces are very sensitive to interference when seen in the same experimental context (non-specific context for all the faces shown in the learning phase). Moreover, this simulation brings water to Davies' (1988) mill, when he suggests that we could enhance context effects in face recognition by "using a smaller number of contexts shared with a number of stimulus persons" (p. 47). In order to test the pertinence of the architecture, we have devised another network without layer 3. Thus, in this case, the constraint of identity constancy imposed in the output layer acts directly on layer 2. So, to satisfy this constraint, the latter network has fewer levels of processing and representation than Facenet. Though it was submitted to exactly the same experimental design with the same learning database, this network failed to show any phenomenon of categorisation during recognition. This result highlights the importance of architecture when one wants to simulate cognitive processes.

GENERAL CONCLUSIONS

Our results show that in old re-paired context conditions (cross-over recognition test), identification performance is impaired. The classical context effect is thus achieved by the system. But it should be noted that this effect varies according to the various encoding conditions of the faces:

---

[4]In our model, decontextualisation does not mean that the context is ignored as noise but that there is a "semantisation" from the various contexts to an identity which becomes independent of context effects. Because the network is able to retrieve the identity and the face from a variable context presented alone at recognition, then we cannot suppose that it has learned to ignore the variable contexts during the acquisition of identity. Moreover, the study of internal representations in layers 2 and 3 (by correlational studies or connection cuttings with faces and contexts presented alone or simultaneously) shows that the configurations of activation are determined by the context as well as by the face.

Only the recognition of faces encoded in non-variable contexts seems affected. These results improve our understanding of why experimentally pre-familiarised faces remain very sensitive to contextual change (Seamon, 1982; Thomson et al., 1982, experiment 6): not only learning frequency but also learning conditions may determine the range of context effects. This hypothesis implies that if we pre-familiarise faces in variable contexts, these faces may acquire the same status as faces already familiar to the subjects, and thus we would observe no context effects as reported in the literature on familiar faces (Davies & Milne, 1982; Thomson et al., 1982). In the same way, everyday failures to recognise familiar faces due to contextual change (Young et al., 1985) may be essentially attributable to people being encoded in relatively non-variable contexts. The discrepancy between familiar and unfamiliar faces could be recouched in terms of contextual conditions of learning and not in terms of dual processing. From a theoretical point of view, we could say that an identity representation can be "semantised" from contextualised episodes, this "semantisation" being possible owing to the variability of encoding contexts. This result is theoretically important, because it puts forward the notion that the contextual history of memory *in itself* might account for the transformation of episodic representations into semantic ones, without supposing several different memory systems (Tulving, 1983). So, as McClelland (1988) and O'Toole, Millward and Anderson (1988) have already underlined, connectionist models provide a very simple framework to explain apparently complex, disparate or incompatible phenomena. In the present model, the crucial issues of the distinction between episodic and semantic memory can be approached, thanks to the inherent characteristics of the connectionist system, which are: distributed representations; the possibility of dynamic face–context interactions (for the creation of contextualised episodic representations); and the existence of several processing levels (which allows for generalisation). But the most important point, which allows us to study the hypothetical "semantisation" process, is that connectionism models learning procedures. In fact, because learning is actually carried out in a network, we are able to study how identity representations are constructed in different encoding conditions. A recognition model must indeed take into account the way information is learned.

The second important result of this simulation is related to the specificity factor. The learning of faces in non-specific contexts induces the creation of categories founded on contextual information. These categories are revealed at recognition by a spreading activation phenomenon, which had previously been put forward to explain the organisation of information in human memory (Anderson, 1983). Facenet can give an account of this phenomenon *without* supposing any semantic network organisation, but simply in terms of the parallel processing of a database of examples with non-specific contexts. Through the control of contextual history during the learning stage, our simulation enabled us to study the intrinsic characteristics of contextual memory. It is worth remembering that by simulating the encoding specificity principle on a connectionist network, the contextual history of memory in itself can account for the transformation of memory traces ("semantisation") as well as their organisation (categorisation).

The reinjection mechanism of the echoes enables the network to simulate in an automatic way the dynamic evolution of the search in memory. These dynamics can lead to positive effects (completion, cued recall, etc.) or negative ones, such as misidentifications. We want to stress here a characteristic of this type of modelling: In the current models of face recognition, there are several stages which are deemed to be sequential. However, it is interesting to note that the connectionist framework enabled us to model these processes in an interactive, parallel and unitary way. Despite this, when presented with a face, Facenet never retrieved the identity before the correct face-echo during reinjections. Thus, assuming that the latency of recognition is directly related to the number of reinjections, this simulation shows that a hierarchy of latencies does not *necessarily* imply a sequential hierarchy of processing modules.

The architecture and the functioning of Facenet led to hypotheses that must be (and are actually being) tested by experiments both on normal and brain-injured patients. First, the parallelism between familiarity feeling, identity feeling and identity content described in Facenet functioning predicts that we should observe dissociations between these three indicators. Secondly, the modelling of the familiarity mechanism implies that the same structures are responsible for mental imaging of a face and for its familiarity estimation (the comparator needs indeed the content of the face-echo at recognition). So, we must expect to observe a priming effect of the mental imaging of a face on a familiarity decision. Thirdly, since the face-echo is influenced not only by the face-specific part but also by the face–context association part, the familiarity estimation of a face can be influenced by the current context. This influence could be related to the semantic priming effect (Bruce & Valentine, 1986), because a face presented can evoke a context which may subsequently facilitate (via the face–context association) the recognition of a face that had been encoded in the same contextual category. So, the model predicts that familiarity is not context-free, *without* supposing feedback from a higher level of processing and *without* invoking a bias on the decision mechanism. Furthermore, some extensions of the system are envisaged in order to integrate other functions such as the study of face memory representations constructed from digitalised pictures, the access to name information and the processing of expression. Finally, the simulation is a useful and necessary adjunct to standard empirical investigations for modelling the cognitive processes underlying face recognition. What should a simulation be if not a model in action?

Manuscript received December 1989
Revised manuscript received August 1990

REFERENCES

Anderson, J. R. (1983). *The architecture of cognition.* Cambridge, Mass.: Harvard University Press.

Baddeley, A. D. & Woodhead, M. (1982). Depth of processing, contexts and face recognition. *Canadian Journal of Psychology, 36,* 148–164.

Bruce, V. & Valentine, T. (1986). Semantic priming for familiar faces. *Quarterly Journal of Experimental Psychology, 38A,* 125–150.

Bruce, V. & Young, A. (1986). Understanding face recognition. *British Journal of Psychology, 77,* 305–327.

Davies, G. M. (1988). Faces and places: Laboratory research on context and face recognition. In G. Davies & D. M. Thomson (Eds), *Memory in context: Context in memory,* pp. 35–53. Chichester: John Wiley.

Davies, G. M. & Milne, A. (1982). Recognizing faces in and out of context. *Current Psychological Research, 2,* 235–246.

Davies, G. M. & Thomson, D. M. (Eds) (1988). *Memory in context: Context in memory.* Chichester: John Wiley.

Deffenbacher, K. A., Carr, T. H. & Leu, J. R. (1981). Memory for words, pictures, and faces: Retroactive interference, forgetting, and reminiscence. *Journal of Experimental Psychology: Human Learning and Memory, 7,* 299–305.

de Schonen, S. & Mathivet, E. (1989). First come, first served: A scenario about the development of hemispheric specialization in face recognition during infancy. *Cahiers de Psychologie Cognitive/European Bulletin of Cognitive Psychology, 9,* 3–44.

Ellis, A. W., Young, A. W., Flude, B. M. & Hay, D. C. (1987). Repetition priming of face recognition. *Quarterly Journal of Experimental Psychology, 39A,* 193–203.

Grossberg, S. (Ed.) (1988). *Neural networks and natural intelligence.* Cambridge, Mass.: Bradford Books.

Hay, D. C. & Young, A. W. (1982). The human face. In A. W. Ellis (Ed.), Normality and pathology in cognitive functions, pp. 173–202. London: Academic Press.

Hintzman, D. L. & Stern, L. D. (1978). Contextual variability and memory for frequency. *Journal of Experimental Psychology: Human Learning and Memory, 4,* 539–549.

Jordan, M. I. (1986). *Serial order: A parallel distributed processing approach.* ICS Report 8604.

McClelland, J. L. (1988). Connectionist models and psychological evidence. *Journal of Memory and Language, 27,* 107–123.

McClelland, J. L., Rumelhart, D. E. & the PDP Research Group (1986). *Parallel distributed processing: Explorations in the microstructure of cognition,* Vol. II. Cambridge, Mass.: Bradford Books.

Memon, A. & Bruce, V. (1985). Context effects in episodic studies of verbal and facial memory. *Current Psychological Research and Reviews,* Winter, 349–369.

Rumelhart, D. E., Hinton, G. E. & Williams, R. J. (1986a). Learning representations by error propagation. In D. E. Rumelhart, J. L. McClelland and the PDP Research Group (Eds), *Parallel distributed processing: Explorations in the microstructure of cognition,* Vol. I, pp. 318–362. Cambridge, Mass.: Bradford Books.

Rumelhart, D. E., McClelland, J. L. & the PDP Research Group (Eds) (1986b). *Parallel distributed processing: Explorations in the microstructure of cognition*, Vol. I. Cambridge, Mass.: Bradford Books.

O'Toole, A., Millward, R. B. & Anderson, J. A. (1988). A physical system approach to recognition memory for spatially transformed faces. *Neural Networks*, *1*, 179–199.

Sayre, K. M. (1986). Intentionality and information processing: An alternative model for cognitive science. *Behavioral and Brain Sciences*, *9*, 121–166.

Seamon, J. G. (1982). Dynamic facial recognition: Examination of a natural phenomenon. *American Journal of Psychology*, *95*, 363–381.

Shepherd, J. W., Davies, G. M. & Ellis, H. D. (1981). Studies of cue saliency. In G. Davies, H. D. Ellis & J. Shepherd (Eds), *Perceiving and remembering faces*, pp. 105–131. London: Academic Press.

Smith, S. M. (1982). Enhancement of recall using multiple environmental contexts during learning. *Memory and Cognition*, *10*, 405–412.

Smith, S. M. (1988). Environmental context-dependent memory. In G. Davies & D. M. Thomson (Eds), *Memory in context: Context in memory*, pp. 13–34. Chichester: John Wiley.

Thomson, D. M., Robertson, S. L. & Vogt, R. (1982). Person recognition: The effect of context. *Human Learning, 1*, 137–154.

Tiberghien, G. (1986). Contextual effects in face recognition: Some theoretical problems. In H. D. Ellis, M. A. Jeeves, F. Newcombe & A. W. Young (Eds), *Aspects of face processing*, pp. 88–105. Dordrecht: Martinus Nijhoff.

Tiberghien, G. (1989). Comment: What is face semantics, what is face processing? In A. W. Young & H. D. Ellis (Eds), *Handbook of research in face processing*, pp. 275–288. Amsterdam: North Holland.

Tulving, E. (1982). Synergistic ecphory in recall and recognition. *Canadian Journal of Psychology*, *36*, 130–147.

Tulving, E. (1983). *Elements of episodic memory*. Oxford: Oxford University Press.

Tulving, E. & Thomson, D. M. (1973). Encoding specificity and retrieval processes in episodic memory. *Psychological Review*, *80*, 352–373.

Young, A. W. & Ellis, H. D. (1989). Semantic processing. In A. W. Young & H. D. Ellis (Eds), *Handbook of research on face processing*, pp. 235–262. Amsterdam: North Holland.

Young, A. W., Hay, D. C. and Ellis, A. W. (1985). The faces that launched a thousand slips: Everyday difficulties and errors in recognizing people. *British Journal of Psychology*, *76*, 495–523.

Young, A. W., McWeeny, K. H., Hay, D. C. and Ellis, A. W. (1986). Access to identity-specific semantic codes from familiar faces. *Quarterly Journal of Experimental Psychology*, *38A*, 271–295.

VISUAL PERCEPTION: Physiology, Psychology and Ecology, 2nd edn.

VICKI BRUCE, PATRICK R. GREEN (University of Nottingham)

Recent theoretical developments and research findings from three different approaches to visual perception are brought together in this book. The first approach is physiological; the evolution of different types of eye and the physiology of mammalian visual pathways are described. The second is the traditional psychological approached; perceptual organisation, the perception of depth and motion, and pattern recognition are discussed in terms of the processing of information contained in retinal images. Emphasis is placed on recent computational work on these processes, and particularly on algorithms for the detection of edges and motion, the computation of stereo disparity, and object recognition.Connectionist approaches to these problems are discussed and contrasted with those of theorists such as Marr. The third perspective considered is ecological; the work of Gibson and his followers is described and applied to problems of animal and human locomotion, event perception and perception of the social world, including the human face.

0-86377-145-9 1990 348pp. $38.75 £24.95 hbk.
0-86377-146-7 1990 348pp. $18.50 £11.95 pbk.

VISUAL COGNITION

Computational, Experimental, and Neuropsychological Perspectives

GLYN W. HUMPHREYS (University of Birmingham) VICKI BRUCE (University of Nottingham)

Vision allows us to do many things. It enables us to perceive a world composed of meaningful objects and events. It enables us to track those events as they take place in front of our eyes. It enables us to read. It provides accurate spatial information for actions such as reaching for or avoiding objects. It provides colour and texture that can help us to separate objects from their background, and so forth. This book is concerned with understanding the processes that allow us to carry out these various visually-driven behaviours.

In the past ten years our understanding of visual processing has undergone a rapid change, primarily fostered by the convergence of computational, experimental and neuropsychological work on the topic. *Visual Cognition* provides the first major attempt to cover all aspects of this work within a single text. It provides a state-of-the-art summary of research on visual information processing, relevant to advanced undergraduates, postgraduates and research workers. It covers: seeing static forms, object recognition, dynamic vision (motion perception and visual masking), visual attention, visual memory, visual aspects of reading.

0-86377-124-6 1989 352pp. $45.95 £24.95 hbk.
0-86377-125-4 1989 $18.95 £9.95 pbk

LAWRENCE ERLBAUM ASSOCIATES
27 Church Road, Hove, East Sussex, BN3 2FA England

Subject Index